From an etching by C. E. Shaw, 1882

THE "COCKPIT", PRESTON, LANCASHIRE
Where the first British Mission Conference was held
(pp. 44-49 and 57).

THE RIVER
Near the spot where the first
were performed (

RICHARD L. EVANS

A CENTURY OF "MORMONISM" IN GREAT BRITAIN

Publishers Press
Salt Lake City, Utah

Preface to 1984 Printing

This book was first published in 1937, the British Mission's centennial year, under the circumstances described in the author's preface. Elder Evans was then thirty-one years of age, had been managing editor of the *Improvement Era* for a year, and had been writing and delivering "The Spoken Word" sermonettes for the weekly nationwide Tabernacle Choir broadcast for seven years.

In the years following its publication there were frequent requests for reprintings, revisions, or updatings of this work, but the demands on Elder Evans's time and talents took him in other directions. In 1938 he was called into the First Quorum of the Seventy, and fifteen years later, at age forty-seven, he was sustained a member of the Quorum of the Twelve Apostles. In addition to this demanding Church service, he continued to write and deliver "The Spoken Word," a service he performed for a total of over forty years until his death in 1971 at age sixty-five. He also published fifteen books of his sermonettes and a selection of quotations gained from a lifetime of reading.

The development of his literary skills made him perhaps too critical of his earlier writing and therefore reluctant to have this book reprinted. As his family, however, we have become aware of a growing demand for this work, a work which when originally published was of considerable significance in Church circles. Accordingly we offer this reprint in the hope that it will be well received by Latter-day Saints everywhere.

The Richard L. Evans Family
October 1984

Author's Preface

The basis of this volume is a series of articles on British Mission History which appeared in the *Millennial Star* in 1928 and 1929, when the author was serving, successively, as Associate Editor of that publication and as Secretary of the European Mission. The series was prepared under the direction and encouragement of Dr. John A. Widtsoe, who was then President of the European Mission and Editor of the *Millennial Star*.

The forepart of the book, giving a detailed account of Gospel "beginnings" in Great Britain, was written essentially as it appears here, nine years ago. The latter part of the book, dealing with summaries, generalizations, and conclusions on the century's British Mission activities, is of more recent origin.

Grateful acknowledgment is here made to Dr. Widtsoe, whose helpful persuasion was responsible for the beginning of the book nine years ago, and for its completion now. Appreciation is also due President Heber J. Grant for his interest in bringing about its publication at this time. Remembered with gratitude also is the late Dr. James E. Talmage, who found the author as a twenty-year-old "Mormon" missionary traveling in England and took him to the European Mission office for a rigorous and invaluable training as Associate Editor of the *Millennial Star*. The research services and editorial assistance of Elder James H. Wallis have also been greatly helpful and appreciated. Gratitude is also hereby acknowledged to Elder Joseph Fielding Smith, Church Historian, for his many kindnesses in making Church records available, and to Elder A. Wm. Lund, Assistant Church Historian, for his helpful attention to the historical accuracy of this volume. The author is also indebted to Elder Melvin J. Ballard and Elder Charles A. Callis for their reading of the manuscript.

June 5, 1937.   R. L. E.

Contents

APPENDIX

ILLUSTRATIONS

(Illustrations are opposite the pages indicated)

Frontispieces: The River Ribble and The "Cockpit";
Preston Market Place, 16; Vauxhall Chapel, 17; 42 Islington,
Liverpool, 80; Arthur's Seat, Edinburgh, 81; The Pierhead,
Liverpool, 96; Durham House, Liverpool, 97; "That Pool of
Water", 112; 23 Booth Street, Birmingham and 43 Tavi-
stock Square, London, 113; No. 10 Holly Road, Liverpool
and No. 5 Gordon Square, London, 128; Loch Brickland, 129;
Deseret, London, 208; Mission Presidents, 1837 to 1864, 209;
Mission Presidents, 1864 to 1906, 224; Mission Presidents,
1906 to 1937, 225.

Introduction

As this book comes from the press, President Heber J. Grant is preparing to leave Salt Lake City for Great Britain to participate in the commemoration of an eventful and fruitful century of activity in the British Mission of the Church of Jesus Christ of Latter-day Saints. And yet, so far as the author is aware, this is the first volume to be published on the story of the British Mission during the entire one hundred years of "Mormon" activity in the United Kingdom. It is earnestly to be hoped that it will not be the last. The contributions of British subjects to the Church and of the Church to British subjects are too numerous and notable to deserve obscurity. A century of "Mormonism" in Great Britain has given many lessons worth knowing and many stories worth telling, and he who contributes further to bringing them to light is serving the perpetuation of worthy tradition and mighty accomplishment.

No writer will ever exhaust the story of the British Mission. Ninety-nine volumes of the *Millennial Star,* averaging more than eight hundred pages each, have fallen far short of telling the complete story, and the voluminous Journal History in the Church Historian's Office leaves much to be recorded and much that is forever lost, so far as perishable and incomplete man-made records are concerned. But even such sources as are available may never be completely sounded by any searcher. Realizing the inexhaustible nature of the task, no attempt has been made in this brief volume to record statistical or chronological detail to any extensive degree. Rather, emphasis has been placed on "beginnings," and after the "beginnings" have been chronicled, the closing pages of the book have been devoted to broad, long-range generalizations and interpretations.

That this Church should preach the Gospel to "every nation, kindred, tongue and people" was a matter of divine injunction, and the most logical starting point, outside the confines of continental America, where the restoration occurred, was Great Britain, the mother country of the world's greatest empire. The contributions of the Church to the British Mission and of the British Mission to the Church have been mutual, and by no means one-sided. A few of those contributions are herein noted and summarized.

The story of "Mormon" activity in Great Britain is almost as old as the story of the restoration itself, and the results of the labors in this field have been vital beyond power of estimation to the welfare and growth of the Church. Nearly six thousand missionaries have been sent by the Church to Great Britain. More than one hundred and twenty-six thousand loyal British subjects have joined the Church, of whom more than fifty-two thousand have emigrated to be closer to its headquarters. A century of such interchange of thought, culture, ideals, principles and man power has been productive of inestimable consequences which deserve a more exhaustive consideration, and which, it is to be hoped, will be given, as future writers and researchers undertake to investigate and write upon this highly worthy field.

CHAPTER 1

WHEN THE GOSPEL CAME TO BRITAIN

The story of the British Mission is an intense human drama of a century's duration. Great characters have played leading roles in its development. Tens of thousands of human lives have been touched, affected, uplifted. The goodness and power of God have been manifest; the sick have been healed; the needy have received their needs; the sorrowing have been comforted; the wayward have been caused to return to paths of righteousness; the troubled and tormented have been given peace; truth-seekers—wanderers on uncertain roads—have found shelter from the storms of life, and soul-satisfying joy.

From the British Isles has ever come stalwart stock —defenders of the faith, carriers of the glad message— men and women who have had the courage of their convictions, and whose convictions have been born of a testimony of truth. They and their children have largely supplied the rank and file of the Church and the majority of its leaders.

Persecution has cast its shadow over the British Mission. The "Mormons" have been perennial subjects of attack by the spoken and written word. Mobbings have occurred; violence has been used. Traveling missionaries and resident members have been shunned, ridiculed, maltreated; but the sustaining hand of the Lord has ever been there to strengthen and bless the faithful.

Achievement and disappointment have entered, retired and reappeared; but steady progress has been certain and unceasing. Tragedy and comedy, with all of life's intermediate experiences, have taken place, as the action has proceeded. The situations have been real, vital, thrilling. Few stories have equal possibilities for human appeal. The story of the British Mission is a story of courageous lives, of strong convictions, of fearless action.

It would be pleasing to record that all was well with the Church when the Gospel first came to Britain in 1837, but history deals with stern realities, and such was not the case.

A financial panic swept over the United States in 1837. Reckless speculation, loose banking and inordinate expansion of paper currency had been in course for two or three years. The crash came soon after Mr. Van Buren became President of the United States in March, 1837. Distress was nationwide. A veritable avalanche of petitions for relief swept into the White House. Financial institutions throughout the country were forced to close their doors. Failures in the city of New York alone during the months of March and April amounted to more than one hundred million dollars. The Church and its members, with the whole nation, were unavoidably drawn into this financial catastrophe, and grievous troubles followed.

At this time Church headquarters were in Kirtland, Ohio. Previously, to render financial aid and facility there, the Prophet and his associates decided to organize a Kirtland Safety Society Bank, for which articles of agreement were prepared in November, 1836. Through prejudice, the State of Ohio refused to grant a bank charter, so in January, 1837, the undertaking was launched merely as the Kirtland Safety Society, complying with all the requisite laws for such an institution. Church leaders and other members subscribed for stock, and the business became operative.

The repeated warnings of the Prophet were not generally heeded, and he, therefore, disposed of his holdings and withdrew from the Society in the late spring, at which time he stated that after five months' experience he was satisfied that "no institution of the kind, established upon just and righteous principles for the blessing, not only to the Church but to the whole nation, would be suffered to continue its operations in such an age of darkness and speculation and wickedness."

Then the cashier, a former trusted clerk of the Prophet, became disaffected because of transgression, and misappropriated over twenty thousand dollars— which he later confessed. Although the stockholders pledged redemption of all outstanding liabilities, the Society was forced to discontinue business, with many others throughout the nation.

Besides this widespread financial disaster, other causes contributed to the distress of the Church at this time. Obligations, with extreme sacrifice, had been incurred during the construction of the Kirtland Temple. The Saints were being persecuted and driven from their homes in other parts of the country, and were moving in poverty to Kirtland for relief. At considerable expense large tracts of land were obtained for their accommodation. Disaffection was contagious; apostasy

was widespread. It was a day of testing for the souls
of men, and only the pure in heart survived. Amid
these grievous scenes the Prophet wrote:

"At this time the spirit of speculation in lands and property of all kinds, which was so prevalent throughout the
whole nation, was taking deep root in the Church. As the
fruits of this spirit, evil-surmising, fault-finding, disunion,
dissension, and apostasy followed in quick succession, and it
seems as though all the powers of earth and hell were com-
bining their influence in an especial manner to overthrow the
Church at once, and make a final end. Other banking institutions refused the Kirtland Safety Society's notes. The
enemy abroad, and apostates in our midst, united in their
schemes; flour and provisions were turned towards other
markets, and many became disaffected toward me, as though
I were the sole cause of those very evils I was most strenuously striving against, and which were actually brought upon
us by the brethren not giving heed to my counsel.

"No quorum in the Church was entirely exempt from the
influence of those false spirits who are striving against me
for the mastery; even some of the Twelve were so far lost
to their high and responsible calling as to begin to take sides,
secretly, with the enemy."—*History of the Church*, Vol. II,
pp. 487-8.

So much by way of introduction, to tie up the
story of the British Mission with the happenings in
Kirtland, and to give insight into the spirit of the times.
The Prophet continues:

"In this state of things, and but a few weeks before the
Twelve were expecting to meet in full quorum (some of
them having been absent for some time), God revealed to me
that something new must be done for the salvation of His
Church. And on or about the 1st of June, 1837, Heber C.
Kimball, one of the Twelve, was set apart by the spirit of
prophecy and revelation, prayer and laying on of hands, of
the First Presidency, to preside over a mission to England,
to be the first foreign mission of the Church of Christ in the
last days. While we were ordaining him, Orson Hyde,
another of the Twelve, came in, and upon listening to what

was passing, his heart melted within him (for he had begun to drink of the cup filled with the overflowings of speculation); he acknowledged all of his faults, asked forgiveness, and offered to accompany President Kimball on his mission to England. His offer was accepted, and he was set apart for that purpose."—*History of the Church,* Vol. II, p. 489.

Heber C. Kimball, be it remembered, was of hardy New England stock, a native son of Vermont, and a potter by trade, who, with Brigham Young, heard and accepted the Gospel at Mendon, New York, and subsequently sold all his possessions and moved to the body of the Church to be near the Prophet, where he devoted most of his time to the service of the Church in traveling throughout the states, preaching, and in doing other important labor. He engaged in his trade as opportunity afforded, for the support of himself and family. At the time the mission call to Great Britain came to him he was in his thirty-sixth year—a vigorous and able minister of the Gospel of Jesus Christ. He had been ordained to the Apostleship two years previous.

Elder Orson Hyde was also New England born, and had been an Apostle for two years when he accepted the British Mission call as a young man of thirty-two. He, too, had served the Church well on former missions, and possessed outstanding abilities.

The feelings of Heber C. Kimball, when he was called to this stupendous task, are well described in his own words, and those of his biographer, Elder Orson F. Whitney, as follows:

" 'On Sunday, the 4th day of June, 1837, the Prophet Joseph came to me, while I was seated in front of the stand, above the Sacrament table, on the Melchizedek side of the Temple in Kirtland, and whispering to me said: "Brother Heber, the Spirit of the Lord has whispered to me: Let my

servant Heber go to England and proclaim my Gospel, and
open the door of salvation to that nation."

"The thought was overpowering. He had been surprised
at his call to the Apostleship; now he was overwhelmed.
Like Jeremiah he staggered under the weight of his own
weakness, exclaiming in self-humiliation: 'O Lord, I am a
man of stammering tongue, and altogether unfit for such
a work; how can I go to preach in that land, which is so
famed throughout Christendom for learning, knowledge and
piety; the nursery of religion; and to a people whose intelligence is proverbial!'

" 'Feeling my weakness to go upon such an errand, I
asked the Prophet if Brother Brigham might go with me. He
replied that he wanted Brother Brigham to stay with him,
for he had something else for him to do. The idea of such a
mission was almost more than I could bear up under. I was
almost ready to sink under the burden which was placed upon
me.

" 'However, all these considerations did not deter me
from the path of duty; the moment I understood the will of
my Heavenly Father, I felt a determination to go at all
hazards, believing that He would support me by His almighty
power, and endow me with every qualification that I needed;
and although my family was dear to me, and I should have
to leave them almost destitute, I felt that the cause of truth,
the Gospel of Jesus Christ, outweighed every other consideration.' "—Whitney's *Life of Heber C. Kimball*, p. 116.

Dr. Willard Richards, also one of New England's
stalwart sons, then in his thirty-third year, had joined
the Church six months before, and shortly after had
been promised by Heber C. Kimball that he should
accompany the Twelve, or those who should go, on
their first mission to Europe, which Elder Kimball had
prophesied would come. Elder Richards had returned
from the Eastern States, where he had been on a business mission for the Church, the day before the departure for Britain, and was set apart to go on the
mission.

The other member of the party from Kirtland was Joseph Fielding, a native of England, born in Bedfordshire in 1797, who emigrated to Canada in 1832 and four years later became a convert to "Mormonism" as a result of the Canadian labors of Parley P. Pratt. Joseph Fielding then moved to Kirtland, soon to return to his native land with the first missionary party, to bear witness of the Gospel restoration to his kinsmen and friends. Through his brother, the Reverend James Fielding of Preston, Lancashire, the first chapel in England in which the Gospel was preached was later opened—and closed.

There was much interest in Canada in the British Mission undertaking. Many, like Joseph Fielding, had left friends and loved ones in the mother country, to better their opportunities in a new land, and had there heard and accepted the Gospel. Like all who are possessed of the true Christ-like spirit, it was their desire to pass on to others this true plan of life that had brought such joy and comfort into their own lives. Many letters bearing Gospel tidings had crossed the sea. Many in England were informed of Gospel truths and of the progress of the Church, and were awaiting with expectancy the coming of authorized servants of the Lord Jesus Christ, who could expound the scriptures with the enlightenment of the Holy Spirit, and perform required ordinances of the Gospel in the name of God. Thus the way for the coming of the Gospel to Great Britain was made easier by the labors of the missionaries in Canada.

Doubtless this Canadian interest was an added argument in favor of opening the mission to Britain at this time; and without doubt affairs in Kirtland brought pressure to bear upon the undertaking; but the fundamental reason does not lie in either of these causes. For seven years the public ministry of the Church had been conducted in America. The time was ripe for the Gospel to go forth to the other nations of the earth. The Lord had so spoken. The particular charge of the Church is to preach the Gospel of Jesus Christ to all the world; and Great Britain, rightly, was designated to be the first benefactor. It was an age when religious feeling ran deep; it was a day when thousands of truth-hungry men and women were waiting and praying that their souls might be fed, as later events testify. The petitions that were sent to heaven were many, and earnest and fervent, from both sides of the water; and the Lord opened up the way for the granting of those petitions.

The day decided upon for the departure from Kirtland, June 13th, 1837, quickly arrived. The Kirtland party of four—Elders Heber C. Kimball, Orson Hyde, and Willard Richards, and Priest Joseph Fielding—were to travel to New York City by way of Buffalo, where they were to meet three missionaries from Canada—Brothers John Goodson, Isaac Russell, and John Snyder—who had been chosen to join the mission, and who were anxious to bear witness to friends and relatives on the other side of the water.

In this day of rapid communication and luxurious travel it is hard to understand the departing feelings of those who undertook such a journey in that day of uncertainty. Had the Prophet let his human desires prevail, he would in all probability have chosen to have these faithful brethren remain. They were leaving well-loved families in uncertain circumstances without visible means of support, and with only remote hopes for a distant reunion. They were leaving homes for a life

PRESTON MARKET PLACE AND OBELISK

From a drawing by John Ferguson. 1844

Here the first "Mormon" missionaries to Great Britain held their outdoor meetings (p. 29).

From a drawing by G. H. Lugsdin, London.

VAUXHALL CHAPEL, PRESTON, LANCASHIRE
In which the first public discourse was preached by the first
"Mormon" missionaries in Great Britain, (pp. 24-26).

of wandering; friends for strangers; the known for the unknown. And to what purpose? The Lord had spoken! That was purpose enough for those men of courage—mighty among men, but humble and weak before God. They were departing upon one of the greatest missionary journeys of all time, to introduce the Gospel, restored anew, into one of the greatest nations of all history. A stupendous task for mere men—but the Lord was with them, and, in their faith and devotion, it never occurred to them to question that He had chosen such a troublous time for this undertaking, nor to doubt the wisdom of the task that had come to them through the Prophet.

The parting of Heber C. Kimball from his family is thus feelingly described by Elder Robert B. Thompson:

"The day appointed for the departure of the Elders to England having arrived, I stepped into the house of Brother Kimball to ascertain when he would start, as I expected to accompany him two or three hundred miles, intending to spend my labors in Canada that season.

"The door being partly open, I entered and felt struck with the sight which presented itself to my view. I would have retired, thinking that I was intruding, but I felt riveted to the spot. The father was pouring out his soul to that 'God who rules on high . . .' that He would grant him a prosperous voyage across the mighty ocean, and make him useful wherever his lot should be cast, and that He who careth for sparrows, and feedeth the young ravens when they cry, would supply the wants of his wife and little ones in his absence.

"He, then, like the patriarchs, and by virtue of his office, laid his hands upon their heads individually, leaving a father's blessing upon them, and commending them to the care and protection of God, while he should be engaged in preaching the Gospel in a foreign land. While thus engaged his voice was almost lost in the sobs of those around, who tried in vain to suppress them. The idea of being separated from

their protector and father for so long a time was indeed
painful. He proceeded, but his heart was too much affected
to do so regularly. His emotions were great, and he was
obliged to stop at intervals, while the big tears rolled down
his cheeks—an index to the feelings which reigned in his
bosom. My heart was not stout enough to refrain; in spite
of myself I wept, and mingled my tears with theirs. At
the same time I felt thankful that I had the privilege of
contemplating such a scene. I realized that nothing could
induce that man to tear himself from so affectionate a family
group, from his partner and children who were so dear to
him—nothing but a sense of duty and love to God and an
attachment to His cause."—Whitney's *Life of Heber C.
Kimball,* pp. 120, 121.

The missionaries had little money. Mary Fielding
gave Heber C. Kimball five dollars with which he paid
his own fare and that of Orson Hyde on the Lake
Erie boat for Buffalo. The Canadian brethren did not
meet them there as prearranged, but joined the party
in New York, which made seven in all. On the way,
Heber C. Kimball and Willard Richards departed from
their companions to call at the home of Elder Richards'
father, where his brother paid him a forty-dollar debt,
which enabled them to continue their journey to New
York, where they arrived on June 22nd.

A good vessel bound for Liverpool was sailing on
the following day, but they did not have sufficient
funds among them to pay for passage and procure the
necessary outfit, which in those days usually included
both bedding and food. Elder Elijah Fordham was the
only member of the Church known to be living in the
great city of New York at that time. He met them,
but having no home of his own, took them to the home
of his sister-in-law, where they did not stay because
of expenses; "and so," says Heber C. Kimball, "we
hired a small room in an unfinished storehouse of
Brother Fordham's father, who was very wealthy, as he

owned many storehouses and buildings, but never invited us into his house to sleep or eat, though he did
invite us to assist him two days in raising a building, as
a compensation for lying on his storehouse floor."

On the 23rd of June the party booked passage
on the *Garrick,* which was to sail on July 1st.   On
Sunday, June 25th, Elder Kimball records:

"We fasted, prayed, administered the Sacrament, held
council for the success of the mission, and had a joyful
time.   In the afternoon two sectarian priests came in, to find
fault, but they were soon confounded and left.

On the 28th we deposited one hundred eighty of Orson
Hyde's *Timely Warnings* in the New York post office,
addressed to the priests and ministers of different denominations in that city. We also distributed many to the citizens,
and at the same time conversed with them on the subject of
the Gospel."—Whitney's *Life of Heber C. Kimball,* p. 123.

At ten o'clock on the morning of July 1st, 1837, the
Garrick, a nine-hundred ton sailing vessel, weighed
anchor.   It was with intermingled feelings of regret and
joy that the brethren saw their homeland sink beyond
the horizon.

Those early missionaries did not wait until they
reached their destination before they began to deliver
their message.   They were ministers of the Gospel
of Jesus Christ, and as such, the world was their field,
and every son and daughter of God their particular
charge.

A sick child on board, whom the ship's doctor had
given up to die, gave Elder Kimball opportunity to
preach the healing power of God to its parents.   They
had prepared to consign their little one to a watery
grave, and were vitally interested. Secretly, Elder
Kimball blessed the child and rebuked the disease that
was preying upon it—this in the name of the Lord

Jesus Christ. From that time on it began to improve, and in three days was playing about the ship in good health. Elder Kimball told the parents what he had done, and they acknowledged the hand of God in the recovery.

On the last Sunday out, July 16th, Brother Kimball sought permission from the captain for one of the brethren to preach on board. It was readily granted, and a meeting was called for the afternoon on the aft quarter deck. Elder Hyde was the speaker, and chose the resurrection for his theme. He spoke eloquently, powerfully and sincerely, to a congregation of between two and three hundred persons, who listened with deep interest to truths that were strange, yet not foreign to their understanding. Witness a picture long to be remembered—mid ocean; the sea and the sky; a frail craft with sails full spread; weather-beaten seamen and seasoned passengers—both Christian and Jew—of English, Irish, Scotch, French, German and other nationalities, all listening to an Apostle of the Lord Jesus Christ—a special witness—declaring truths that feed the hungering souls of men—truths that the Master declared, but that the world has undervalued and lost. Men of many nations heard convincing testimony that day. A committee was appointed by the congregation to return thanks to the missionaries for their service.

The passage had been favorable. The coast of Ireland was sighted on the 18th, and at daybreak on the 20th the *Garrick* anchored in the River Mersey opposite Liverpool, twenty days out of the harbor at New York. The *South America*, another packet ship that had left New York at the same time, arrived a few lengths behind, thereby losing a wager of ten thousand dollars that had been made between the operators of the ships on the day of starting.   Elder Kimball recorded:

"When we first sighted Liverpool I went to the side of the vessel and poured out my soul in praise and thanksgiving to God for the prosperous voyage and for all the mercies which He had vouchsafed to me, and while thus engaged, and contemplating the scene presented to my view, the Spirit of the Lord rested down upon me in a powerful manner, and my soul was filled with love and gratitude. I felt humble, while I covenanted to dedicate myself to God, and to love and serve Him with all my heart.

"Immediately after we anchored, a small boat came alongside, when several of the passengers, with Brothers Hyde, Richards, Goodson and myself, got in and went to shore. When we were within six or seven feet of the pier, I leaped on shore, followed by Elders Hyde and Richards, and for the first time in my life I stood on British ground, among strangers, whose manners and customs were different from my own. My feelings at that time were peculiar, particularly when I realized the importance and extent of my mission—the work to which I had been appointed and in which I was shortly to be engaged. However, I put my trust in God, believing that He would assist me in publishing the truth, give me utterance, and be a present help in time of need."—Whitney's *Life of Heber C. Kimball*, pp. 130-131.

Such, in brief, are the conditions under which the restored Gospel of Jesus Christ first made its entrance upon British shores in modern times. Such is the manner in which the prophetic world-wide mission of the Church of Jesus Christ of Latter-day Saints first began its reach beyond the shores of continental America.

CHAPTER 2

TRUTH PROCLAIMED IN VAUXHALL CHAPEL

Humility is a virtue that well becomes servants of the Lord. Humility and a message of truth were virtually the entire stock-in-trade of Heber C. Kimball and his associates when they arrived in the port of Liverpool on July 20th, 1837. Brother Heber, Brother Orson Hyde and Brother Willard Richards were penniless. The means of the other four members of the party were very limited.

They were strangers in a strange land, upon their own resources, separated from home aid and home news by a month's travel, with no precedent to follow, no headquarters in Britain to communicate with, no human source of advice or direction. The work was before them. The task loomed mountain-high—everything to do, no trails broken, no paths beaten. With these prospects, if they may be termed such, the brethren walked the streets of Liverpool—and only the poor and downcast may know how depressing the streets of Liverpool may be. Says Elder Kimball of this time:

"Elders Hyde, Richards, and myself, being without purse or scrip, wandered in the streets of Liverpool, where wealth and luxury abound side by side with penury and want. I there met the rich attired in the most costly dresses, and the next minute was saluted with the cries of the poor, with scarce covering sufficient to screen them from the weather. Such a wide distinction I never saw before. Looking for a place to lodge in, we found a room belonging to a widow in Union Street, which we engaged for a few days."
—Whitney's *Life of Heber C. Kimball,* p. 131.

Under such conditions, depression of spirit is un-derstandable. Under such conditions God-fearing men are led to turn unrestrainedly towards the God of heaven, the only Friend who is always approachable, who always gives comfort, who always aids and coun-sels. And to this all-wise heavenly Friend the brethren turned at this time as the bar of highest and last appeal.

During the brief time spent in Liverpool, council meetings were held, during which hearts were opened, souls were unburdened, and the Lord was earnestly sought, for direction and for success. The appeals of the brethren were not unheeded. They felt the spirit and power of God with them; they were encouraged and lifted from a passing shadow of doubt and gloom. Al-though of themselves they continued to feel as weak in-struments, they did not discount that they were on the business of the Master, and that as His commissioned servants they were entitled to comfort, protection, sup-port and guidance. These they received. The answer came: Go to Preston.

Preston, Lancashire, England, a manufacturing town on the River Ribble and about thirty miles in a northerly direction from Liverpool, was now their des-tination. On Saturday, July 22nd, they took coach from Liverpool and arrived at their journey's end about four o'clock in the afternoon.

It was election day in Preston. Queen Victoria had ascended the throne but a short time before their arrival in Britain, and had called for a general election of members of Parliament. The town was at its gayest. Bands were playing; flags were flying; men, women and children were parading and frolicking; streets were be-decked with varicolored streamers and ribbons, bearing mottoes and catch-phrases such as one would expect to

see on occasions of great political movements. Sup-
porters of candidates apparently had left nothing un-
done that could reasonably have added to the day's
festivities.

Just as the coach carrying the missionaries reached
its destination, a large banner was unfurled almost
above their heads. In bold gilt letters it bore the inscription: *"Truth Will Prevail."* With joy in their hearts
the stalwart messengers of truth caught the spirit of
the favorable omen, and cried aloud: "Amen! Thanks
be to God! Truth *will* prevail!"

With the exception of Joseph Fielding the brethren
took lodgings in Wilfred Street at the home of a widow.
Joseph Fielding went in search of his brother, the Reverend James Fielding, pastor of a vigorous congregation
and modest chapel in Preston. Joseph was received
kindly, joyfully, and accepted an invitation for other
members of the party to call at the home that evening.
Elders Kimball, Hyde and John Goodson, with Joseph
Fielding, filled the appointment. Besides the Reverend
Mr. Fielding, they were met by his brother-in-law,
Mr. Watson, also a minister, who lived in Bedford.
The evening was not of the chatty, gossipy variety
that is sometimes indulged in while more important
matters wait. The time was spent in serious and earnest
discussion of the Gospel of Jesus Christ and its restoration, and the small gathering did not break up until
well into the night. There some deep impressions were
made.

The next morning Mrs. Watson—Mr. Fielding's
sister—sent each of the brethren a half crown; and,
it being the Sabbath, they received and gladly accepted
an invitation from Mr. Fielding to hear him address
his own congregation in Vauxhall Chapel at the morning service.

Mr. Fielding had been informed by letter of the restoration of the Gospel, of the progress of the Church in America, and of the newly-restored doctrines, taught by the Master, but not generally accepted by religionists. He had likewise been informed, and had advised his congregation, of the coming of the missionaries from America. He had assured his flock that they could place unrestrained confidence in the statements of his brother, Joseph Fielding, concerning the Church. Many of his following, particularly the more earnest and devout, had been praying for the coming of the message and messengers of light and new hope. They were prepared and expectant.

Of the first service attended in Vauxhall Chapel Heber C. Kimball says: "We sat before him, praying to the Lord to open up the way for us to preach."

The prayer was answered. Without any request for the privilege having been made, of his own accord, at the close of his service, Mr. Fielding announced that an Elder of the Latter-day Saints would preach in Vauxhall Chapel at three o'clock that afternoon. An unusually large congregation assembled at the given hour. As first speaker, Elder Kimball describes this initial public meeting in Great Britain:

"I declared that an angel had visited the earth, and committed the everlasting Gospel to man; called their attention to the first principles of the Gospel, and gave them a brief history of the work which the Lord had commenced on the earth; after which Elder Hyde bore testimony to the same, which was received by many with whom I afterwards conversed; they cried "Glory to God!" and rejoiced that the Lord had sent His servants unto them. Thus was the key turned and the Gospel dispensation opened on the first Sabbath after landing in England."—Whitney's *Life of Heber C. Kimball*, p. 137.

A place of worship had been opened; truth had been proclaimed from the pulpit; a large congregation had listened and had been impressed. The work was actually under way. But a few days before in Liverpool this progress would have seemed incredible. But all things are possible with God, and mighty works can be accomplished by His servants.

The labors of the first meeting bore fruit. Invitations were given and accepted to preach from the same pulpit at the Sunday evening service, and on the following Wednesday evening. On Sunday evening Elder Goodson spoke and Joseph Fielding bore testimony. On Wednesday Elder Hyde spoke and Elder Richards bore testimony. On both occasions audiences overfilled Vauxhall Chapel. Many were convinced, and rejoiced. As the Reverend James Fielding later said—when he was less friendly: "Kimball bored the holes; Goodson drove the nails, and Hyde clinched them." But the Lord was directing, and the honest in heart never knowingly turn their faces from truth.

and notwithstanding his former kindness he soon became one of our most violent opposers.

"However, his congregation did not follow his example, they having some time been praying for our coming, and having been assured by Mr. Fielding that he could not place more confidence in an angel than he did in the statements of his brother Joseph, respecting this people. Consequently they were in a great measure prepared for the reception of the Gospel, probably as much so as Cornelius was anciently.

"Having now no public place to preach in, we began to preach at night in private houses, which were opened in every direction, when numbers came to hear and believed the Gospel."—Whitney's *Life of Heber C. Kimball,* pp. 141-143.

When the time for the first baptism was set, the powers of evil marshalled their forces together in a determined effort against the lives and plans of the missionaries. Elder Kimball continues:

"Saturday evening it was agreed that I should go forward and baptize the next morning in the River Ribble, which runs through Preston.

"By this time the adversary of souls began to rage, and he felt determined to destroy us before we had fully established the kingdom of God in that land, and the next morning I witnessed a scene of satanic power and influence which I shall never forget.

"Sunday, July 30th, about daybreak, Elder Isaac Russell (who had been appointed to preach on the Obelisk in Preston Square that day) who slept with Elder Richards in Wilfred Street, came up to the third story, where Elder Hyde and myself were sleeping, and called out: 'Brother Kimball, I want you should get up and pray for me that I may be delivered from the evil spirits that are tormenting me to such a degree that I feel I cannot live long, unless I obtain relief.'

"I had been sleeping on the back of the bed. I immediately arose, slipped off at the foot of the bed, and passed around to where he was. Elder Hyde threw his feet out, and sat up in the bed, and we laid hands on him, I being mouth, and prayed that the Lord would have mercy on him, and rebuked the devil.

"While thus engaged, I was struck with great force by some invisible power, and fell senseless on the floor. The first thing I recollected was being supported by Elders Hyde and Richards, who were praying for me; Elder Richards having followed Russell up to my room. Elders Hyde and Richards then assisted me to get on the bed, but my agony was so great I could not endure it, and I arose, bowed my knees and prayed. I then arose and sat up on the bed, when a vision was opened to our minds, and we could distinctly see the evil spirits, who foamed and gnashed their teeth at us. We gazed upon them about an hour and a half (by Willard's watch). We were not looking towards the window, but towards the wall. Space appeared before us, and we saw the devils coming in legions, with their leaders, who came within a few feet of us. They came toward us like armies rushing to battle. They appeared to be men of full stature, possessing every form and feature of men in the flesh, who were angry and desperate; and I shall never forget the vindictive malignity depicted on their countenances as they looked me in the eye; and any attempt to paint the scene which then presented itself, or portray their malice and enmity, would be vain. I perspired exceedingly, my clothes becoming as wet as if I had been taken out of the river. I felt excessive pain, and was in great distress for some time. I cannot even now look back on the scene without feelings of horror; yet by it I learned the power of the adversary, his enmity against the servants of God, and got some understanding of the invisible world. We distinctly heard those spirits talk and express their wrath and hellish designs against us. However, the Lord delivered us from them, and blessed us exceedingly that day."—Whitney's *Life of Heber C. Kimball,* pp. 143-145.

In seeking an explanation of this manifestation some years later from the Prophet Joseph Smith, Heber C. Kimball received this axiom of truth:

"The nearer a person approaches the Lord, a greater power will be manifested by the adversary to prevent the accomplishment of his purposes."—Whitney's *Life of Heber C. Kimball,* p. 146.

Therein lies at least partial explanation for the

bitter opposition to the Church and people of God in
this dispensation and in former times.

Reverend James Fielding had taken his stand, and
from then on let it be said of him that at least he was
consistent—consistent in opposition. When he learned
that the missionaries meant to go forward with the
baptismal service, in anger he went to the lodge of the
brethren and forbade Elder Kimball to carry out his
plans. Said the latter:

"They are of age, and can act for themselves; I shall
baptize all who come unto me, asking no favors of any man."
—Whitney's *Life of Heber C. Kimball*, p. 147.

This terse reply left no doubt in the reverend gentleman's mind as to the effect of his unauthoritative
injunction upon the actions of the missionaries. In the
above reply are embodied the principles of religious
freedom and worship according to the dictates of conscience, as also the doctrine of man's inalienable right
to free agency, which is fundamental and which is God-
given—the very cornerstone of the plan of salvation.
There is no predestination—no superimposed divine
will upon the actions of men; neither is it right or just
that one man should hedge about the freedom of another
in matters that pertain only to him and the Lord. This,
and more, was all implied in the brief retort that an
Apostle of the Lord gave to a minister of the world
who commanded that God's will should not be done.

The baptism proceeded as planned. Speaking of
the services, Elder Kimball records:

"Notwithstanding the weakness of my body from the
shock I had experienced, I had the pleasure, about 9 a. m.,
of baptizing nine individuals and hailing them brethren and
sisters in the kingdom of God. These were the first persons

baptized into the Church in a foreign land, and only the eighth day after our arrival in Preston.

"A circumstance took place which I cannot refrain from mentioning, for it will show the eagerness and anxiety of some in that land to obey the Gospel. Two of the male candidates, when they had changed their clothes at a distance of several rods from the place where I was standing in the water, were so anxious to obey the Gospel that they ran with all their might to the water, each wishing to be baptized first. The younger, George D. Watt, being quicker of foot than the elder, outran him, and came first into the water.

"The circumstance of baptizing in the open air being somewhat novel, a concourse of between seven and nine thousand persons assembled on the banks of the river to witness the ceremony. It was the first time baptism by immersion was administered openly, as the Baptists in that country generally have a font in their chapels, and perform the ordinance privately."—Whitney's *Life of Heber C. Kimball*, p. 149.

The River Ribble rises well to the north in West Riding, flows by factories and fields, picturesquely, through Preston, Lancashire, and shortly opens into a long river-mouth off the Irish sea. The traveler by its banks today may well imagine that most unusual and inspiring sight, when commissioned servants of the Lord baptised by immersion, as the Lord prescribed, the first European converts of this dispensation—this, as thousands of spectators thronged the banks of the river on that memorable Sunday morning.

The names of the nine—the first fruits of British labors—follow: George D. Watt, Brother Charles Miller, Thomas Walmesley, Ann Elizabeth Walmesley, Miles Hogden, George Wate, Henry Billsbury, Mary Ann Brown and Ann Dawson.

Ann Elizabeth Walmesley, wife of Thomas Walmesley, was a consumptive invalid, and had been given up by the doctors to die. She was promised that if she would believe, repent and be baptized, she

A nucleus had been formed to which other truth-seekers would gather. It was now thought expedient to branch out into other parts. With this purpose in view the missionaries assembled on the day following the baptism. They remained together, fasting, praying, and rendering thanks to God for His many mercies, until two o'clock on the following morning. At this meeting Brothers Willard Richards and John Goodson were appointed to labor in the city of Bedford. Brothers Isaac Russell and John Snyder were assigned to the region of Alston, in Cumberland. It was agreed that Orson Hyde, Heber C. Kimball and Joseph Fielding should remain in the vicinity of Preston for a time. Those who were to travel departed for the new fields of labor within a day or two.

The brethren realized their chief duty—to carry Gospel tidings to those who were in ignorance of the restoration. It was not their custom to remain longer in any field than was necessary. Granted, to do so would have been the easiest course. Where friends are, and where ties have already been made, is always the inviting place; but personal comfort was not their concern; they were vigorous, alert—seeking new friends, new methods, new opportunities for delivering their message. They used the means and conveniences of their day to advantage. Branches, districts, and even missions, were entrusted largely to the care of the resident members, while the traveling ministry was left free to carry on active campaigns in untouched territory. Their success in part is thus accounted for.

As would be expected, however, they were frequent visitors at the homes of those who had embraced the Gospel. Conversions often had their beginnings at these visits—friends and relatives would meet the missionaries, hear of the latter-day work, and investigate further.   One case of this kind is here related:

As a visitor at the home of Brother Thomas Walmesley, one of the first to be baptized in Preston, Heber C. Kimball met Miss Jennetta Richards, a friend of the Walmesley family and a daughter of an independent order minister of Walkerfold, a village about fifteen miles from Preston.   The subject of the conversation turned, as it invariably did in the presence of these brethren when there were any willing to listen, to the restored Gospel of Jesus Christ.   Miss Richards was impressed, and attended two small gatherings at which Brother Kimball spoke, on the evening of their meeting and on the following evening.   The next day, August 4th, she applied for baptism.   The ordinance was performed the same day in the River Ribble by Heber C. Kimball, who, assisted by Orson Hyde, also confirmed Miss Jennetta Richards at the water's edge.   This was the first confirmation in the British Isles in this dispensation of the Gospel.

When the time for her return home arrived, Miss Richards had some misgivings as to the effect the tidings —to her, joyful and glorious—would have upon her father.   Speaking in the spirit of prophecy, as it was frequently given him to do, Elder Kimball assured her that her father would not only receive her kindly, but would open up his chapel and request him, Elder Kimball, to preach in it.   This shortly occurred.

At this time the services of the brethren were sought for in many quarters.   They filled appointments to preach nearly every night and frequently during the day.   At times they were under the necessity, so crowded were they, of declining invitations to speak before gatherings. Because of their strenuous labors and irregular habits of living, their health was not the best, but they continued diligent and met with success.

Often they held forth at the Obelisk, Preston Square, where they were always assured a large gathering. At this place, on Sunday, August 6th, a clergyman, an advocate of infant baptism, began to oppose them and their doctrines. The audience would not let him be heard until Elder Hyde intervened, assuring them that he was prepared to meet all arguments, and asking their permission for the reverend gentleman to express his views. When the clergyman had stated his objections, Elder Hyde answered them to the satisfaction of his auditors. The general reaction of that gathering toward the interrupter was such that the meeting could not proceed until someone had led the infant baptism advocate out of the crowd.

By this time, which was only the third Sunday in England, many persons had been baptized in Preston, but only one of these had been confirmed. A meeting was called at the home of Sister Ann Dawson, one of the first baptized, with whom the Elders lodged. At this meeting, Sunday, August 6th, between forty and fifty Preston converts were confirmed, and further instructed in their duties, obligations and privileges as members of the Church of Jesus Christ. Here the Preston Branch, the first branch of the Church of Jesus Christ of Latter-day Saints in Great Britain, was organized. The Spirit of the Lord was felt in power and abundance, and all were led to rejoice.

In the early part of the ensuing week, two letters —one from Miss Jennetta Richards and one from her father—arrived. The latter read:

"Mr. H. C. Kimball,
   Sir:
      You are expected to be here next Sunday. You are given out to preach in the forenoon, afternoon and evening. Although we be strangers to one another, yet I hope we are not strangers to our blessed Redeemer, else I would not have given out for you to preach. Our chapel is but small and the congregation few, yet if one soul be converted, it is of more value than the whole world.
      I remain, in haste,
                              JOHN RICHARDS."
—Whitney's *Life of Heber C. Kimball*, p. 154.

To fill this appointment, Heber C. Kimball traveled by coach the next Saturday to Walkerfold, where he arrived towards evening, to be warmly received and hospitably entertained by John Richards and his family. The next morning Elder Kimball went with Mr. Richards to his chapel and preached. He also filled the afternoon and evening appointments, one on Monday evening, and, at the request of the congregation, another on Wednesday evening. At these times many shed tears of joy, and on Thursday, August 17th, six members of Mr. John Richards' flock applied for baptism.

Mr. Richards felt that he must close his chapel to the preaching of Elder Kimball, as a matter of self-preservation; but, unlike the Reverend Fielding, he did not oppose the work, but continued to treat his guest with respect. Following the procedure that had been observed at Preston, Brother Kimball continued preaching, in private houses or wherever there were auditors. Before he left he had baptized most of the younger and more vigorous members of Mr. Richards' congregation. Personally, he felt regard and pity for the old gentleman, but he was not one to let personal affections or feelings stand between him and his duty in proclaiming the Gospel. Had he been, he would never have set out upon his mission to Great Britain. Those of Mr. Richards' flock who answered truth's call, also, did so in spite of personal regard for the tender old man who had for over thirty years ministered to them in love and kindness.

Jennetta Richards was grieved when Mr. John Richards closed his chapel to Elder Kimball, but she was assured by the latter that her father would again open it for him to preach in. This happened two weeks following the first appointment. Heber C. Kimball accompanied John Richards to his chapel in the morning, and that worthy old clergyman gave out an appointment for him to occupy the pulpit in the afternoon and evening, which he gladly did.

On the day following this preaching engagement, August 28th, Heber C. Kimball left for Preston, where the brethren were anxiously awaiting his return, with letters from his home in Kirtland and with news from the other missionaries. Elder John Goodson had returned from Bedford, and reported that he and Willard Richards had already been successful in raising up a branch of nineteen there.

The brethren in Bedford were befriended and aided by a minister, Timothy R. Matthews, a brother-in-law of Joseph Fielding, who invited them to preach in his chapel. This they did on several occasions. Many, including Mr. and Mrs. Matthews, were convinced. Mr. Matthews himself bore testimony to his congregation and invited them to accept baptism at the hands of the Elders. The time was set for his baptism; but before it arrived, contrary to positive counsel, Elder Goodson read to Mr. Matthews and some of his followers the vision of Joseph Smith and Sidney Rigdon

(*Doctrine and Covenants,* Section 76), which these new
friends apparently were not yet prepared to receive.
Mr. Matthews did not appear for baptism at the appointed time and place, but received the ordinance
elsewhere, and soon after denounced the missionaries,
saying that their doctrines were false. He then began
to preach those very doctrines on his own account.

There is a lesson of deep import to be derived from
this unfortunate occurrence. It is one of unnumbered
instances in which evil consequences have followed the
disobeying of counsel by missionaries and others.

Brother Snyder, who had been laboring with
Brother Russell in Cumberland, returned in late summer
and reported that although opposition had been strong,
thirty had been baptized, and others were investigating.

Soon after this Brothers Goodson and Snyder departed for Liverpool, from whence they sailed for
America on about the 1st of October. Urgent business
was the reason given for this action. Elder Goodson
took with him two hundred copies of the *Book of Mormon* and *Doctrine and Covenants,* despite Heber C.
Kimball's request that he leave them, and despite his
offer to pay for them. These, writes Elder Kimball,
he burned soon after he reached Iowa Territory, at
which time he apostatized and left the Church.

An interesting comment on Elder Goodson, written by the Prophet Joseph Smith, appears in the
History of the Church, Vol. 2, p. 498; it may serve
as a clue to his difficulties. Writing of the first landing
of the missionaries at Liverpool on July 20th, 1837, the
Prophet says:

"While the passengers were going on board a steamer,
Elders Kimball, Hyde, Richards and Goodson jumped into
a small boat and were rowed toward shore. When within
leaping distance Elder Kimball sprang from the boat as if im-

pelled by some superior power, and alighted on the steps of
the dock, followed instantly by Elders Hyde and Richards, all
three of whom had not one farthing on earth at their command, while Elder Goodson, *having a heavy purse of silver
in his hand, waited until the vessel touched shore.*

"A heavy purse" has been the undoing of many.
It was so with Judas in the day of the Master. It has
been so countless times before and since that day.
"Heavy purses" do not ordinarily contribute to the best
in human endeavor. Particularly is this true of those
engaged in the service of the Lord.

Three clergymen of this early period may well
bear comment: Mr. Timothy Matthews, of Bedford,
was well educated, and a man of some talent. Formerly
he had been a minister in the established Church of
England, but realizing its inconsistencies and contrary
doctrines, and feeling its lack of authority and vitality,
had separated from that organization and as an independent preacher had raised up a moderately large
congregation.

A similar story may be told of Mr. Fielding. He
had been a clergyman of the Methodist faith, but became dissatisfied, and withdrew from that body for
like reasons. He gathered his own following in Preston.

Another independent reform clergyman, the Reverend Robert Aitken, played a prominent part in the
early labors of the missionaries in Great Britain. He
had vigorously opposed the established Church of England, and, being an eloquent preacher, had been successful in establishing and supporting chapels in Liverpool,
London, Manchester, Preston, Burslem and elsewhere.
The restoration of a church in the latter days in fulfilment of inspired prediction was one of his much-used

themes. He capitalized the idea, and had a numerous following. Many of his members in various places left his order and joined the Church of Jesus Christ of Latter-day Saints.

In a state of deep concern and agitation, caused by the loss of many of his best members, this leader of the Aitkenites, as his followers were called, went to Preston with the avowed purpose of "exposing 'Mormonism' " and discrediting the *Book of Mormon.* Of this action Heber C. Kimball writes:

"He made a very long oration on the subject, was very vehement in his manner, and pounded the *Book of Mormon* on the pulpit many times. He then exhorted the people to pray that the Lord would drive us from their coast; and if the Lord would not hear them in that petition, that He would smite the leaders.

"The next Sunday Elder Hyde and myself went to our meetingroom, read the thirteenth chapter of First Corinthians, and strongly urged upon the people the grace of charity, which is so highly spoken of in that chapter, and made some remarks on the proceedings of the Reverend Robert Aitken, who had abused us and the Book of Mormon so very much. In return for his railing we exhorted the Saints to pray that the Lord would soften his heart and open his eyes that he might see that it was hard to "kick against the pricks." This discourse had a very good effect, and that week we had the pleasure of baptizing fifty into the kingdom of Jesus, a large number of whom were members of Mr. Aitken's church."—Whitney's *Life of Heber C. Kimball,* p. 164.

Mr. Aitken was one of the first—probably the first in Great Britain—to thus "expose 'Mormonism'." Since his day thousands of carping critics, false religionists, pseudo-reformers, hireling lecturers and sensational journalists, by press, by public discourse, and in private conversation, have, with like results, "exposed 'Mormonism'." But still it persists—not only persists, but grows and prospers; and the penetrating searchlight of world scrutiny has not yet "exposed" anything but truth and good works in the "Mormon" Church.

The cry of this unhappy trio of disconcerted clergymen—Mr. Fielding, Mr. Matthews and Mr. Aitken—was this: Our best members have left us. So wrote Mr. Matthews to Mr. Fielding; so bitterly declared Mr. Fielding on more than one occasion; such was the condition that roused the ire of Mr. Aitken. The missionaries made no defense, nor does the Church today. It was true then. It is true today. It was and is as it should be. The choicest of the flock continue to be the harvest of the Church of Jesus Christ of Latter-day Saints.

CHAPTER 5

THE "COCKPIT" AND THE TEMPERANCE MOVEMENT

As soon as their presence and their message were heralded, private houses, small meetingrooms and chapels were thrown open to the first missionaries to Great Britain. Opportunities to preach in such places were thankfully received and utilized to the utmost. Of the first five or six weeks of this procedure Heber C. Kimball writes:

"Calls from all quarters to come and preach were constantly sounding in our ears, and we labored night and day to satisfy the people, who manifested such a desire for the truth as I never saw before. We had to speak in small and very crowded houses, and to large assemblies in the open air. Consequently our lungs were often very sore, and our bodies worn down with fatigue. Sometimes I was guilty of breaking the priestly rules—I pulled off my coat and rolled up my sleeves and went at my duty with my whole soul, like a man reaping and binding wheat, which caused the hireling priests to be very much surprised."—Whitney's *Life of Heber C. Kimball*, p. 169.

Many thousands heard the word at these smaller indoor gatherings, and at the larger outdoor gatherings; scores believed and were baptized. Much effective preaching was done beneath humble roof and open sky; but the brethren realized that there were advantages to be gained by having a large and central meeting place in which services could be held regularly. Such a place was the "Cockpit," Preston, Lancashire. The use of it was obtained, and on the first Sunday in

September, 1837, the members of the Church in Preston began to hold regular meetings in that spacious auditorium.

The acquisition of the "Cockpit" calls forth an interesting story. The building was erected about 1801 by the then Lord Derby, the twelfth earl. It was originally used for the purpose revealed by its name. Its location in Preston was ideal—near Stoneygate, at the bottom of St. John's Place and Greystock's Yard, near the center of town, close to the market place. It was neither the first nor the only building in Preston devoted to a sport once popular and widely patronized but now virtually extinct, but of all such places it was the largest and most famous. It had seating room for approximately eight hundred persons.

The "Cockpit" is now demolished. It fell in, old-timers say, late in the nineteenth century. At the time of the author's last visit there, nearly nine years ago, only a portion of one wall, with a window casing or two, remained standing. The ground upon which it stood was then used for the storing of contractor's tools and equipment, and occasionally to accommodate a small fair or circus.

Of its acquisition and of the building itself, Elder Kimball records:

"We obtained a large and commodious place to preach in, called the 'Cockpit,' which had formerly been used by the people to witness cocks fight and kill one another, and where hundreds of spectators had shouted in honor of the barbarous sport which was once the pride of Britons. And now, instead of the huzzas of the wicked and profane, the Gospel of Christ and the voice of praise and thanksgiving was heard there. The building had also been used for a temperance hall."—*Heber C. Kimball's Journal*, pp. 27 and 28.

"The space for cock-fighting was an area of about twelve or fifteen feet in the center, around which the seats formed a circle, each seat rising about a foot above another, till they reached the walls of the building. When we leased it the area in the center was occupied by the singers, and our pulpit was the place where the judges formerly sat, who awarded the prizes at cock-fights. We had to pay seven shillings per week for the use of it, and two shillings per week for lighting; it being beautifully lit up with gas."— Whitney's *Life of Heber C. Kimball*, p. 166.

"It is situated about twenty rods from the 'Old Church,' probably the oldest in Lancashire. This church has twelve bells which are rung at every service, the noise of which was so great that we were unable to proceed in our services until they had done ringing them.

"Our meeting was once disturbed by some ministers belonging to the Methodist Church; however, we got our place licensed, and two gentlemen, who were constables, proffered their services to keep the peace, and protect us from any further disturbances, which they continued to do as long as we stayed in that land."—*Heber C. Kimball's Journal*, p. 28.

Although the name "Cockpit" was the first given to the building in question, and although that name stayed with it as long as it existed (and still lingers), sheltering cock-fights had ceased to be one of its functions. When "Mormon" missionaries first went to Preston in 1837, it was the official meeting place of the Preston Temperance Society.

A brief digression may be pardonable at this point. An account of early British labors, dated March 24th, 1841, which appeared in the first volume of the *Millennial Star* over the names of Heber C. Kimball, Orson Hyde and Willard Richards, makes the following comment concerning the "Cockpit" and the temperance movement:

"Some years previous, the principles of the Temperance Society (originally established in America) were introduced into England, and Preston was the first town to receive them [the total abstinence pledge]. Among the many interesting and valuable items held forth by the temperance people, it was often remarked by them that temperance was the forerunner of the Gospel, which prophecy proved true, for when the fulness of the Gospel came from America to England, it was first preached in Preston, and through the influence of the Temperance Society the Latter-day Saints procured the use of the Temperance Hall in Preston (a commodious building, originally erected for cock-fighting) for their chapel, and commenced meeting there on the 3rd of September, 1837, and continued until they were ejected through the influence of others, the Temperance Society not having it entirely at their control. Similar favors have been received from several other Temperance Societies in England, for which, the Lord reward them."—*Millennial Star*, Volume I, p. 294.

In his private journal, Heber C. Kimball further states:

"In almost every place we went where there was a Temperance Hall, we could get it to preach in, many believing that we made men temperate faster than they did; for as soon as any obeyed the Gospel they abandoned their excesses in drinking; none of us drank any kind of spirits, porter, small beer, or even wine; neither did we drink tea, coffee, or chocolate."—Whitney's *Life of Heber C. Kimball*, p. 165.

According to authorities the temperance movement in Great Britain did not begin in Preston, but "teetotalism" did begin there; and, what is more remarkable and noteworthy, not only the initial steps of the movement in Britain, but the coinage of the word itself— "teetotal"—occurred in Preston, in the "Cockpit" of which we are speaking, and at the hands of the very society of men through whose influence that commodious assembling place was opened to the first missionaries.

The coinage of the word and the impetus of the movement are said to have come about as follows: Technically there is a distinction between temperance and total abstinence; and, although the two terms are used somewhat synonymously in this day, formerly there were distinct movements upholding the two degrees of abstinence, and there was some quibbling about the merits of each. Mr. Joseph Livesey, then the leader of the Temperance Society in Preston, and an outstanding figure in the temperance movement in Great Britain and in the world, was a pioneer of the total abstinence agitation. Quoting *Chambers Encyclopedia,* 1892 edition:

"In British North America abstinence from all alcoholic beverages was common even under the old form of pledge, and on May 25th, 1832, at St. John, New Brunswick, a society was formed with a constitution expressly committing its members to abstinence from all intoxicating liquors, save as a medicine. It was, however, reserved for the Preston Temperance Society in England to apply such missionary power in the diffusion of the total abstinence principle as to justify for it the supremacy in the advocacy of the new reform. On September 1st, 1832, seven members of the Preston Society allowed Mr. Joseph Livesey to attach their names to a pledge of total abstinence, and in later days it became common to speak of the "seven men of Preston" as having commenced the new crusade."

A year later, in September, 1833, Richard Turner, a reformed drinker and a member of the Preston Temperance Society, better known as "Dicky" Turner, was attending a temperance meeting in the "Cockpit" at which the relative merits of "total abstinence" and the "moderation system" were being discussed. "Dicky" Turner, who is described as a rough, humorous speaker, was a staunch disciple of the "total abstinence" faction, and wishing to express himself in emphatic terms, he exclaimed in broad Lancashire: "I'll have nowt to do wi' this moderation botheration pledge; I'll be reet down out-and-out tee-tee-total for ever and ever!"*

Chamber's Encyclopedia, 1892 edition, Temperance, W. & R. Chambers, Edinburgh.

This brought cheers from the audience and the following comment from Mr. Livesey: "Well done, Dicky! That shall be the name of our new pledge." In his reminiscences, Mr. Livesey assures us that "Dicky" did not stutter, and that if he ever lacked an expressive word, he was nothing loath to coin a new one. Repeating the first letter—"tee-tee"—was his way of emphasis. And "tee-total" it has continued to be.

Four years later, to the month, "Mormon" missionaries were proclaiming the Gospel of Jesus Christ in the same town, in the same building, by courtesy of the same society of men to whom credit is given for giving impetus to the total abstinence movement. Extending this privilege to the servants of the Lord is another service that the "Cockpit" and the Preston Temperance Society rendered humanity.

CHAPTER 6

SUCCESS IN SCATTERED FIELDS—THE FIRST BRITISH CONFERENCE

Opposition to the Church of Christ in Britain grew with its progress in 1837. Heber C. Kimball and his associates were repeatedly threatened with expulsion and with physical violence, but little was done. What disturbances did occur were incited by opposing ministers, whose services were not in demand where the Gospel of Jesus Christ was being preached by divinely commissioned messengers of truth.

Following September 3rd, 1837, the first Sunday on which meetings were held by the Church in the "Cockpit"—the work seemed to gain momentum, and to roll forth with greater power and breadth.

Shortly before this, a letter sent by Heber C. Kimball to his wife, who was in Kirtland, showed that plans were being considered by others of the Twelve to leave for Britain the following spring. In this epistle Brother Kimball advised his brethren, should they come to England, to leave their families at home, because of the uncertainty of means and the poor living conditions that the unremunerative nature of their work forced them to accept. Part of the letter read:

"We have hired our lodgings since we have been here, and bought our own provisions. We eat but one meal a day at home, for the brethren invite us to dinner and supper with them, and they frequently divide their last loaf with us. They do all in their power, and I feel to bless them in the name of the Lord. There are fifty-five baptized in Preston, and it is as much as they can do to live, and there are but two or three that could lodge us over night if they should try; in fact, there are some that have not a bed to sleep on themselves. The Lord says 'take no thought for the morrow' and this is the way I feel for the present. I commit myself into His hands, that I may always be ready to go at His command. I desire to be content with whatsoever situation I am placed in."—Whitney's *Life of Heber C. Kimball,* p. 167.

Elder Kimball returned to Walkerfold early in September, and found that those who had joined the Church were being severely persecuted. He left them with renewed courage and conviction of truth, and later returned to find them prospering. Several more were there added to the Church by baptism. Following the later Walkerfold visit the Gospel was taken to Barshe Lees, where two persons were baptized. By invitation, Brothers Kimball and Hyde took a journey into the country about ten miles, where they preached twice to very large assemblies.

The three missionaries in Preston, Brothers Orson Hyde, Joseph Fielding and Heber C. Kimball, and Brother Willard Richards in Bedford and Isaac Russell in Alston, were pursuing their labors diligently and using to the fullest the time and services the local brethren were able to give. Brother Kimball went on a short journey to the villages south of Preston in company with a newly-baptized Church member. The people flocked in great numbers to hear them. At Longbridge five preachers were among those who believed the doctrines they advanced. At Eccleston they preached in a Methodist Chapel. On the journey ten persons were baptized, two of them Methodist preachers.

At Barshe Lees, on October 7th, 1837, the first child in Great Britain, Mary Smithies, infant daughter of James and Nancy Smithies, was blessed by Heber C. Kimball.

The Church in Preston had grown rapidly. Although a loose branch organization had previously been effected there, to operate under the immediate supervision of the missionaries, it now became expedient to divide the Preston members into five branches, and to ordain Priests and Teachers to take charge. This was done on October 8th, 1837, at which time arrangements were made for the entire membership to meet in the "Cockpit" on the Sabbath to partake of the Sacrament. Thursday evenings were devoted to prayer meetings, at which times the branches met separately in private homes or in smaller meetingrooms. Harmony prevailed in the branches. The resident brethren and sisters worked in unity and love, and largely conducted their own affairs, in accordance with general instructions, thus leaving the missionaries free a greater part of the time to proclaim their message to others, which they willingly and effectively did.

On October 12th Heber C. Kimball wrote from Preston to Brother Willard Richards at Bedford, a letter, advising the latter to preach first principles, and giving other instructions and information. His words may be taken to heart by those who are called to preach the Gospel in this day; they follow in part:

"Brother Hyde and myself have labored all the time, night and day, so that we have not had much time to sleep. There are calls on the right and left. In Preston there are about one hundred and sixty members. At Walkerfold I have built up one branch; one in Barshe Lees, in Yorkshire; one in Ribchester; one in Penwortham, and one in Thornley.

.   .   .

"The harvest is ripe and many are thirsting for the word of life. May God give you energy to go forth in His name, and cry aloud and spare not; and I say unto you, Brother Richards, if you stay in that place much longer there will be contentions arise, until the little branch will be broken

Following the labors in this section, Elder Kimball and Joseph Fielding went to the northeast of Preston, where they labored for a short season with much success. At Clithero a preacher, Thomas Smith, and six members of the Methodist Church, were baptized immediately after they had heard the Gospel preached the first time.

In Ribchester a mob often gathered to pelt the brethren with stones when they went to baptize. On one occasion, to thwart their evil designs, Elder Kimball arranged to have the applicants go singly to the appointed place. He followed quickly and baptized them all. As he was baptizing the last one, the mob arrived on the scene, disappointed; they were unable to find out how many were baptized, or to discomfort them.

It was decided to take the Gospel into Downham and Chatburn. Many well-meaning friends advised the brethren against going to those places, as they had a reputation for wickedness, and it was said that for over thirty years ministers of many sects had attempted to raise up churches there without success. This convinced Elder Kimball that those were the very places to which he wished to go.

The next day came a pressing invitation from Chatburn for the brethren to preach there that evening. Another appointment in Clithero conflicted, but those who were sent to request the favor were insistent, and so Joseph Fielding went to Clithero alone, and Elder Kimball to Chatburn. Of this occasion Heber C. Kimball says:

"In Chatburn I was cordially received by the inhabitants, who turned out in great numbers to hear me preach. They procured a large tithing barn, placing a barrel in the center, upon which I stood. I preached to them the first principles of the Gospel. . . . When I concluded I felt someone pulling at my coat, exclaiming: 'Maister! Maister!' I turned around and asked what was wanted. Mrs. Elizabeth Partington said: 'Please, sir, will you baptize me?' 'And me!'—'And me!' exclaimed more than a dozen voices. Accordingly I went down into the water and baptized twenty-five. I was engaged in this duty, and confirming them and conversing with the people until after midnight.

"The next morning I returned to Downham and baptized between twenty-five and thirty in the course of the day." —Whitney's *Life of Heber C. Kimball*, pp. 183, 184.

The next evening Elder Kimball returned to Chatburn. This night the congregation was so large that he had to preach outdoors from a stone wall; he afterwards baptized several. On this journey the brethren were absent from Preston five days, during which time Brothers Kimball and Fielding baptized one hundred ten persons and organized branches in Downham, Chatburn, Clithero and Waddington. On one occasion when they were traveling through Chatburn to Downham, the noises from the looms in the village were hushed, and the people flocked to their doors to welcome them. Brother Kimball records:

"More than forty young people of the place ran to meet us; some took hold of our mantles and then of each others' hands; several having hold of hands went before us, singing the songs of Zion, while their parents gazed upon the scene with delight, and poured their blessings over our heads and praised the God of heaven for sending us to unfold the principles of truth and the plan of salvation to them. The children continued with us to Downham, a mile distant."— Whitney's *Life of Heber C. Kimball*, p. 184.

Who knows where the truth-hungry are waiting! Had the brethren listened to hearsay, Downham and Chatburn would have been shunned. To follow the promptings of the Spirit of the Lord and the counsel of presiding officers is the only safe course in such matters.

At length it was decided to hold a conference—the first general conference of the Church of Jesus Christ of Latter-day Saints in Great Britain—in the "Cock-pit," Preston, on Christmas day, 1837. Branches had been raised up in Preston, Walkerford, Alston, Bedford, Eccleston, Wrightington, Hexton, Euxton Bath, Daubers Lane, Chorley, Whittle, Leyland Moss, Ribchester, Thornley, Clithero, Waddington, Downham, Barshe Lees, Askin, Hunter's Hill, Stoney Gate Lane, Chatburn, Penwortham, and other places.

About three hundred Saints, representing a much larger membership residing in branches extending thirty miles and more around Preston, attended that first conference. Priest Joseph Fielding was ordained an Elder. Ten Priests and seven Teachers were ordained to minister in the various branches; one hundred little children were blessed at this time, and the Word of Wisdom, which had heretofore been taught more by example than by precept, was first publicly proclaimed in Great Britain.

A glorious day of glorious deeds! It was fitting that such a body of Saints should meet under the direction of two of the Lord's Apostles on the day that is celebrated as that of His birth. And on that day it was fitting that a hundred little children should be blessed. It was fitting, too, that in the old "Cockpit," the cradle of "teetotalism," the Word of Wisdom—the Lord's law of health and vigor, life and vitality—should first be publicly proclaimed in Great Britain.

CHAPTER 7

THE SECOND BRITISH CONFERENCE—AND PARTING

The first British Mission Conference—Christmas Day, 1837, in the "Cockpit," Preston, Lancashire—was a success. No one could or cared to deny that fact. The missionaries had been in England scarcely over five months, and yet the fruits of their labors were shown forth in a manner that must have exceeded anticipation.

Immediately after that memorable day, Elders Orson Hyde and Heber C. Kimball went to Longton, a village near the sea, and declared their all-important message. Brothers Hyde and Goodson had preached there before. Many had believed; but no baptisms had been performed. On this occasion, however, after the first meeting ten were baptized, and others followed the next morning. The notable feature of this occurrence, besides the severity of the weather, was the faith of the converts, which gave them courage to be born of the water in the cold brine of the open sea when the temperature was such that fresh-water streams were frozen thick with ice.

That winter was characterized by inclement weather to a degree that caused abnormal economic conditions; and the poor, as always under such circumstances, were called upon to bear the brunt of the suffering. Describing those bitter months, Elder Kimball records:

"This was very extraordinary weather for that country, as I was informed that some winters they had scarcely any insistent and exacting.   Call after call, of necessity, went unanswered.

Elder Willard Richards returned from Bedford to Preston on March 7th.   Ill health and other unfortunate conditions had prevented the spread of the work there to the same extent as in Preston; but he had been successful in raising up two small branches of about forty members—which is by no means an inconsequential accomplishment for seven months of missionary endeavor.   He left these, happy and prosperous, in charge of Elder James Lavender, whom he had ordained.

It was thought advisable to spend the remaining time in strengthening and further organizing the branches that had already been established—a means of entrenching and fortifying the territory that had already been claimed from the enemy of righteousness. To do this in a short time was a tremendous task.   It meant visiting a branch nearly every night.

During this strenuous "wind-up" campaign, a pressing invitation to preach came from a Baptist congregation of a village between Burnley and Downham. The time at their disposal being already overfilled, the brethren declined this invitation, or attempted to; but further insistence led them to go.

When they arrived at the chapel they found a large congregation already assembled. Elder Hyde addressed them, followed by Elder Kimball, who says: "During the services the congregation was overjoyed; tears ran down their cheeks, and the minister could not refrain from clapping his hands for joy, while in the meeting." He took the brethren to his home and entertained them.

The next morning, when they were about to leave, a large number of the inhabitants of the place gathered about, and, with tears in their eyes, requested that they

preach again. News of their coming departure having
spread, a number of factories suspended operations to
enable their employees to hear, but previous appointments forced the brethren to refuse them at this time.

Many touching farewell scenes were to be witnessed on this final circuit of the branches—final so far
as they knew. The temptation to elaborate rather
than condense the details of this period is great. All
that has been recorded—both of journal entries and
discourses—could well bear reprinting. Such material
is fraught with interesting accounts, words of counsel
and other valuable information. But there is much
ahead in the story of the British Mission.

The second general conference of the Church in
Great Britain was held Sunday, April 8th,* 1838, in the
"Cockpit," Preston. In the early hours of the day the
members began to gather from the surrounding countryside, and by nine o'clock between six and seven hundred had assembled. The branches represented were as
follows: Preston, Penwortham, Walkerfold, Thornley,
Ribchester, Chatburn, Clithero, Barshe Lees, Waddington, Leyland Moss, Leyland Lane, Eccleston, Hunter's
Hill, Euxton, Whittle, Dauber's Lane, Bamber Bridge,
Longton, Southport, Downham, Burnley, Bedford, Alston, Brampton, Bolton, Chorley and others. The membership of the Mission at that time was between fifteen
hundred and two thousand. There were about four
hundred in the Preston Branch alone. The five missionaries from America who still remained in England were
in attendance, Brother Isaac Russell having recently
returned from Alston, where, in spite of much opposition, he had left a membership of about sixty under the
care of Elder Jacob Peart.

---

*This date is according to the *Journal History of the Church.*

Several Elders, Priests, Teachers and Deacons were ordained and given special assignments. Again little children were blessed, and about forty persons who had previously been baptized were confirmed.

In view of the impending departure it was necessary to leave someone in charge of the Mission. Accordingly it was proposed that Elder Joseph Fielding be sustained as President of the British Mission, with Willard Richards as first and William Clayton as second counselor. These brethren were sustained by the members, and set apart to these positions of great responsibility. At about five p. m. the conference adjourned, having continued without intermission since nine in the mornng. Another meeting was called for seven o'clock, following which the brethren who had been called for special work, about eighty in number, met for instructions and remained together until about one o'clock in the morning.

Elder Joseph Fielding, a member of the first missionary party and second President of the British Mission, it will be remembered, was a native of Honeydon, Bedfordshire, England, where he was born in March, 1797. His devoted service to God and his countrymen was acknowledged in this appointment.

Willard Richards, two years later, became the only Apostle ever to be ordained in Great Britain. One account of his appointment states that he returned from Bedford with the intention of going home with Brother Kimball, until the conference Sunday, at which time he willingly, as always, agreed to stay where he was needed.

William Clayton was born July 17th, 1814, a native of Penwortham, near Preston. He had been baptized soon after the arrival of the missionaries. Shortly after he was made second counselor to Joseph Fielding he discontinued all other business and devoted his entire time to the ministry of the Gospel, in which he was eminently successful.

On Sunday, April 8th,* the brethren delivered their farewell testimonies in the "Cockpit." The scene at this time was one of joy in the Gospel, and sorrow in parting. Those who were to leave and those who were to stay were in tears. Severing the ties of friendship and brotherhood was an ordeal. It would almost seem that a necessary part of our earth experience is to meet, to enjoy kindred company, and to part—to meet again under happier conditions, the Gospel of Jesus Christ assures us.

On the 9th Elders Kimball, Hyde and Russell took their leave from Preston for Liverpool by coach. They were waved farewell by a sorrowing multitude. Those good Saints had provided them with means sufficient to pay their transportation back to Kirtland. Elder Kimball writes:

"Notwithstanding the variegated scenery of the country, which in England is very beautiful, my mind reverted back to the time when I first arrived in that country, and the peculiar feelings that possessed me when I traveled from Liverpool to Preston eight months before. Then I was a stranger in a strange land, and had only to rely upon the kindness and mercy of that God who had sent me there. While I mused on these things, my soul was humbled within me, for I had now hundreds of brethren to whom I was united in bonds the most endearing and sacred, and who love me as their own souls, and whose prayers would be continually offered up for my welfare and prosperity."—Whitney's *Life of Heber C. Kimball,* p. 207.

In about four hours—the ride of an hour to-day—they reached Liverpool, and found that because of

---

*This date is according to the *History of the Church.*

storms the ship on which they had planned to sail would not leave as early as expected. The opportunity to counsel longer with Elders Fielding and Richards, who had accompanied them to Liverpool, was welcomed. But when word reached Preston that they had been detained, Elder Clayton and others hastened to Liverpool, and largely filled their time. Before embarking Brother Kimball wrote several letters of encouragement, counsel and warning to the branches. On April 20th Elders Kimball, Hyde and Russell boarded the *Garrick,* the same sailing vessel that had brought the seven to British shores nine months before—Brothers Goodson and Snyder had previously departed; Elders Richards and Fielding were remaining.

The forepart of the passage was stormy. After twenty-two and one-half days at sea, during which time they preached on board again, the brethren landed in New York on May 12th—after an absence of nearly ten and one-half months. There they had left only one member of the Church. Returning, they found a large branch. There they met Elder Elijah Fordham, who had waved them farewell.

So ends the first period of the British Mission story. The Gospel seed was planted in British soil. It was cultivated by able gardeners of the Lord. In less than nine months it yielded a glorious harvest. It has borne fruit each succeeding year.

CHAPTER 8

THE "JOSEPH FIELDING PERIOD"

From April, 1838, to April, 1840, may conveniently be termed the "Joseph Fielding Period" in the British Mission account; for between these approximate dates that earnest disciple of truth—Joseph Fielding—held presidency there, with Willard Richards and William Clayton as counselors.

As the winds carried the good ship *Garrick*—with Heber C. Kimball, Orson Hyde and Isaac Russell aboard—out of the River Mersey, and out of sight, on April 20th, 1838, a sense of heavy responsibility settled upon the shoulders of the three brethren in whose charge had been left the duties and cares of presidency. A stout support upon which they had leaned heavily had been removed—for Apostle Heber C. Kimball had been both father and brother, both spiritual and temporal adviser to them.

They, true men of God that they were, realized, however, that it was not in any man or group of men that their strength lay. It was an opportune time to demonstrate that the cause they represented was not of man's making, but of God's bidding. Their further labors in Great Britain were fraught with success, but by no means were they characterized by tranquility.

Enemies of the Church in Great Britain at that time made the same mistake that enemies of the Church of Christ have always made. They planned the time and nature of their attacks according to the movements and supposed strength of men, not admitting as a factor in their calculations the vital force—the power of God, which verily has carried this work until now, and which insures its ultimate triumph.

The time was ripe, so thought mischief-makers, to launch an attack. Before Heber C. Kimball and his fellow travelers had sailed, the first onslaught came. Previous to this time the brethren had been frequently, sometimes violently, opposed. Falsehood and calumny concerning them and their work had been circulated. Comments upon their activities had appeared in the press; but few of the now well-known slanderous lies had found their way into print. However, about the 15th of April, 1838, in the region near Longton, Lancashire, a Methodist minister, known as the Reverend Richard Livesey, offered for sale an anti-"Mormon" pamphlet. Speaking of the incident, a later account published in the first volume of the *Millennial Star* over the names, Heber C. Kimball, Orson Hyde and Willard Richards, makes the following comment:

"When Elders Fielding and Richards had returned to Longton (after April 20th, the day on which farewells were said in Liverpool) they found a pamphlet purporting to be by the Reverend Richard Livesey, a Methodist minister who had spent some time on a mission in the United States, as he says; and having nothing more important to attend to during his mission, it appears that he spent his time gathering up a heap of lies and filth from the American papers, and imported them to England on his return; and finding that the work of God had commenced in his native land, and was likely to destroy his craft, set himself at work to (compile) his heterogeneous mass of trans-Atlantic lies, and form the wonderful production of the Reverend Richard Livesey's attack against the Latter-day Saints, it being the first thing of the kind that the enemy of all righteousness had found means to export from America, and circulate in England, but since which he has found servants in abundance to assist in this nefarious merchandise of his heart's delight."—*Millennial Star*, Vol. 1, p. 295.

The Reverend Livesey's pamphlet did not enjoy a ready sale, however, as he contradicted himself several times in introducing it before a public congregation. At first he had denied any knowledge of the Latter-day Saints in America. Later, when he thought the time opportune, he brought the pamphlet forth and publicly declared that he had found the subject matter accidentally in some old papers in his trunk. In the course of the same address he stated that he wished the people to buy it because he had "been at great expense to procure the materials for writing it." It is said that his hearers retired.

Such works fall with their own weight.

The members in Great Britain at this time were comparatively young in the faith, and uninformed as to the doctrines and procedure of the Church, beyond the first principles and ordinances. To instruct them, and to put the machinery of the great Church organization into working order, were the first tasks of Joseph Fielding and his brethren. For some months this occupied their time to such an extent that they were hindered in the work of proclaiming the Gospel. Consequently growth was not as rapid as formerly; but the branches continued to gain numbers steadily.

An incident that culminated in early October is amusing, despite its serious nature. Sister Alice Hodgin of the Preston Branch was the first member of the Church in Great Britain to die. She passed away September 2nd, 1838. The usual services incident to death were attended to by the Latter-day Saint missionaries. An entry from the 1840 *Millennial Star* account, page 295, quoted above, makes the following comment:

"Sister Alice Hodgin died at Preston on the 2nd of September, 1838, and it was such a wonderful thing for a

Latter-day Saint to die in England, that Elder Richards was arraigned before the mayor's court at Preston, on the 3rd of October, charged with 'killing and slaying' the said Alice with a 'black stick,' etc.; but was discharged without being permitted to make his defense as soon as it was discovered that the iniquity of his accusers was about to be made manifest."

Mistaken notions of the doctrines and practices of the Church, and of the authority of the brethren in whose care the Mission had been left, coupled with differences of a personal nature, contributed to the disaffection of some. This ultimately led, when the offenders made no show of repentance, to the excommunication of several. Among this number was one Thomas Webster. He had been a member of the Preston Branch in good standing, and is described as a man of ability, pleasing personality and apparent integrity. On April 13th, just a few days before sailing for America, the spirit of prophecy rested upon Heber C. Kimball and he was led reluctantly to pen a few lines to the effect that Brother Webster would depart from the faith and become an enemy to the people of God. When he did, instructions were given that the prophecy should be opened and read to the congregation as a warning to all.

This letter was read by Joseph Fielding and Willard Richards, and then sealed, so that no others should know of its contents until its fulfilment. The sealed epistle was marked and examined by Brothers William Clayton and Arthur Burrows, and placed in safe keeping.

Because of this foreknowledge, Brothers Fielding and Richards were particularly anxious for the welfare of Brother Webster. They earnestly instructed him and prayed for him. He grew in wisdom and favor.

Soon, however, a change was apparent. He became
ambitious for office and authority, and began to criticize
affairs in general. At length he brought open charges
against the presiding brethren, which he could not
substantiate, or which were of no consequence. He was
then called upon to acknowledge his error or to cease
officiating in his calling, both of which he refused to do.

On the Sunday following, he administered the
Sacrament in a private home to six people, one of whom
had not been baptized, and one of whom had been excommunicated. For this defiant action, and other counts,
he was excommunicated.

Because of his popularity, Thomas Webster might
have carried many of the Saints into error with him,
but the sealed prophecy was opened and read to the
congregation, the witnesses of its genuineness testify-
ing of its origin. This voided the influence of Thomas
Webster with the members, and further strengthened
their faith in the divine direction of the Church. This
disturbance occurred in September and October, about
six months after Heber C. Kimball had left the Mission.

Having formerly ignored opportunity to state his
case in public meeting, his subsequent request to do so
was refused. He then felt it his duty to "expose 'Mormonism'." Placards to the following effect soon appeared about Preston: "A lecture will be delivered at
Mr. Giles' Chapel, to expose 'Mormonism,' by Thomas
Webster." This appointment he filled, but with neg-
ligible effect.

Unrighteous ambition and malicious criticism of
authority were ever the forerunners of downfall.

On October 19th, 1838, William Clayton gave up
his business pursuits and devoted himself wholly to
Church activities. His first move after this worthy

action was to proceed to Manchester. To him is accredited the first preaching of the Gospel message in that great manufacturing town of the English Midlands. The Lord prospered him in his labors. Many believed and were baptized, and a healthy, vigorous branch was soon organized.

Willard Richards had been designated by revelation given to Joseph Smith at Far West, Missouri, July 8th, 1838, as one to be ordained an Apostle. This information was not transmitted by letter, but had been made known to Elder Richards also by revelation. Of the calling, however, he told no one; "but it appeared from that time," says the Prophet Joseph Smith, that "the devil seemed to take a great dislike to him, and strove to stir up the minds of many against him."

To begin with, Elder Richards was in poor health for a time. For this he was criticized. Then, in September, 1838, he had married Miss Jennetta Richards —the first person confirmed in the British Mission, it will be remembered. The following entry appears in his journal:

"September 24th, 1838, I married Jennetta Richards, daughter of the Reverend John Richards, independent minister at Walkerfold, Chaigley, Lancashire. Most truly do I praise my Heavenly Father for His great kindness in providing me a partner according to His promise. I receive her from the Lord, and hold her at His disposal. I pray that He may bless us forever. Amen."

This marriage tried the shallow faith of many, and called forth cutting criticism. Under entry of March 9th, 1839, the Prophet Joseph Smith wrote:

"Some were tried because his wife wore a veil, and others because she carried a muff to keep herself warm when she walked out in cold weather; . . . to gratify their feelings she wore the poorest clothes she had, and they were too good, so hard was it to buffet the storm of feeling that arose from such foolish causes. Sister Richards was very sick for some time, and some were dissatisfied because her husband did not neglect her entirely and go out preaching; and others, that she did not go to meeting when she was not able to go so far.

"From such little things arose a spirit of jealousy, tattling, evil-speaking, surmising, covetousness, and rebellion, until the Church but too generally harbored more or less of those unpleasant feelings; and this evening (March 9th, 1839) Elder Halsal came out openly in council against Elder Richards and preferred some heavy charges, none of which he was able to substantiate."—*History of the Church*, Vol. 3, pp. 276-277.

Such petty meanness is not consistent with membership in the Church of Christ. From the pulpit Elder Richards invited any who had grievances against him or his wife to come to him and state them, and let him acknowledge the fact if he had erred. Only one came, and he to acknowledge his own error in passing judgment without cause.

During this period the Church in America was experiencing bitter trials and persecutions. The Saints were being driven and mobbed, particularly in Ohio and Missouri, and apostasy claimed many, among whom was Elder Isaac Russell.

Loving his British brethren as a father would his children, and fearing lest Isaac Russell should influence them for ill, Heber C. Kimball sent a message to the presidency of the British Mission, which reached them early in May, 1839. It follows in part:

"I have only received two letters from you since I came here. If you knew the feelings I have for the welfare of that people your pen would not be so idle. May God stir you up to diligence to feed His sheep; for they are the children of my begetting through the Gospel. Think it not strange that I speak thus, for you know the feelings that a father has for his children.

. . .

"Mobs are common in this country; it is getting so that there is no safety anywhere in this land. Prepare yourselves for trouble wherever you go, for it awaits you and all others that love the Lord and keep His commandments.

"Brethren, I want you to go to the north where Brother Russell labored, and see what situation the Saints are in, for I have some fears about them. Go and strengthen them in the name of the Lord, for I think that Russell is leading them astray.

"Brethren, I can truly say that I have never seen the Church in a better state since I have been a member of it. What there are left are firm and steadfast, full of love and good works.

"They have lost all their earthly goods, and are now ready to go and preach the Gospel to a dying world!"— Whitney's *Life of Heber C. Kimball*, pp. 258, 259.

Upon receipt of the above, Willard Richards departed for Alston, to find that Elder Russell had written a misleading letter to the Saints there, a copy of which he secured. The Prophet Joseph Smith writes:

"Elder Richards, being led by the Spirit of God, soon unfolded the sophistry and falsehood of this letter to the convincing of the Saints in Alston and Brampton, so as to entirely destroy their confidence in the apostate Russell, although they had loved him as a father."—*History of the Church*, Vol. 3, p. 344.

While the hardships of the Saints in Britain at this period may not be compared for severity with those of the Saints in America, still, there was much to contend with in Britain. But then, hardship, dealt by an unbelieving world, has ever been the lot of truth's allies. Progress in the face of stubborn opposition is one of the things that puts the very stamp of divinity upon this work.

Steady gains were made by the Church in the United Kingdom, despite all difficulties. Besides the organization of the large Manchester Branch, through the efforts of the presiding brethren and local missionaries, among the latter being John Moon, Thomas Richardson and Elder Wilding, the Gospel was established in the vicinity of Stockport, Bolton, Salford and Burslem.

During this period, too, the Gospel was taken into Scotland, an account of which appears in the succeeding chapter.

In April, 1840, the brethren who labored for the cause of truth in Great Britain during the "Joseph Fielding Period," were able to report increased membership, more branches and a sound spiritual condition throughout the British Mission. Although Joseph Fielding was not formally released until July 6, 1840, the active direction of the mission was largely taken over as Brigham Young and other members of the Council of the Twelve began to arrive in Great Britain between January and April, 1840.

CHAPTER 9

SCOTLAND HEARS THE GOSPEL

It was reserved for two of Scotland's valiant sons
to carry the Gospel into that fair and rugged land.
Elders Samuel Mulliner and Alexander Wright were
the men thus to serve their Church and their countrymen. Both were born in Scotland in the early nineteenth century; both emigrated to Canada and there
embraced the Gospel, later to return and bear witness
that God had spoken again from the heavens—a service
that was appreciated by many in their day, and for
which untold thousands have since blessed their memory.

Samuel Mulliner was born in Haddington, East
Lothian, Scotland, on January 15th, 1809. His youth
was spent in Dunbar, where he became a shoemaker.
Shortly following his marriage in 1830 he made plans
to emigrate to Australia, but financial considerations
led him to change his choice to Canada. There he
went in 1832, and located near the city of Toronto.
Five years later he heard the Gospel, and, with his
wife, was baptized at the hands of Elder Theodore
Turley, September 10th, 1837. Desiring to be with
the body of the Church, the next spring, he, with
his family, set out for Missouri, but stopped with
a temporary settlement of Saints in Springfield, Illinois.
In the late spring of 1839 the call came to Elder Mulliner
—as calls do come in this Church and Kingdom—to
prepare for an overseas mission. True Latter-day
Saint-like, within two months he was on his way. He
visited Kirtland, preached as he traveled eastward, and

was in readiness to sail from New York by the first week in November.

The preliminary story of Elder Alexander Wright is very similar. He was a native of the parish of Marnoch, near Banff, Banffshire, Scotland, where he was born January 27th, 1804; he emigrated to Canada in 1835, joined the Church in 1836 and removed to Kirtland. His mission call came early in 1839. By March 14th of the same year he was on his way with several companions. They traveled eastward afoot about twenty miles a day, and preached along the way. In New York Elder Wright halted for some of the Twelve, who were also preparing to leave for distant lands. In early August he was joined by Elder Samuel Mulliner. From then their stories run together for a time.

They preached and labored on the Atlantic seaboard until they had accumulated means sufficient to pay for passage. On November 6th, 1839, they sailed, in company with Elder Hiram Clark, for British shores.

For nearly a month they were tossed on the high seas. Finally, on December 3rd, Liverpool was reached. During the voyage some of their identification papers were mislaid, and they experienced difficulty in landing, but were admitted. They reached Preston on December 8th, and after eleven days of visiting with Joseph Fielding, Willard Richards and members of the branch in Preston—exchanging news and experiences and receiving instructions—they again set out on December 19th, this time for Glasgow. On December 20th, 1839, they reached that city as the first Latter-day Saint missionaries to Scotland.

This much is by way of introduction, to follow two native Scotsmen on a round trip from land of birth, half a world away, back to land of birth. The Gospel

brought them together.   The Gospel brought them
back to the homeland. Each had left in the interest of
material comforts and financial prosperity. Both returned without thought of worldly aggrandizement,
each being the possessor of that which he would not
exchange for the gold and glory of men—a testimony
of the Gospel of Jesus Christ, and the peace of soul
and fulness of living that come with it. They earnestly
strove to help their fellows gain like knowledge; in that
undertaking they enjoyed more than meagre success.

The day after their arrival in Glasgow the brethren continued their journey to Edinburgh by canal
boat, to visit the parents of Elder Mulliner. There
they were joyfully received and comfortably housed.

Elder Wright limited his stay to three or four days.
He was anxious to reach his parents and other friends
and relatives in the north of Scotland. Inquiry showed
that no boats were running that way during the winter
season. This knowledge, however, did not change his
plans—he was a hardy Scot and a true "Mormon"
missionary—a happy combination to produce stead-
fastness of purpose. He crossed the Firth of Forth
and set out on foot for Northern Scotland in mid-
winter.

Exposure, irregularity and poor food began to tell
on him. Some nights he slept in the open—in a Scotch
winter, and with little or no covering. In spite of a
persistent illness, the nature of which he did not know,
he doggedly covered the distance to Aberdeen, more
than one hundred miles. There a druggist diagnosed
his ailment as smallpox—before the days of rigid quar-
antine, of course. On the strength of this information
he rested, but not for long. Within two or three days,
still afoot, he continued his journey to his father's house

in the neighborhood of Banff. After a brief rest he was well again, with no apparent permanent ill effects.

Despite his illness and other difficulties and discomfortures incident to traveling afoot in winter weather, on the journey northward Elder Wright had proclaimed the Gospel on many occasions, wherever there were any who would listen. Many times he had borne testimony to old friends and to chance acquaintances met in travel. Such procedure is characteristic of Latter-day Saints abroad in the world, for they who have the spirit of the Gospel have also the missionary spirit. Every person encountered is a subject for the message of "Mormonism."

To return to Elder Mulliner in Edinburgh: He had remained with his parents until early January, 1840, and had explained his mission as often as opportunity afforded. He then began systematic missionary work, making Bishopton, a village near Paisley, the starting point. A member of the Church from England, a Brother James Lea, was employed in Bishopton at the time. Through him Brother Mulliner was introduced to the family of Alexander Hay. On January 10th, 1840, in a small meetingroom that had been procured for the purpose, Elder Samuel Mulliner first proclaimed the Gospel in public meeting in Scotland.

Four days later, on the evening of January 14th, 1840, Alexander Hay and his wife, Jessie Hay, were baptized in the River Clyde, near Bishopton. These two were the first fruits of Scottish labors.

On January 19th they were confirmed; their children were blessed, and the Sacrament was administered in their home. It was the initial administration in Scotland of each of these ordinances. The blessings of the Lord were with that little gathering. Peace and joy entered the home and the hearts of the Hays. That the Lord approved the action of that evening and the labors of the humble missionary was made known by spiritual manifestation; Elder Mulliner spoke in tongues. The tiny assembly that was to form the nucleus of the Church in Scotland was led to praise God and rejoice.

But truth was not long permitted to proceed on its way unopposed. As interest in the Gospel message grew, so did resistance to its messengers. Clergymen began publicly and vehemently to denounce the doctrines of the Master—for such are the doctrines taught by Latter-day Saint missionaries.

On one occasion in late January Elder Mulliner engaged in public debate with a Mr. Crowley. The result was an overwhelming victory for the former—with no apparent results, save it were increased opposition. The experience of the Church has proved that few souls are saved in public debate, or, in fact, in argument of any description. A humble testimony that God lives, that Jesus is the Christ, and that Gospel truth has been restored through the Prophet Joseph, touches, mellows and convinces where eloquent persuasion and bombastic oratory and argumentation can do nought but thicken the wall of resistance around stubborn hearts.

By this time Elder Wright had accomplished his purpose in going North, and so the two missionaries planned to continue their labors together. Elder Wright plodded and preached his way from Banff, as he had done on the northward journey—still in winter weather. According to appointment the two met in Edinburgh on January 31st, 1840, and began to spend their united efforts for the advancement of the Lord's work.

At a cottage meeting held in Edinburgh in early February two young men, Messrs. Gillispie and Mc-

Kenzie, received an irresistible conviction of truth. Both impelled to action, they stood upon their feet and bore testimony of their belief in the message of the restoration. That same evening both were baptized in the open waters near Leith harbor. The Gospel of Jesus Christ works wonders. Out of the congregation assembled that evening faulty human judgment would probably have considered Messrs. Gillispie and McKenzie the least likely so to humble themselves. None can tell who will be touched, nor how; but blessed is he who is so favored, and who yields himself with full purpose of heart to the message of truth. Thereby lives are transformed and made joyous and meaningful.

In February Elders Mulliner and Wright returned to Bishopton, and commenced activities in the neighborhood of Glasgow, Paisley, Bridge-of-Weir, Kilpatrick, Houston, Johnston, Kilbarchan, Kilmalcolm and elsewhere. Public meetings were regularly held in a rented hall in Paisley. The missionaries were forced to leave Kilpatrick under shower of stone and rubbish, ably projected by a mob. They experienced rebuffs, tongue-lashings, slanders, successes, and surpassing peace and joy in the knowledge of duty well-performed—all incident to the life of a "Mormon" missionary.

When Elder Orson Pratt arrived in Scotland, in early May, 1840, to coordinate the work of Elders Mulliner and Wright, he found there about eighty members of the Church. On May 8th, 1840, the Paisley Branch was organized under his direction, as the first organized branch in Scotland, Robert McArthur, a local brother, was chosen to preside over the branch.

On May 18th, Elder Pratt with Elder Mulliner traveled to Edinburgh, and hired a hall for public meetings, in

42 ISLINGTON, LIVERPOOL

Headquarters of the British and European Missions for
over threescore years (formerly 36 Chapel Street—p. 143).

ARTHUR'S SEAT ("PRATT'S HILL"), EDINBURGH

The prominence faintly seen in the background was ascended by Orson Pratt when he petitioned the Lord for 200 converts (p. 81).

which on the 24th of the same month, Elder Pratt preached the first public Gospel discourse in that city. The previous activities of Elders Mulliner and Wright had
been carried on privately among friends and acquaintances. Baptisms followed the arrival of Orson Pratt,
and among the number baptized were the parents of
Elder Mulliner, with whom the brethren lodged during
their stay. On a high level, above the Castles of Holy-
rood and Edinburgh, one sees in the distance a majestic,
rugged hill. It is known as "Arthur's Seat." There
Orson Pratt retired the morning after his arrival in
Edinburgh, and earnestly pleaded with the Lord to give
him two hundred souls. That number and more was the
answer to the earnest prayer of that humble servant
of the Lord. The Saints in those early days referred
to the elevation on which this prayer was uttered as
"Pratt's Hill."*

Elder Reuben Hedlock arrived in Paisley on May
26th, 1840, and took up his labors with Elder Wright.
Under his direction, on June 6th, a branch was organized at Bridge-of-Weir, consisting of twenty-seven
members. Much opposition was quickly aroused in
Scotland. Ministers warned their flocks. One em-
ployer of a large cotton mill threatened to discharge
any who went to the "Mormon" meetings—but despite
all threats and warnings, many heard and were baptized.

Elder Hedlock began to labor in Glasgow on June
17. With the aid of a friend, Mr. John McAuley, he
was able to secure a large hall in Anderson University.
Concerning the incident Elder Hedlock wrote:

"I told the trustees I had no means to pay for the hall,
only what I collected at the door; I was a stranger, and could

---

*Millennial Star, Vol. 96, p. 332.

not give them security, but if they would let me have the hall I would pledge my word that they should have their rent; this they did, though it was the first time they had let it on such conditions. Having procured a place to preach in, I put up bills through the city that an angel of God had appeared and restored the everlasting Gospel again to the earth. This excited the curiosity of about one hundred people to come and hear. After the first Sabbath my hearers dwindled to about twenty in number, but having agreed for the hall for five months I was determined to preach my time out, if I had only two hearers. I soon began to baptize."

Orson Pratt did not feel justified in spending the time or money required to attend the general conference of the Church on July 6th, 1840, in Manchester, The progress of the work was reported at the conference by Elder Hedlock, who represented five branches and nearly one hundred and twenty members.

Elder Orson Pratt remained for some time in Scotland. At the conference of the Church held in Manchester, October 6, 1840, he and Elder Samuel Mulliner represented the Scottish branches, reporting a membership of nearly two hundred fifty members in the region of Glasgow, Edinburgh and Ancrum.

Elders Samuel Mulliner and Alexander Wright had laid the Gospel ground-work in Scotland, upon which the Lord's laborers who followed have built. Before they left, many persons had been baptized, and many more were friendly and were seeking further knowledge. Thus two of Scotland's own sons rendered mighty service to God and their fellowmen.

Since these two humble and worthy missionaries first trudged into their beloved Scotland, thousands of the honest in heart have been gathered from the highlands and the lochs and the heather-covered hills. The membership of the Church in Scotland was reported as high as 3291 back in 1853, according to available records.

From the coal mines of Hunterfield, Midlothian, Scotland, came Charles W. Nibley, an emigrant lad, who later became successively Presiding Bishop of the Church and a member of the First Presidency, and who, by his business canniness, became also a wealthy industrialist and financier in his own right.

From Caithness, Scotland, came David McKay, father of President David O. McKay. From Scotland, also, as a "Mormon" emigrant lad, came the late David Eccles, who later became one of America's wealthy men, and whose son, Marriner S. Eccles, Governor of the Federal Reserve Board of the United States, himself returned to Scotland, the land of his fathers, to serve for two years as a "Mormon" missionary. Another notable Scotch convert was William Budge, who later was president of the European Mission, president of the Bear Lake Stake, and president of the Logan Temple. He was in the presidency of the European Mission before emigrating to Utah in 1860.

And so, the notable Scottish contributions to the Church could be multiplied by many score, but the greatest contribution is yet to be mentioned: the contribution of clean blood, of noble heritage, of honest frugality and independence, of worthy traditions and unshakable loyalty to truth. These have been fused into the ranks of modern Israel from the great Scottish clan whose plaid is the fabric of the Gospel and whose banner is truth at any price.

Recently, called to the bedside of an ailing and aged Scottish widow, the writer heard the story of her fourteen "bairns," some of whom had died, others of whom were scattered over the world, save for one young daughter who cared for her mother as best she could while earning for both a living. Asking nothing, and still willing to give much, this woman who had left her highland home for the Gospel's sake, and who had fared poorly in the way of finding material comfort, knew not whether this illness would be her last. But with bright, clear eyes and steady gaze she looked full into the countenance of her visitor and said in broad Scotch: "Aye, but it's been worth it, lad. And if I ken what I hae to go through before I started, I would go through it all again, and mair for what I ken to be true."

And of this ilk from the northern bulwark of the United Kingdom, have come to the Church clean and honest and loyal men and women. What more could any land give to any cause!

CHAPTER 10

THE OVERSEAS CALL OF THE TWELVE APOSTLES

To Joseph Smith the Prophet the word of the Lord came on July 8th, 1838, at Far West, Missouri, as follows:

"Verily, thus saith the Lord: Let a conference be held immediately; let the Twelve be organized; and let men be appointed to supply the place of those who are fallen.

"Let my servant Thomas remain for a season in the land of Zion, to publish my word.

"Let the residue continue to preach from that hour, and if they will do this in all lowliness of heart, in meekness and humility, and long-suffering, I, the Lord, give unto them a promise that I will provide for their families; and an effectual door shall be opened for them, from henceforth.

"And next spring let them depart to go over the great waters, and there promulgate my gospel, the fulness thereof, and bear record of my name.

"Let them take leave of my saints in the city of Far West, on the twenty-sixth day of April next, on the building-spot of my house, saith the Lord.

"Let my servant John Taylor, and also my servant John E. Page, and also my servant Wilford Woodruff, and also my servant Willard Richards, be appointed to fill the places of those who have fallen, and be officially notified of their appointment."—*Doctrine and Covenants,* Section 118.

The stormy scenes of Kirtland, Ohio, and regions round about, shortly preceded the receiving of this revelation. Most of the Saints had relinquished homes and property and had left Ohio because of severe persecution. A temporary refuge was found in Missouri, although uprisings and mobbings had already occurred there. Disaffection had claimed many; but just at this time at Far West there was a brief lull in the storm.

More than two months previous, April 26th, 1838,

the Lord had accepted Far West as a gathering place for the Saints, and had commanded that a house holy to His name be built there. On the 4th day of July, 1838, the site for the Lord's house was to be dedicated, and a beginning to be made. One year from April 26th, 1838, the laying of the foundation was to be recommenced. (See *Doctrine and Covenants,* Section 115.) The requirements of this revelation were fulfilled in detail up to and including the date of the divine instruction given above, July 8th, 1838.

It appeared for a time that all would be well in Far West. But it was not to be. Before the specified time had arrived for the Twelve to take their mission to distant lands from the building spot in Far West, a storm broke with pent-up fury, and changed conditions materially. The blackest, most hateful of the Missouri persecutions intervened. Between July 8th, 1838, and April 26th, 1839, the Haun's Mill massacre occurred; the President of the Church, members of the Twelve and many of the brethren were falsely imprisoned and unlawfully detained for months at a time; death and apostasy had claimed some; others were driven from their homes, and scattered—forced to flee for their lives because of the Boggs "exterminating order."

By the 20th of April, 1839, the last of the Saints had departed from Far West, leaving homes and other property, fleeing before point of gun on threat of death for non-removal. In fact, the situation appeared hopeless for the Twelve to leave from the building site on the 26th, and to recommence building the foundations. It seemed probable that Satan had personally supervised the mob activities, and had left no detail uncared for in making fulfilment of the revelation impossible.

It was rather unusual for a definite date and a particular place to be given for such an appointment. In
most revelations of the Lord are given words of counsel,
eternal principles and general rules of conduct, while
men are left to use their God-given faculties for application, and for arrangement of details. The reason for
this exception was not made known directly, but the
conditions under which it was fulfilled justify the inference that it was both to prove the fidelity of the
Twelve Apostles and to demonstrate to the enemies of
truth that the Lord's word would be carried out.

Mobocrats had sworn that if all of "Joe" Smith's
other revelations came true, this one would not be
fulfilled. An entry in the *History of the Church*, under
date of April 5th, 1839, twenty-one days before the
Twelve were to leave, reads as follows:

"Eight men—Captain Bogart, who was the county
judge, Dr. Laffity, John Whitmer, and five others—came into
the committee's room (i. e., the room or office of the committee on removal) and presented to Theodore Turley the
paper containing the revelation of July 8th, to Joseph Smith,
directing the Twelve to take their leave of the Saints in Far
West on the building site of the Lord's house on the 26th of
April, to go to the isles of the sea, and then asked him to
read it. Turley said: 'Gentlemen, I am well acquainted
with it.' They said: 'Then you, as a rational man, will give
up Joseph Smith's being a prophet and an inspired man?
He and the Twelve are now scattered all over creation;
let them come here if they dare; if they do, they will be
murdered. As that revelation cannot be fulfilled, you will
now give up your faith.'

"Turley jumped up and said: 'In the name of God that
revelation will be fulfilled.' They laughed him to scorn."—
History of the Church, Vol. III, pp. 306-307.

It was fulfilled. But even faithful members of
the Church had their doubts beforehand. Surely,
argued some, the Lord will take into consideration pre-

vailing conditions—will accept the labors of the Twelve
and appoint another time and place for departure. This,
however, was weak argument for weak men, which
phrase is not descriptive of any member of the Twelve.
Those who were at Liberty and in the vicinity met at
Quincy, Illinois, on the 24th of April, and when the
proposition was placed before them they were in favor,
to a man, of fulfilling the revelation, and trusting in
the Lord to deliver them.

In the early morning hours of April 26th, 1839,
while it was yet dark, Brigham Young, Heber C. Kimball, Orson Pratt, John Taylor and John E. Page met
on the designated spot. Other members of the Council
were absent because of death, imprisonment and apostasy. Wilford Woodruff and George A. Smith, who
had previously been called, and accepted by the body
of the Church, were ordained Apostles. This made
seven, or a majority of the Quorum, in attendance.

Many other members of the Church were there.
Some ordinations to the Priesthood were attended to.
Several persons who had proved false to the Church
were excommunicated. The Twelve prayed in the
order of their standing in the Quorum; and a song was
sung. A stone near the southeast corner of the Lord's
house was rolled into place under the direction of
Alpheus Cutler, the master workman. When the business at hand had been disposed of they departed for
Quincy, taking their families with them from Tenney's
grove, where they had sought temporary refuge. Quoting from the *History of the Church*:

"As the Saints were passing away from the meeting,
Brother Turley said to Elders Page and Woodruff: 'Stop
a bit, while I bid Isaac Russell good-bye;' and knocking
at the door, called to Brother Russell. His wife answered:
'Come in, it is Brother Turley.' Russell replied: 'It is not;

he left here two weeks ago;' and appeared quite alarmed; but on finding it was Brother Turley, asked him to sit down; but the latter replied: 'I cannot, I shall lose my company.' 'Who is your company?' inquired Russell. 'The Twelve.' 'The *Twelve!*' 'Yes, don't you know that this is the 26th, and the day the Twelve were to take leave of their friends on the foundation of the Lord's house, to go to the islands of the sea? The revelation is now fulfilled, and I am going with them.' Russell was speechless, and Turley bid him farewell."—*History of the Church*, Vol. III, pp. 339-340.

The command was obeyed and the word of the Lord vindicated, despite mob threats to the contrary.

It was the purpose of the Twelve to leave at the earliest possible date for distant lands; but they had first to locate their families, who were homeless, in poverty and without visible means of support. Many settled in the region of Commerce—later Nauvoo, Illinois—and Montrose, just across the Mississippi River in Iowa Territory. Exposure, short rations, and unhealthful, damp living conditions in rude log huts and tents induced widespread disease. Malarial fever and other ailments were prevalent, and caused many deaths and much suffering and hardship.

Council meetings were frequently held with the Prophet, who had gained his freedom shortly before the 26th of April. On the 2nd of July, 1839, the First Presidency met with the Twelve and some of the Seventy, to set them apart for their missions to Europe and to the islands of the sea. The following are some of the many words of counsel and instruction given them by the Prophet at this time:

"Then, O ye Twelve! notice this Key, and be wise for Christ's sake, and your own souls' sake. Ye are not sent out to be taught, but to teach. Let every word be seasoned with grace. Be vigilant; be sober. It is a day of warning, and not of many words. Act honestly before God and man. Beware of Gentile sophistry; such as bowing and scraping unto men in whom you have no confidence.

Be honest, open and frank in all your intercourse with mankind.
"I will give you one of the Keys of the mysteries of the Kingdom. It is an eternal principle that has existed with God from all
eternity: That that man who rises up to condemn others, finding fault
with the Church, saying that they are out of the way, while he
himself is righteous, then know assuredly, that that man is in the
high road to apostasy; and if he does not repent will apostatize,
as God lives."—*History of the Church*, Vol. III, p. 385.

This was followed by a discourse on Priesthood,
in which many fundamental points of Church doctrine
are contained.

It was a momentous occasion. The Twelve Apostles of the latter-day Church of Christ receiving commission by revelation to preach to all the world! The
first time since the Twelve of the former-day Church
of Christ had received like commission direct from the
lips of the Master!

It was neither possible nor desirable that all should
travel together. The first of the Twelve to start for
the mission overseas were John Taylor and Wilford
Woodruff—two giants in spiritual strength, two of the
Lord's noblemen, both of whom later became presidents
of the Church, successively.

John Taylor was a native of England. He was
born on November 1st, 1808, at Milnthorpe, West-
moreland County, where his parents were the owners of
a small estate. In boyhood he was raised as a member of the Church of England. At fifteen years he
joined the Methodist sect and later became a local
preacher. In 1829 he emigrated to Canada and settled
near the city of Toronto, where he met Parley P. Pratt,
heard the Gospel, and, with a number of friends of the
Methodist society, was baptized in 1836.

During the succeeding years of persecution and
apostasy, John Taylor ever defended the Prophet of
the Lord, frequently at the risk of his life. After having

been called to the Apostleship by revelation, he was ordained to that holy office in Far West on December 19th, 1838, at the hands of Brigham Young and Heber C. Kimball. A year later he returned to his native land to bear witness of truth's restoration.

Wilford Woodruff was born March 1st, 1807, at Farmington (now Avon), Hartford County, Connecticut. He was the hardy son of a New England miller. In his youth he was deeply religious, but held aloof from the inconsistencies of sectarianism throughout his most eventful life. He moved to New York State in 1833, and there heard the Gospel from two "Mormon" missionaries, Zera Pulsipher and Elijah Cheney. He was baptized later that same year. In 1834 he was advised by Parley P. Pratt to remove to Kirtland, which he did. Throughout the dark and troublous days that followed, he, too, supported the Prophet upon all occasions. His call and ordination to the Apostleship are related above.

On the morning of August 8th, 1839, John Taylor and Wilford Woodruff separately left their homes in Montrose. They crossed the river, met in Nauvoo, and proceeded on their way together. Elder Taylor left his family in log barracks, scarcely fit for human habitation. He dedicated his wife and family to the care of the Lord and departed. Of his reflections on leaving he wrote:

"The thought of the hardships they had just endured, the uncertainty of their continuing in the house they then occupied—and that only a solitary room—the prevalence of disease, the poverty of the brethren, their insecurity from mobs, together with the uncertainty of what might take place during my absence, produced feelings of no ordinary character. These solicitations, paternal and conjugal, were enhanced also by the time and distance that was to separate us. But the thought of going forth at the command of the God of Israel to revisit my native land, to unfold the principles of eternal truth and make known the things that God had revealed for the salvation of the world, overcame every other feeling."—Roberts' *Life of John Taylor*, pp. 67-68.

The conditions under which Wilford Woodruff left his family are described by himself thus:

"The 7th day of August was the last day I spent at home in Montrose. Although sick with chills and fever most of the day, I made what preparations I could to start on the morrow on a mission of four thousand miles, to preach the Gospel to the nations of the earth; and this, too, without purse or scrip, with disease resting upon me, and an attack of fever and ague afflicting me once every two days.

"Early upon the morning of the 8th of August I arose from my bed of sickness, laid my hands upon the head of my sick wife, Phoebe, and blessed her. I then departed from the embrace of my companion, and left her almost without food or the necessaries of life. She suffered my departure with the fortitude that becomes a saint, realizing the responsibilities of her companion. I quote from my journal: 'Phoebe, farewell! Be of good cheer; remember me in your prayers. I leave these pages for your perusal when I am gone. I shall see your face again in the flesh. I go to obey the commands of Jesus Christ.'

"Although feeble, I walked to the banks of the Mississippi River. There President Young took me in a canoe— having no other conveyance—and paddled me across the river. When we landed, I lay down on a side of sole leather by the post office, to rest. Brother Joseph, the Prophet of God, came along and looked at me. "Well, Brother Woodruff, you have started upon your mission| 'Yes,' said I, 'but I feel and look more like a subject for the dissecting room than a missionary.' Joseph replied: 'What did you say that for? Get up and go along; all will be right with you.'

"I name these incidents that the reader may know how the brethren of the Twelve Apostles started upon their missions to England in 1839. Elder John Taylor was going with me. We were the first two of the Quorum of the Twelve who started upon that mission. Brother Taylor

was about the only man in the Quorum who was not sick."
—Cowley's *Life of Wilford Woodruff*, p. 109.

The two traveled by team and wagon, on foot, or
by any means that presented itself.   On the first lap of
the journey they met Parley P. Pratt, who was hewing
logs for a cabin.   He had no money, but gave Elder
Woodruff a purse.   A few paces further they came to
Heber C. Kimball, who was engaged in like occupation.
He gave them a dollar he had to put in the purse.

Both were repeatedly ill.   On September 2nd they
parted company; Elder Woodruff was afforded a
means of transportation, and was advised by John Taylor to accept it, and to leave him behind to recover.
After much sickness, and many experiences in preaching the Gospel along the way, they next met in New
York City on December 13th, in company with Elder
Parley P. Pratt.   At a conference held on that day in
New York, Parley P. Pratt prophesied that the mission
of the Twelve to Great Britain would be known to all
nations of the earth.   It has been fulfilled.

Brother Woodruff booked passage on the packet
ship *Oxford* for himself, John Taylor and Theodore
Turley, who arrived on the scene and asked to sail with
them.   The latter two had no money, but Elder Taylor
was assured that it would come before the boat sailed.
It did—enough to pay for two steerage passages at fifteen dollars each.

Elder Theodore Turley's prominence in early British Mission activity deserves brief biographical comment at this point.   He was born April 10, 1801, at
Birmingham, England, and married Frances Kimberley
there, from which place they emigrated to Canada.   Their
first children were born in Toronto.   He accepted the
Gospel there, and then joined the main body of the

Church in Missouri. He was a prominent figure in the early history of the Church before going on his mission. He later laid the logs for the first house built by the Saints in Nauvoo, and figured in the events that culminated in the martyrdom of the Prophet and his brother Hyrum. He was a lieutenant-colonel in the Nauvoo Legion. He carried the Prophet's last letter to Governor Ford.

On the 19th of December the party embarked, and after a stormy passage of twenty-three days arrived in Liverpool on the 11th of January, 1840. Two days later they left for Preston, where a happy reunion with Willard Richards and Joseph Fielding occurred.

On the 17th of January, 1840, a council was held at the home of Willard Richards. It was decided that Elders John Taylor and Joseph Fielding should go to Liverpool; Elder Wilford Woodruff to the Staffordshire Potteries; Elder Theodore Turley, to Birmingham, his native city; Elder Willard Richards, wherever the Spirit might direct him, and Elder William Clayton, to preside over the branch in Manchester. At early dates the brethren left for the fields assigned.

These men were among those who in the weeks and months to come converted the inhabitants of whole towns and villages, and who baptized entire congregations and their preachers.

CHAPTER 11

JOHN TAYLOR—GOSPEL MESSENGER TO LIVERPOOL

No account of the introduction of the Gospel to Great Britain would be complete should it fail to dwell at some length upon the labors of Elder John Taylor, a native of England, an Apostle of the Lord Jesus Christ, and later the earthly head of the latter-day Church of God.

When John Taylor arrived in Liverpool aboard the packet ship *Oxford* on January 11th, 1840, in company with Elders Wilford Woodruff and Theodore Turley, Elder Taylor called at the home of George Cannon, the brother of his wife, Leonora Cannon Taylor.

It would not be well to pass on without briefly commenting upon Leonora Cannon Taylor and the part she and her family connections played in the labors of John Taylor in Liverpool and on the Isle of Man.

This family of Cannons, illustrious members of which have played many parts of leadership and service in the subsequent history of the Church, were natives of Peel, Isle of Man. Leonora, whose father was Captain George Cannon, had gone to Canada as the companion of an intimate friend who had married the secretary to the Governor of Canada. Leonora had intended to return soon, but during her Canadian sojourn the inevitable happened—two kindred souls met, and began a new life together.

The kindred souls in this instance were Leonora

Cannon and John Taylor. Both were devout members of the same Methodist society. Both were not quite satisfied with that sect. Both heard the Gospel of Jesus Christ from the lips of Apostle Parley P. Pratt, and together they joined the Church and spent their lives in service for the cause of truth.

In earlier years her brother George, who lived in Liverpool, had refused Leonora's invitation to join the Methodist sect on the ground that it could not satisfy his spiritual needs. He was searching for truth, and truth alone. For this reason she felt confident that he would accept the message of the restored Gospel of Christ when it was presented to him. With this end in view John Taylor made the call mentioned above. George Cannon was not home at that time; but as Elder Taylor left the house after a brief visit, George's wife spoke to her twelve-year-old son, George Q.— who later served as first counselor in the First Presidency of the Church to Presidents Taylor, Woodruff and Snow, respectively—and said: "Your uncle is a man of God."

As related before, at a special consultation meeting held in the home of Willard Richards in Preston on January 17th, among other matters it was decided that John Taylor should take up his labors in the city of Liverpool, to be accompanied by Elder Joseph Fielding.

It is peculiar to note that although every missionary who had arrived from or departed for America had done so by the port of Liverpool, yet not one missionary of the Church of Jesus Christ of Latter-day Saints during the three years that the Mission had been opened felt prompted to engage there in the serious business of bearing witness of the Gospel restoration to the inhabitants. Acting on the promptings of the Holy

THE PIERHEAD, RIVER MERSEY, LIVERPOOL

Where generations of "Mormon" missionaries and converts have come and gone.

DURHAM HOUSE, 295 EDGE LANE, LIVERPOOL, ENGLAND
Headquarters of the European Mission from 1906 to 1933.

Spirit all had been led elsewhere, and it seemed that the public introduction of the Gospel to that particular city had been reserved by a Master Executive for the especial charge of John Taylor. Considered in the light of his connections there, and in the light of subsequent results, why it should be so is not hard to understand.

Delaying no longer than was necessary after their destination had been decided upon, John Taylor and Joseph Fielding traveled to Liverpool on January 22nd, 1840, and began work in earnest.

A character to whom we have been previously introduced, but who has been forgotten for some time, enters again—the Reverend Timothy R. Matthews. It will be remembered that Mr. Matthews was a brother-in-law of Joseph Fielding; that he was a non-conformist preacher of Bedford in 1837; that he had opened his chapel then to the preaching of Willard Richards and his companion; that he had been convinced of the truth of their message, had borne witness of it to his congregation, had himself arranged to be baptized at their hands at a given time and place; and had then closed the shutters of his mind to the light of the Gospel, denounced the missionaries and their doctrines as being of the devil, and had gone his way, preaching the same doctrines in a distorted form, administering the same ordinances without authority—crying the while that his best members had left him to join the "Mormons."

But Mr. Matthews had not been inactive during the two or three years intervening. Financially, materially, numerically speaking, he had been a success. He had assumed the role of a religious founder, and had instituted a new sect, congregations of which had grown up in several cities, Liverpool among them.

On a Sabbath shortly following the January 22nd return to Liverpool, John Taylor and Joseph Fielding attended services at the chapel in Hope Street in which Mr. Matthews' Liverpool congregation met. Mr. Matthews was not present on this occasion, but one of his devout young followers conducted the services. His remarks were in the nature of regrets for the woeful state of the religious world, for the absence of spiritual power and authority, for the pride and worldliness of churches in general. He prayed for the gifts of the Holy Ghost and for the second coming of Christ.

Such a frame of mind on the part of preacher and congregation was an opportunity not to be passed by. As the meeting was breaking up, John Taylor arose and asked permission to speak. He was directed to the vestry, where about a score of the local leaders of the sect gave him audience and requested to know what denomination he represented. Without answering them directly, he spoke as follows:

"Gentlemen, friends and brethren: I have listened with deep interest to the things that I have heard this morning. I have observed with peculiar emotions the deep anxiety, the fervent prayer and the strong solicitude manifested by you in relation to obtaining the Holy Ghost. I have been pleased with the correct views you entertain in regard to the situation of the world. We believe in those things as you do. We hear that you believe in baptism and the laying on of hands; so also do we. Brethren and friends, we are the humble followers of Jesus Christ and are from America. I lately arrived in this place, and have come five thousand miles without purse or scrip, and I testify to you, my brethren, that the Lord has revealed Himself from heaven and put us in possession of these things you are so anxiously looking for and praying that you may receive. ('Glory be to God' was shouted by many present, and great emotion manifested.)

"The thing has taken place which is spoken of by John in the Revelations, where he says: 'I saw another angel fly in the midst of heaven, having the everlasting Gospel

to preach unto them that dwell on the earth, and to every
nation, and kindred, and tongue, and people, Saying with a
loud voice, Fear God and give glory to him, for the hour of
his judgment is come.'   Brethren, we the servants of God are
come to this place to warn the inhabitants of their approaching danger, and to call upon them to repent and be baptized
in the name of Jesus Christ, and they shall receive the gift
of the Holy Ghost.

"I feel an anxious desire to deliver this testimony. I feel
the word of the Lord like fire in my bones and am desirous
to have an opportunity of proclaiming to you those blessings
that you are looking for, that you may rejoice with us in
those glorious things which God has revealed for the salvation of the world in the last days."—Roberts' *Life of John
Taylor*, pp. 77-78.

These words caused much excitement in the little
gathering. Some believed and were led even to weep
for the joy of it. The power of evil led others to
bitter anger. To all, the doctrines and message sounded
familiar, and the brethren were asked if they were
"Mormons." To this query Elder Taylor replied: "No,
we belong to the Church of Jesus Christ of Latter-day
Saints, called by our enemies the 'Mormon' Church."

This confirmation of a fact they all suspected
brought to the minds of the company vivid and untrue
tales told them by Mr. Matthews, and circulated by
hearsay, concerning the "Mormons." The brethren
were refused permission to preach in the chapel.

In the afternoon of the same Sabbath they attended
a service of non-communion Baptists, following which
they asked permission of the leader of that congregation for the use of the meeting place. All they wanted,
they told him, was to speak—he could make the collection and keep the money. He treated them in a friendly
manner and politely refused their request.

Nothing daunted, they returned to Mr. Matthews'
chapel for evening services. John Taylor prophesied

that many of the congregation would shake off the
influence of the priests, who held them in error, and
become members of the Church of Christ. The first
steps for the fulfilment of this prophecy occurred immediately after the meeting. Mr. William Mitchell,
a preacher of the sect, came forward and invited Elder
Taylor to his home, which, within the next week, was
opened for small gatherings. The congregation of Mr.
Matthews' were strenuously exhorted by their religious leaders not to attend these gatherings. Despite
warnings the house was repeatedly filled. Following the
first of these informal meetings Mr. and Mrs. Mitchell
expressed their desire to join the Church.

A hall in Preston Street, with accommodations to
seat three hundred, was rented for regular meetings.
It was filled on the first night. In his address at this
time Elder Taylor paid his respects to the work of fearless religious reformers, from Luther down. He lauded
the efforts of those great men, and showed how their
accomplishments laid the ground-work for the restoration of the Gospel of Jesus Christ, through the Prophet
Joseph Smith.

His auditors were deeply affected; many friends
were raised up; ten offered themselves for baptism.
Mr. Matthews sent a letter of warning to his flock
against all things "Mormon." The warning did not
accomplish its purpose, however. The ten baptisms
were performed, and among the number were Mr. and
Mrs. William Mitchell. Of Church progress in Liverpool,
in particular, and throughout the Mission in general, at
this time, John Taylor wrote the following to his wife,
under date of March 16th, 1840:

"As regards the situation of things here, they are still
progressing. I told you about our coming to Liverpool.

The first time I preached, ten came forward. We have been baptizing since. Last week we baptized nine. We are to baptize to-morrow; how many I know not. The little stone is rolling forth. One of the brethren dreamed he saw two men come to Liverpool; they cast a net into the sea and pulled it out full of fishes. He was surprised to see them pick the small fish out first and then the large; well, if we get all the fish I shall be satisfied.

"Brother Woodruff has written to the editors, and another letter has gone from here, so I suppose you will know all things pertaining to the Church. Elder Woodruff has lately left the Potteries where he was, and has gone to another neighborhood and is making Methodist preachers scarce. He baptized thirty-two persons in one week; thirteen of them were Methodist preachers. I received a letter from him two days since with this intelligence. He is well.

"Elder Clark is preaching and baptizing in and about Manchester. The latest account from Elder Turley, he was well, preaching and baptizing in the Potteries."—*Times and Seasons*, Vol. I, pp. 110-11.

During the labors of Elder Taylor in Liverpool we may be reasonably sure that he spent much time with the near relatives of his well-beloved wife. George Cannon, her brother, read the *Book of Mormon* through twice before he was prepared for baptism. Upon completing the second reading he said: "No wicked man could write such a book as this; and no good man would write it, unless it were true and he were commanded of God to do so."

Some idea of the joy George Cannon's acceptance of the Gospel gave to a loving sister may be gained by the following excerpt of a letter from Leonora to John Taylor. The writing was dated April 14th at Montrose, Iowa Territory, North America:

"My dear husband: I went over the river yesterday, and I got a letter from you, dated 15th February. I never received a letter that gave me so much real comfort as it has done. I do rejoice and praise God for what He has done in bringing

my dear brother George, and sister Ann, into the Church—
the only Church with which the Lord is well pleased. I do
hope that the rest of our dear scattered ones may yet be
gathered into the fold, and yet live and reign with our blessed
Lord and Savior.

"Give my kindest love to all my dear friends; I hope to
see many of them yet in time, and also spend a glorious
eternity with them.

"I feel my heart bowed down before the Lord, and filled
with thanksgiving and praise for His providential care of you
and your companions in crossing the waters, and in supplying
your wants; and, above all, that He condescends to bless and
crown your labors with success.

"I do pray that his work may roll on, and that hundreds
of the sincere in heart out of every church and people may
be added to it, such as shall be eternally saved.

"It will not be long before the Church of Christ will
arise 'bright as the sun, fair as the moon, and terrible as an
army with banners.' I saw Sisters Pratt, Kimball, Young,
Woodruff, Turley, Smith, Thomson, Clark, and Hedlock;
also Dr. Richards, and father John Smith. They and their
families are well. . . . It is said that the Indians are breaking
out and committing many outrages in Upper Missouri. Several families have left in consequence, and came here. They
are calling out the militia. . . . My love to all my dear
friends, as if I mentioned them by names. Believe me, as
ever, your affectionate wife.

"LEONORA TAYLOR."
—*Millennial Star*, Volume I, pp. 64-65.

Some time later, June 18th, 1840, three of the children of George Cannon were baptized.

Elder John Taylor continued to make it his business to labor among people of all stations of life in
Liverpool. He shunned no one. He made it a special
duty to call upon the ministers of the city, to bear witness to them as well as to those who wore not the
clerical garb. He was sometimes harshly, sometimes
kindly, sometimes indifferently received.

On one occasion he held a long and interesting
conversation with a Mr. Radcliff, agent for the Bible

Society and superintendent of the School of Arts. True to type, this learned gentleman admitted the case of "Mormonism" up to the opening of the heavens, the restoration of divine authority, the renewal of direct revelation. Of these he said: " 'Mormonism' leads to tremendous conclusions."

Tremendous conclusions, indeed! These are the truthful claims that stir up the resentment of all unbelievers. Any statement to the effect that the Lord has spoken in this latter day is accepted by the world as a challenge, and is responsible for all opposition to this work since its inception—this, regardless of opinions that opposition has come because of polygamy and other peculiar doctrines and practices. Polygamy had not been introduced into the Church when the first missionaries went to Great Britain, but this fact did not free them from evil hatred, slander and bitter resistance. Belief in communication with the Father in heaven is the veritable bone of contention—has ever been, and ever will be until humanity accepts the truth.

On April 6th, 1840, when Apostles Brigham Young, Heber C. Kimball, Parley P. Pratt, Orson Pratt, George A. Smith and Elder Reuben Hedlock landed in Liverpool from the *Patrick Henry,* they found John Taylor mightily engaged in his labors—overjoyed that already nearly thirty in Liverpool had been baptized and more were soon to follow.

CHAPTER 12

WILFORD WOODRUFF—IN THE POTTERIES

The story of the early British Mission labors of Wilford Woodruff is a notable example of whole-hearted resignation to the will and direction of God. The bounteous success resulting from this pursuance of the Lord's work in the Lord's way is eloquent in its testimony of the wisdom of such resignation to and support of the Lord's word.

In a previous chapter we have followed Wilford Woodruff from his New England boyhood to his early manhood in New York State, where he encountered two "Mormon" missionaries, accepted their message and moved to the body of the Church. His call and ordination to the Apostleship, his departure from his family, his journey to British shores, his arrival in Liverpool on January 11th, 1840, and his presence at the Preston consultation held in the home of Willard Richards on January 17th, have also been noted. At this last named gathering it was decided that Wilford Woodruff should take up his labors in the Potteries of Staffordshire.

He was a stranger to England and to the territory assigned. He had no friends there known to him. There was work to be done, however, and Wilford Woodruff was not one to let time slip by in inactivity. On the following day he bade adieu to Elders Fielding, Richards and Taylor in Preston, and set out for the designated field, accompanied by Elder Turley, who was bound for Birmingham. We may well suppose that parting from his brethren and from the organized body

of the Church was hard on this occasion, but throughout his life Gospel interests were paramount in the
actions of Wilford Woodruff.

Elders Turley and Woodruff took their journey
by way of Manchester, where they visited for a day
or two. There Wilford Woodruff and William Clayton
met for the first time. The formalities of introduction
had scarcely passed, when Elder Clayton requested
Elder Woodruff to join him in administering to a woman possessed of an evil spirit.

They found the unfortunate lady in a rage, with
three men attempting to quiet her. Many, among them
both members of the Church and unbelievers, had gathered to see the devil cast out. "Had I acted upon my
own judgment," wrote Wilford Woodruff, "I should
have refrained from administering to her in the company of those present; but as I was a stranger there,
and Brother Clayton presided over the branch, I joined
with him in administering to the woman."

The unbelief of those present had the effect of
building up resistance to the workings of the Spirit of
God, which seldom, in such cases, forces itself upon
unwilling, unworthy company, unless there be purpose
in so doing. The administration was void of effect,
except to increase the writhings and sufferings of the
afflicted lady.

All but the few who waited upon her were requested to leave the room. In this smaller, more re-
ceptive, more believing company the missionaries laid
their hands upon her head a second time. In the name
of the Lord Jesus Christ and by virtue of the Holy
Priesthood of God, Wilford Woodruff, a latter-day
Apostle, rebuked the evil spirit and commanded it to
depart. The afflicted woman relaxed into a restful

sleep. The next day, the Sabbath, she stood before a large audience in public service, healed, and bore witness of the blessings of the Lord in her behalf, acknowledging His hand in her deliverance from the powers of evil.

This manifestation of the power of God greatly increased the numbers who attended gatherings of the Church in that vicinity. True, curiosity and a desire to be entertained were the motives that brought many. But at least, witness was borne to them of the Gospel restoration, and it frequently happened that those who came to scoff or to be amused, stayed to worship.

On the Monday following, the evil power, apparently incensed at being cast out from the woman, and loath to depart from the realm of mortality, entered into her little child—a babe of but a few months. From its infant victim it was commanded to depart by the laying on of hands of the Elders. That household was no more troubled with such occurrences. During this Manchester visit of Wilford Woodruff about a score of persons suffering from sickness and disease were blessed and healed by the power of God.

Brother Woodruff continued his journey and reached Burslem in the Potteries on January 21st, only four days after the Preston council. The region commonly known in England as the Potteries lies in North Staffordshire. It covers an area about nine miles in length by three in width, and includes Burslem, Hanley, Newcastle-under-Lyne, Stoke-upon-Trent, Tunstall, and other towns. It is the center of British earthenware manufacture. The territory had previously been visited by Latter-day Saint missionaries, but little had been done there before the arrival of Brother Woodruff.

Success attended the Pottery labors of that servant

of the Lord.   He ministered there nearly six weeks on his first visit—January 22nd to March 2nd.   Many believed, and were baptized and confirmed members of the Church of Jesus Christ of Latter-day Saints.   The brethren were enabled to obtain excellent meeting places.   Frequently town halls were placed at their disposal for public gatherings.   The usual resistance accompanied the successful preaching of the Gospel, but nothing of a serious or unusual nature is recorded. Within the few short weeks Elder Woodruff was well established, with many friends and acquaintances, with many doors opened in welcome to him.   Many praised God and rejoiced in the knowledge of truth that had lately come into their lives.   The Gospel had gained fair foothold in the region round about.

Being aware of this success, knowing that he had many appointments ahead, and that he had no thought of leaving the territory, it was, therefore, with wonder and surprise that Wilford Woodruff received an irresistible impression to leave a field so fruitful for a destination unknown to him.   The occurrence is described by himself as follows:

"March 1st, 1840, was my birthday; I was thirty-three years of age. It being Sunday, I preached twice during the day to a large assembly in the city hall, in the town of Hanley, and administered the Sacrament to the Saints.   In the evening I again met with a large assembly of the Saints and strangers, and while singing the first hymn the Spirit of the Lord rested upon me and the voice of God said to me: 'This is the last meeting that you will hold with this people for many days.'   I was astonished at this, as I had many appointments out in that district.   When I arose to speak to the people I told them that it was the last meeting I should hold with them for many days.   They were as much astonished as I was.   At the close of the meeting four persons came forward for baptism; we went down into the water and baptized them.

"In the morning I went in secret before the Lord, and asked Him what was His will concerning me. The answer I received was that I should go to the south; for the Lord had a great work for me to perform there, as many souls were waiting for His word. On the 3rd of March, 1840, in fulfilment of the directions given me, I took coach and rode to Wolverhampton, twenty-six miles, spending the night there. On the morning of the 4th I again took coach, and rode through Dudley, Stourbridge, Stourport, and Worcester, then walked a number of miles to Mr. John Benbow's, Hill Farm, Castle Frome, Ledbury, Herefordshire. This was a farming country in the south of England, a region where no Elder of the Latter-day Saints had visited."—Cowley's *Life of Wilford Woodruff*, p. 116.

Blessed is he who places the word of God before the wisdom of man. The events which followed Wilford Woodruff's willingness so to be led are among the most fascinating, most colorful, most far-reaching for good in all British Mission history.

CHAPTER 13

WILFORD WOODRUFF AND THE UNITED BRETHREN

Hill Farm, Castle Frome, Ledbury, Herefordshire —such is the mail address of the one-time habitation of Mr. John Benbow—God bless his memory!—to whom Wilford Woodruff was directed by the power of God in the early spring of 1840. It is not difficult for any stranger who has tried to find the old Benbow farmstead to believe that Wilford Woodruff would never have reached John Benbow or the United Brethren had not the Lord been his Guide.

Hill Farm just does not happen to be on the road to anywhere in particular. It lies between Worcester and Ledbury by an indirect and circuitous route, about six miles from the latter town. The nearest village— virtually a road crossing, which does not lend any dignity to the term "village" for having been applied there—is Froome's Hill, roughly a mile from Hill Farm. Froome's Hill was plaintively described by one old inhabitant as a "one-'pub' village"—which would probably correspond to the "one-horse town" of America. The same old-timer harked back with pride to the days when the village boasted two public houses instead of only one.

Froome's Hill, with its surrounding acreage, is not without distinguishing history, however. It was once the center—and a most fruitful center—of intensive "Mormon" activity. No one lives there today who personally remembers Wilford Woodruff or his associates, but the country folk even yet review tradition

and unwritten history concerning "Mormon" days.
Many of the stories, which have been oft-whispered
through three or four generations, and which have
gained notably in color and peculiar twists at each
whispering, have now assumed strange and distorted
characteristics quite out of keeping with the original
versions. But considering the remarkable nature of
the actual happenings it is not surprising that this
should be so, after the lapse of a near-century period.
The simple and truthful story, without any borrowed
elaboration, has enough of romance, enough of adven-
ture, enough of the miraculous, enough of achievement
and success, to hold the interest of the most indifferent reader.

The descendants of those who early received the
latter-day message of truth in that vicinity may well
give praise and thanksgiving to the God of heaven and
earth. Froome's Hill and Hill Farm were then tucked
away from the world except for the few who happened
to live there. Even on a more recent journey there
numerous inquiries proved that inhabitants of nearby
towns and cities are unable to direct the traveler to
Froome's Hill village—nor have many ever heard of
the place. Only by a troublesome number of direct
questionings at frequent points along the road is it to be
reached by strangers in private conveyance. How then,
in 1840, must Wilford Woodruff, who had never
before been in England, who had never before
heard of Froome's Hill or Castle Frome or John Benbow, who had no intention of leaving the Potteries,
no intention of going south—how must he have reached
John Benbow, Hill Farm, Castle Frome, Ledbury, Herefordshire? There is only one answer, and that is the
right one, the one that the Lord gave him when he

inquired in the town of Hanley on March 2nd, 1840:
Many souls were waiting and praying for truth.

To fulfill the divine directions received at this time
Wilford Woodruff left Hanley in the Potteries by coach
on March 3rd. The first day he traveled to Wolverhampton, about twenty-six miles, and spent the night.
On March 4th he completed the journey by coach to
Worcester, and from there proceeded afoot, about fifteen miles, to the home of John Benbow, where he was
entertained, and where happenings of far-reaching nature quickly transpired.

John Benbow proved to be a wealthy and independent farmer who lived in a rural mansion with his
good wife, Jane Benbow. The couple were childless.
They were members of an independent church body
that had severed relations with the Wesleyan Methodists
and had taken upon themselves the name "United
Brethren." There were approximately six hundred in
the society—truth-seekers almost without exception.
Among their number were forty-five licensed preachers.
At their disposal were many licensed meetingrooms.
At their head stood Mr. Thomas Kington, a capable,
sincere, truth-loving shepherd of a searching flock.

The above information was imparted to Elder
Woodruff on the first night of his stay at Hill Farm.
Of his introduction into the worthy household of Ben-
bow he wrote:

"I presented myself to him (John Benbow) as a missionary from America, an Elder of the Church of Jesus
Christ of Latter-day Saints, who had been sent to him by
the commandment of God as a messenger of salvation, to
preach the Gospel of life to him and his household and
the inhabitants of the land. He and his wife received me
with glad hearts and thanksgiving. It was in the evening
when I arrived, having traveled forty-eight miles by coach

and on foot during the day, but after receiving refreshments
we sat down together, and conversed until two o'clock
in the morning. Mr. Benbow and his wife rejoiced greatly
at the glad tidings which I brought them."—Cowley's *Life
of Wilford Woodruff*, pp. 116-117.

Upon arising on the morning after his arrival
Elder Woodruff informed Mr. Benbow of his desire
to begin at once upon the business that brought him
there—that of bearing witness of the Gospel restoration. He had not far to go nor long to wait. In the
Benbow home was a commodious room licensed by law
for preaching. The use of this room the worthy Mr.
Benbow proffered. He did more than that—tidings
were sent from farm to farm that a missionary from
America would hold forth at the Benbow home that
evening. Elder Woodruff continues:

"As the time drew nigh many of the neighbors came in,
and I preached my first Gospel sermon in the house. I also
preached at the same place on the following evening, and
baptized six persons, including Mr. John Benbow, his wife,
and four preachers of the United Brethren. I spent most of
the following day in clearing out a pool of water and preparing it for baptizing, as I saw that many would receive that
ordinance. I afterwards baptized six hundred persons in
that pool of water."—Cowley's *Life of Wilford Woodruff*,
p. 117.

The punctuating points of Wilford Woodruff's
ministry in the John Benbow country, and the summary
of his successes, are best told in his own words:

"On Sunday, the 8th, I preached at Froome's Hill in
the morning, at Standley Hill in the afternoon, and at John
Benbow's, Hill Farm, in the evening. The parish church that
stood in the neighborhood of Brother Benbow's, presided
over by the rector of the parish, was attended during the
day by only fifteen persons, while I had a large congregation,

"THAT POOL OF WATER" ON THE BENBOW FARM IN HEREFORDSHIRE
Here Wilford Woodruff baptized hundreds of the United Brethren (pp. 112 to 118).

Photographs by Rulon T. Jeffs.

Top: NO. 23 BOOTH STREET, HANDSWORTH,
BIRMINGHAM
British Mission Headquarters from 1929 to 1932
Bottom: 43 TAVISTOCK SQUARE, LONDON
British Mission Headquarters from 1932 to 1934

estimated to number a thousand, attend my meetings through the day and evening.

"When I arose to speak at Brother Benbow's house, a man entered the door and informed me that he was a constable, and had been sent by the rector of the parish with a warrant to arrest me. I asked him: 'For what crime?' He said: 'For preaching to the people.' I told him that I, as well as the rector, had a license for preaching the Gospel to the people, and that if he would take a chair I would wait upon him after the meeting. He took my chair and sat beside me. For an hour and a quarter I preached the first principles of the everlasting Gospel. The power of God rested upon me, the Spirit filled the house, and the people were convinced.

"At the close of the meeting I opened the door for baptism, and seven offered themselves. Among the number were four preachers and the constable. The latter arose and said: 'Mr. Woodruff, I would like to be baptized.' I told him I would like to baptize him. I went down into the pool and baptized the seven. We then came together. I confirmed thirteen, administered the Sacrament, and we all rejoiced together.

"The constable went to the rector and told him if he wanted Mr. Woodruff taken for preaching the Gospel, he must go himself and serve the writ; for he had heard him preach the only true Gospel sermon he had ever listened to in his life. The rector did not know what to make of it, so he sent two clerks of the Church of England as spies, to attend our meeting, and find out what we did preach. They both were pricked in their hearts, received the word of the Lord gladly, and were baptized and confirmed members of the Church of Jesus Christ of Latter-day Saints. The rector became alarmed, and did not venture to send anybody else.

"The ministers and rectors of the south of England called a convention and sent a petition to the Archbishop of Canterbury to request Parliament to pass a law prohibiting 'Mormons' from preaching in the British dominions. In this petition the rectors stated that one 'Mormon' missionary had baptized fifteen hundred persons, mostly members of the English Church, during the past seven months. But the Archbishop and council, knowing well that the laws of England afforded toleration to all religions under the British flag, sent word to the petitioners that if they had the worth

of souls at heart as much as they valued ground where hares,
foxes and hounds ran, they would not lose so many of their
flock.

"I continued to preach and baptize daily. On the 21st
day of March I baptized Elder Thomas Kington. He was
superintendent of both preachers and members of the United
Brethren. The first thirty days after my arrival in Herefordshire, I had baptized forty-five preachers and one hundred
and sixty members of the United Brethren, who put into my
hands one chapel and forty-five houses, which were licensed
according to law to preach in. This opened a wide field for
labor, and enabled me to bring into the Church, through the
blessings of God, over eighteen hundred* souls during eight
months, including all of the six hundred United Brethren,
except one person. In this number there were also some
two hundred preachers of various denominations. This field
of labor embraced Herefordshire, Gloucestershire and Worcestershire, and formed the conferences of Garway, Gadfield
Elm, and Froome's Hill. During this time I was visited by
President Young and Dr. Richards.

"The power of God rested upon us and upon the Mission in our field of labor in Herefordshire, Worcestershire and
Gloucestershire. The sick were healed, devils were cast out,
and the lame made to walk."—Cowley's *Life of Wilford
Woodruff*, pp. 117-119.

That John Benbow was a sincere truth-seeker was
proved by means more tangible and lasting than words.
To begin with he, a man of position and wealth in his
farming community, humbled himself and complied with
the initial requirements of the Gospel of the Master.
His good works did not stop there. Without obligation
or condition he advanced three hundred pounds* to
print the first British edition of the *Book of Mormon*.
Soon after that time he emigrated to the body of the
Church in America. Before so doing he left certain
properties, including the Gadfield Elm Chapel, for the

---

*This number is given at a lower estimate in other accounts.
It is approximate only.

disposal of the Church in Britain and for the benefit of emigrating poor. At a later date he was among those who stood bond for the Prophet Joseph Smith when evil-designing judges had set bail so high that they felt sure no one would guarantee it. John Benbow was also captain of fifty in the 1848 company of Brigham Young. Due to exposure suffered in being driven from their home in Nauvoo, his wife, Jane Benbow, was laid at rest in the winter of 1846-7 at Winter Quarters. He later married in 1851, Rosetta Wright Peacock, a widow, of South Cottonwood. Unto them was born in 1852 a daughter, Isabella Benbow Erickson. John Benbow sent his team and hired man six times across the plains, 1000 miles, to haul "Mormon" emigrants to Utah. He died in Provo, Utah, May 12, 1874, in full faith. This Church and kingdom has ever been better for the services of John Benbow.

Wilford Woodruff labored in Herefordshire territory until early August, 1840, when he traveled to London with Heber C. Kimball and George A. Smith to introduce the Gospel into the metropolis. His Herefordshire labors were broken by the general conference of the Church in Preston, April, 1840, attended by a majority of the Quorum of the Twelve, and by the general conference gathering in Manchester on July 6th, 1840. Concluding in his own words:

"The whole history of this Herefordshire mission shows the importance of listening to the still small voice of the Spirit of God, and the revelations of the Holy Ghost. The people were praying for light and truth, and the Lord sent me to them. I declared the Gospel of life and salvation, and some eighteen hundred* souls received it. . . . In all these things we should ever acknowledge the hand of God and

---

*This number is given at a lower estimate in other accounts. It is approximate only.

give Him honor, praise and glory, forever and ever. Amen."
—Cowley's *History of Wilford Woodruff*, p. 120.

"That Pool of Water" on the farm of John Benbow, spoken of by Wilford Woodruff, appeared in
1928, when the author last saw it, much the same,
according to those who are in a position to know, as
it was in the day of Wilford Woodruff's sojourn at
Hill Farm. Nature, it would almost appear, prepared
such a place with designing intent. Fed by clear
water, screened by natural leafage, situated but a few
score yards from the house of Hill Farm, it offers itself
as an admirable baptismal font.

The acres once tilled by John Benbow's men are
little changed. Methods of agriculture and the crops,
possibly, have altered much—hops are the chief prod-
uct today. But the sheds, and even the farm villa
itself, have changed remarkably little as to exterior.
Breaks and irregularities in the barnyard wall have
been left, and even the sag in the old front gate appears
to be the same—except that it may tilt a degree or two
more now. In fact, the outward appearance of Hill
Farm has changed so little that it was by means of an
old photograph, reproduced in the *Juvenile Instructor*
some years ago in connection with an account of Brigham Young's missions by Sister Susa Young Gates,
that the old farmstead was located at all. Few in the
village remembered John Benbow, but the old-timers
in the "pub" at Froome's Hill immediately recognized
the farm by the photograph, and one of them gladly
accompanied the inquirer to it.

Hill Farm was not all they recognized by the
photo. The *Instructor*, which was freely passed around,
was printed in Salt Lake City, and Brigham Young's
name appeared on its pages in bold type, which name

connotes much to the inhabitants of that region. Word quickly spread—as word will spread in villages, and elsewhere—that someone was inquiring for places visited by Brigham Young. An interested group—transient hop-pickers, and residents—gathered and whispered. Century-old tales were resurrected and aired. No attempt was made to conceal the fact that the stranger was a "Mormon" missionary, much to the consternation of a few who had "confidentially" related to him some shady rumors of former years, before they were aware of his identity. The farm was reached and audience sought with the master of the house. He came—a well-dressed, upstanding, tolerant, obliging young man of about thirty. The photograph mentioned before, and accompanying explanations, called forth surprise, warm interest and a pressing invitation to step in and meet the lady of the house—the gentleman's young wife. This couple—modern in every particular —had heard the village rumors concerning previous " 'Mormon' goings on" in their home. They wanted facts. Facts were given them.

In answer to earnest inquiry they were assured —as it seems every new inquirer into "Mormonism" must be assured—that polygamy is not practised among the Latter-day Saints today.

Since more pretentious living has become the vogue in farmerdom, the interior of the house has been altered much, and the arrangement that existed in the days of John Benbow cannot now be determined with any degree of certainty. Tradition has it, however, that some old " 'Mormon' branch records" were hidden in a particular place in a particular wall. To satisfy a certain feminine curiosity the lady of the house decided to have that portion of the wall demolished when next it was papered, to prove or disprove the rumors. She was assured that the odds are strongly in favor of disproving them.

An inspection tour of "that pool of water" was then conducted by the master of the house. It had been rumored, he stated seriously, that formerly the "Mormons" had actually submerged people in there as a religious rite. Was it true? It then became a "Mormon" missionary's pleasant duty to explain that baptism by immersion is still practised in the Church of Jesus Christ just as it was in Biblical times. It seems strange that people who have access to the holy scriptures should ask if baptism by immersion is really required for admittance into the Church of God!

CHAPTER 14

A MAJORITY OF THE TWELVE APOSTLES
IN BRITAIN

The British Mission of the Church of Jesus Christ of Latter-day Saints, as a coordinated, unified, widely-functioning institution, virtually dates back to April 14th, 15th and 16th, 1840, when a majority of the Twelve Apostles convened in Quorum capacity and in general conference at the "Cockpit", Preston, Lancashire.

By this statement there is no intent to minimize the accomplishments of the three-year period preceding the dates given above. It is not to be forgotten that the Mission was formally opened in July, 1837. It is not to be denied that the work had taken root quickly and had spread with power and rapidity. It is not to be thought a little thing that more than thirty branches had been established, that near two thousand members had been raised up, that the increase had continued steadily.

Under any conditions such accomplishments are noteworthy, but, considering that until July, 1837, there was not a member of the Church in all of Great Britain, that there was no treasury to draw upon, that there was a loose organization only, that there was no official publication or other well-established means of general communication, that there was a veritable dearth of missionaries—considering these facts and allowing them their full weight, such accomplishments are beyond the power of mere men to explain. It soon became evident, however, that these deficiencies must be overcome for the good of the Lord's work. To do this was the chief concern of the Twelve during the meetings of April, 1840. The dispatch and foresightedness, the deliberate manner, ease and order with which the business was disposed of at this time, have stirred the wonder and admiration of many who deem themselves wise in such matters.

There sat those men—eight of them—unschooled, untrained in business or literary pursuits, but the power of God made them mighty. They had no superior officer in Great Britain, save the Lord only; they had no one from whom to seek advice, save the Lord only; they had to account for the use of their time to none, save the Lord only. The work was there to be done. They did it, and the hours were not allowed to slip by in passing the time of day, nor in exchanging gossipy news, nor in discussing inconsequential matters of any description.

During those three days, questions of a momentous nature to the latter-day work of the Lord in the United Kingdom were presented, considered and disposed of. Undertakings that have endured to our day, and that will reach far beyond it, were visualized, projected and organized. Prior to 1840 the work was haphazard at best. Following April, 1840, it expanded with purpose and order. During the first six months following these gatherings more were received into the Church than during the three years preceding.

The concise, matter-of-fact minutes of the general conference and of the Council meetings reveal the nature and extent of the business. They formed, in large measure, the permanent foundation upon which the work of the British Mission has since been built. They merit reprinting at this point in the British Mission story. First, however, it may be well briefly to review the movements of the Twelve shortly preceding their arrival on British shores.

The overseas call and departure of the Twelve from the Temple site of the Lord's house at Far West, Missouri, have previously been related. The eastward journey and arrival in Liverpool of Apostles John Taylor and Wilford Woodruff have also been recounted.

Of his own departure for the mission, with Brigham Young, Heber C. Kimball has written:

"September 14th, 1839, President Young left his home at Montrose to start on the mission to England. He was so sick that he was unable to go to the Mississippi, a distance of thirty rods, without assistance. After he had crossed the river he rode behind Israel Barlow on his horse to my house, where he continued sick until the 18th. He left his wife sick with a babe only three weeks old, and all his other children were sick and unable to wait upon each other. Not one soul of them was able to go to the well for a pail of water, and they were without a second suit to their backs, for the mob in Missouri had taken nearly all he had. On the 17th Sister Ann Young got a boy to carry her up in his wagon to my house, that she might nurse and comfort Brother Brigham to the hour of starting.

"September 18th, Charles Hubbard sent his boy with a wagon and span of horses to my house; our trunks were put into the wagon by some brethren; I went to my bed and shook hands with my wife who was then shaking with a chill, having two children lying sick by her side; I embraced her and my children, and bade them farewell. My only well child was little Heber P., and it was with difficulty he could carry a couple of quarts of water at a time, to assist in quenching their thirst."—Whitney's *Life of Heber C. Kimball*, pp. 275-276.

Parley P. Pratt, with his family, his Brother Orson, and Hiram Clark, started east by carriage a few days earlier from Nauvoo, August 29th. He made his home for a time in New York, preaching, writing and publishing the while. Apostle George A. Smith left Nauvoo in September, 1839. Elder Reuben Hedlock was also traveling eastward about the same time.

These men performed mighty works as they traveled, and the Lord prospered their labors and cared for their wants. After many conversions, providential escapes, miraculous healings and timely providings of material needs, the party of six found themselves together in New York with means to engage steerage passages aboard the *Patrick Henry,* a sailing vessel on which they embarked for Liverpool, March 9th, 1840. The happenings from this point on are best told in a letter to the Church in America, sent by Brigham Young:

"Preston, England, April 17th, 1840.

"To the Saints in the United States of America: For the comfort of the Church in general, in that country, I attempt to address a few lines to you, to let you know where we are, and what we are doing in this country.

"The work of the Lord is progressing here, and has been ever since Elders Orson Hyde and H. C. Kimball left this country. According to the account that the Elders give of their labors, there have been about eight or nine hundred persons baptized since they left. The Gospel is spreading, the devils are roaring. As nigh as I can learn, the priests are howling, the tares are binding up, the wheat is gathering, nations are trembling, and kingdoms tottering; men's hearts failing them for fear, and for looking after those things which are coming on the earth. The poor among men are rejoicing in the Lord, and the meek do increase their joy. The hearts of the wicked do wax worse and worse, deceiving and being deceived.

"But I rejoice that I am counted worthy to be one of the number to carry salvation to the poor and meek of the earth. Brethren, I want to say many things, but I shall not have room on this paper, as I design giving the minutes of our conference below.

"After a long and tedious voyage of twenty-eight days on the water, we landed in Liverpool. Elders Heber C. Kimball, Parley P. Pratt, Orson Pratt, George A. Smith and

Reuben Hedlock were in the company. We soon found a room that we could have to ourselves, which made our solemn assembly glorious. We blessed each other and prepared for our labor. The next day we found Elder Taylor in the city. There had been about thirty baptized. On Wednesday went to Preston; met with the Church on Sunday, and bore testimony to the things the Lord is doing in these last days. President Joseph Fielding gave out an appointment for a conference for the Church on Wednesday, the 15th."—*History of the Church,* Vol. 4, pp. 114-115.

In this same letter the following minutes of the Council and conference meetings were given:

"At a council of the Twelve, held in Preston, England, on the 14th of April, 1840, it being the 9th day of the 1st month of the 11th year of the rise of the Church of Jesus Christ, Elders Brigham Young, Heber C. Kimball, Parley P. Pratt, Orson Pratt, Wilford Woodruff, John Taylor and George A. Smith being present, Elder Brigham Young was called to preside, and Elder John Taylor chosen secretary.

"The council was opened by prayer by Elder Brigham Young. Elder Willard Richards was ordained to the office of an Apostle, and received into the Quorum of the Twelve by unanimous vote, according to previous revelation. Elder Brigham Young was unanimously chosen as the President of the Twelve.

"Resolved, that he who acts as the secretary of the Quorum, shall prepare the minutes of the conference of the Quorum, and deposit them in the hands of the president for keeping.

"Moved by Elder Kimball, and seconded by Elder Richards, that twenty of the Seventies be sent for, and that it be left discretionary with the President of the Twelve to send for more if he think proper. Conference adjourned. Benediction by Elder Kimball.

GENERAL CONFERENCE MINUTES

"At a general conference of the Church of Jesus Christ of Latter-day Saints, held in the Temperance Hall, Preston, Lancashire, England, on the 15th of April, 1840, President Joseph Fielding called upon Elder Kimball to preside, and Elder William Clayton was chosen clerk, it being the 10th day of the 1st month of the 11th year of the rise of the Church.

"The meeting was opened by singing, and prayer by Elder Kimball. Elder Kimball then called upon the Elders to represent the different branches of the Church."

The names of the various official brethren representing the branches are here given. Reports showed that there were in the British Mission 36 Elders, 54 Priests, 36 Teachers, 11 Deacons, 1,686 members, all contained in 34 branches.

"The meeting was then adjourned for one hour. The conference again assembled at half-past one o'clock. Meeting opened by prayer, and business commenced.

"Elder John Moon represented the Church at Leyland Moss, consisting of six members, one Priest.

"Elder Willard Richards, having been previously ordained into the Quorum of the Twelve, according to previous revelation, it was moved by Elder Young, and seconded by Elder Taylor, that Elder Hiram Clark be appointed as a counselor to Elder Fielding in the place of Elder Richards; carried unanimously.

"Moved by Elder Fielding, seconded by Elder Young, that a hymn-book should be published; carried. Moved and seconded, that the publishing of the *Hymn Book* shall be done by the direction of the Twelve; carried.

"Moved and seconded that a monthly periodical shall be published under the direction and superintendence of the Twelve, for the benefit and information of the Church, as soon as a sufficient number of subscribers shall be obtained; carried.

"Moved and seconded that Brother John Blazard, of Sainsbury, be ordained to the office of a Priest; carried.

"Elder Kimball then laid before the conference the importance and propriety of ordaining a Patriarch to bestow patriarchal blessings upon the fatherless, etc.; referred to the Twelve, whose business it is to select one, and ordain him according to the directions of the Spirit.

"After various remarks and addresses given by the Elders, President Fielding and his counselors proceeded to ordain Brothers Blazard and Cobridge to their offices, as stated above.

"Elder Kimball then called upon the clerk to read over the minutes of the conference, which being done, they were received by the unanimous voice of the conference.

"Moved by Elder Young, and seconded by Elder Parley P. Pratt, that this conference be adjourned until the 6th of July next, to be held in Preston, at 10 o'clock a. m.; carried. Meeting then adjourned.

"HEBER C. KIMBALL, President of the Conference.
"WILLIAM CLAYTON, Clerk."

COUNCIL MEETING OF THE TWELVE

"The council met pursuant to adjournment, April 16th, 1840. The number of the Quorum the same as on the 14th.

"Moved by Elder Young, seconded by Elder Taylor, that Elder Parley P. Pratt be chosen as the editor of the monthly periodical for the Church.

"Moved by Elder Orson Pratt, and seconded by Elder Wilford Woodruff, that Elders Brigham Young, Parley P. Pratt, and John Taylor form the committee for that purpose.

"Moved by Elder Willard Richards, seconded by Elder George A. Smith, that the name of the paper or periodical be the *Latter-day Saints' Millennial Star*.

"Moved by Elder Brigham Young, seconded by Elder Orson Pratt, that the size of the paper, its plan, and price be left at the disposal of the editor.

"Moved by Elder Brigham Young, seconded by Elder Heber C. Kimball, that the Saints receive a recommend to the Church in America to move in small or large bodies, inasmuch as they desire to emigrate to that new country.

"Moved by Elder Brigham Young, seconded by Parley P. Pratt, that we recommend no one to go to America that has money, without assisting the poor according to our counsel from time to time.

"Moved by Elder John Taylor, seconded by Elder Parley P. Pratt, that the copyright of the *Book of Doctrine and Covenants* and the *Book of Mormon* be secured as quickly as possible.

"Moved by Elder Woodruff, seconded by Elder Willard Richards, that Elders Brigham Young, Heber C. Kimball and Parley P. Pratt be the committee to secure the copyright.

"Moved by Elder Heber C. Kimball, and seconded by Elder Willard Richards, that Elder Peter Melling be ordained an evangelical minister (Patriarch) in Preston.

"Moved by Elder Heber C. Kimball, that the Twelve meet here on the 6th of July next, seconded by Elder Wilford Woodruff; and carried.

"Moved by Elder Willard Richards, and seconded by Elder Wilford Woodruff, that the editor of the periodical keep an account of all the receipts and expenditures connected with the printing, general expense, etc., and the books at all times be open for the inspection of the Council.

"The above resolutions were unanimously adopted. The conference closed by prayer.

"JOHN TAYLOR, Clerk."
—*History of the Church,* Vol. IV, pp. 118-119.

The above minutes and letter were followed by this shorter one from Brigham Young.

"To President Joseph Smith and Counselors:

Dear Brethren: You no doubt will have the perusal of this letter, and minutes of our conference; this will give you an idea of what we are doing in this country. If you see anything in or about the whole affair that is not right, I ask, in the name of the Lord Jesus Christ, that you would make known unto us the mind of the Lord, and His will concerning us. I believe that I am as willing to do the will of the Lord, and take counsel of my brethren, and be a servant of the Church, as ever I was in my life; but I can tell you, I would like to be with my old friends; I like new friends, but I cannot part with my old ones for them.

"Concerning the *Hymn Book*—when we arrived here we found the brethren had laid by their old hymn books, and they wanted new ones; for the Bible, religion, and all is new to them. When I came to learn more about carrying books into the States, or bringing them here, I found the duties were so high that we never should want to bring books from the States.

"I request one favor of you, that is, a letter from you that I may hear from my friends. I trust that I will remain your friend through life and in eternity. As ever,

"BRIGHAM YOUNG."

—*History of the Church*, Vol. IV, pp. 119-120.

The greatness of these Latter-day Apostles of the Lord Jesus Christ is nowhere shown more clearly than in their humility and willingness to take counsel from those in authority, even though they, admittedly, were leaders, with power and influence among their fellows.

Many items noted in the minutes reprinted above are worthy of a treatise in themselves, and have been productive of far-reaching results in the British Mission.

CHAPTER 15

AN EVENTFUL THREE MONTHS

Meetings with old friends are among life's most cherished experiences—especially when those old friends have become endeared through bonds of the Gospel of Jesus Christ.

It will be remembered that Heber C. Kimball arrived friendless on British shores in July, 1837. When he departed ten months later, after successful and eventful labors, hundreds loved him as brother and father, as spiritual and temporal adviser, and wept at his leaving. During the two-year absence that followed, those invisible bonds that draw the hearts of kindred children of God together had not slackened their hold, but, despite the many miles that separated shepherd from flock, had grown more real. These conditions made the second meeting of Heber C. Kimball with British friends a time of rejoicing and praise to God.

Being anxious to cast doubt where there was room for doubt, enemies of the Church in Britain pretended to scoff at the idea that Heber C. Kimball would ever return to Great Britain after his first departure. This "doubt campaign" was carried on to destroy confidence in the servants of the Lord. Such rumors were not received with credence by those who knew the men of God, but they introduced depressing elements into the minds of all, which were only removed by the actual revisit, on April 9th, 1840, when Heber C. Kimball, with his traveling companions, returned to the town of Preston, two years to the day from the time of the first reluctant departure.

With his brethren of the Twelve, Elder Kimball surveyed the conditions of the British Mission, and weighed and considered the progress of two years' labor. Having the advantage of comparison, he was able more fully to recommend at the Council meetings and general conference, April 14th to 16th, where the permanent business foundation of the British Mission was projected. During the second day of the conference Elder Kimball presided. Throughout the meetings his wisdom and experience contributed to the dispatch of the work. His recommendations are outstanding, by the records, during those days of notable accomplishment.

Putting aside personal preference, as always when the welfare of the Lord's work was a counter consideration, immediately following the conference meetings the brethren separated and traveled to designated fields of labor—Orson Pratt to Scotland (the results of which assignment have been previously noted in the chapter on Scotland); John Taylor to continue in Liverpool; Parley P. Pratt to take up the work in Manchester; George A. Smith to visit the Potteries; Brigham Young and Willard Richards to travel with Elder Wilford Woodruff to his most fruitful field of labor—Herefordshire.

Heber C. Kimball, rightly, was given the pleasant duty of surveying the branches formerly organized under his direction, of sounding the spiritual condition of those who had been brought to a knowledge of the truth through his preaching.

For a few days he was accompanied by Elder Richards, prior to the latter's departure for Herefordshire. The first visit was to the branch at Walkerfold, the home of the Reverend John Richards, of whom

NO. 10 HOLLY ROAD, LIVERPOOL, Headquarters of the British and European Missions during the administration of President Heber J. Grant, 1904-1906. Headquarters moved here from 42 Islington.

NO. 5 GORDON SQUARE, LONDON. Headquarters of the European Mission since February, 1933, and since June, 1934 of the British Mission and *Millennial Star*. This structure rises four stories from the street.

LOCH BRICKLAND, IRELAND

Where the first baptism of the Restoration was performed in the Emerald Isle (p. 152).

much has been said before. The worthy Reverend John Richards had struggled between spiritual and material forces for nearly three years. He admittedly recognized truth in the latter-day message, but he was old and untrained except in the ministry. His flock was his means of livelihood. Their loss meant, possibly, the loss of his daily bread. Should he accept truth full-heartedly and trust to God to provide the necessities of life? Or should he outwardly deny what he inwardly knew to be right, and cling to a comfortable living?

John Richards is by no means the only man who has had to decide this vital question in these latter days. Tens of thousands have been called upon to make just this decision. Thousands have decided wisely for their soul's salvation and happiness. Others, among whom, unfortunately, was the Reverend John Richards, have chosen to fight a losing battle—to shun what cannot be shunned, to doubt what cannot be doubted, to deny the truth of Jesus Christ, which inwardly convicts whether men will or no. Like all who in their unwisdom have followed this course, John Richards lost happiness, peace of mind, sweetness in living, and the majority of his flock—his stock-in-trade, so to speak, from a worldly minister's point of view.

Jennetta Richards was lying ill in the house of her father. After being administered to by her husband and Elder Kimball, she immediately began to mend, and was shortly restored to health. The Reverend John Richards, however—by this time heatedly angry—ordered Elder Kimball from his house, with which order Elder Kimball complied—much to the subsequent grief of the entire household.

Members of the branch in Walkerfold, who were only few in number, had suffered many indignities for their membership in the Church of Christ. Despite many hardships, however, they had almost without exception remained firm-rooted in the faith. There seems to be that in mankind which makes them love best that for which they endure most. The history of Christian people everywhere bears out this statement. It was so in Walkerfold. In other branches, which had been less persecuted and more prosperous, there had been some departures from the faith.

Return visits were made to Downham and Chatburn—the villages which, prior to the first visit of Latter-day Saint missionaries, had been given up as hopeless by ministers so far as religion was concerned. Apostasy had claimed a few there. Some who had fallen away were mellowed by the return of Elder Kimball, and offered themselves for baptism again into the Church with hearts truly repentant, as their later actions proved.

At this point in the narrative of the British Mission, Brother Peter Melling, the first Patriarch of the Church in Great Britain, is mentioned. His ordination to that office had been recommended by Heber C. Kimball at the Preston General Conference, April 15th, 1840. He was ordained and instructed in his duties. Members of the Church rejoiced at being able to receive patriarchal blessings under the hands of an "evangelist" commissioned of God to bestow them. Thereby they received much needed comfort and encouragement.

On one occasion a meeting was held in Penwortham, to which the local Saints gathered to receive their patriarchal blessings from Brother Melling. Brother Kimball was with them at the time, and gave the group in general, and Brother Melling in particular, such instructions and cautions as are ever necessary in such matters. A comment concerning the ministry of Peter Melling may well be inserted at this point. The following appears as a footnote in the *History of the Church*:

"Peter Melling was the first Patriarch ordained in a foreign land, that is, a foreign land from America where the latter-day dispensation of the Gospel was opened. He was the son of Peter Melling, born in Preston, England, on the 14th day of February, 1787. He was, therefore, in his sixty-fourth year. He was evidently a man of great force of character, for he proceeded at once with great diligence and ability to fulfil the duties of his high office, all of which is evidenced by the record of the patriarchal blessings given under his hands, and now in the Historian's office."
—*History of the Church,* Volume 4, p. 120.

John Albertson was the second Patriarch to be ordained in Great Britain. His ordination occurred April 17, 1840, under the direction of Brigham Young. Since that early day of these first two commissions no Patriarch was authorized to function in his office in Great Britain until the appointment and ordination of Patriarch James H. Wallis as Traveling Patriarch for the British Mission, in which office he functioned from June 2, 1931, to July 23, 1933, during the administration of Dr. John A. Widtsoe. Elder Wallis is the only Patriarch to have been sent from the headquarters of the Church to Great Britain, or any other foreign mission, for the specific purpose of giving Patriarchal blessings.

It was disturbingly noticeable to Heber C. Kimball on his second visit to Great Britain that many who had joined the Church had been reduced in circumstances, materially and financially. Some even at that early day had lost positions because of their affiliation. It was hard for them to understand. It was hard for Elder Kimball to understand. Not an infrequent question was this: "Why do the wicked prevail and prosper?" But do they? If by "prevailing" we mean selling the eternal values of life for temporary advantage and material gain, the answer may be affirmative. But if by "prevail" is meant gaining a philosophy that carries through prosperity and adversity, with joy in living here, and a confident knowledge of happiness in the hereafter—if prospering and prevailing mean this, then only the righteous and obedient prosper and prevail. Material advantages are blessings from God, but they are only part of this earth's existence. Happiness need not depend upon them—and does not if men have the true spirit of the Gospel, and dwell in peace and love with neighbors and friends. So ran the thoughts of Heber C. Kimball, and so have run the thoughts of many British Mission sojourners who have followed in his footsteps.

Although details are not given, there is reason to believe that Elder Kimball revisited all the branches of his former acquaintance, and put his findings to good use. A trip to Manchester in connection with the publication of the *Millennial Star,* the *Book of Mormon* and the *Hymn Book,* and business negotiations and arrangements with members who were emigrating, took some of Heber C. Kimball's attention. With Brigham Young he was instrumental in arranging for the emigration of the first body of Saints from Great Britain to America under Church direction on June 6th, 1840.

This revisiting of earlier scenes, and other business duties, occupied the time of Heber C. Kimball until the next general conference of the Church in Britain, which was held in Carpenter's Hall, Manchester, on the 6th of July, 1840.

Conference times are clearance times in the latter-day Church of Christ. Reports of past labors are made; finished jobs are cleared off the board; new en-

deavors are projected. It was so in the early days of
the British Mission—and, member for member, missionary for missionary, resource for resource, probably
not as much of lasting consequence has ever been
accomplished in a period of equal length in all British
Mission history, as during the three-month period from
April to July, 1840. Without again going into the
details of the April conference recommendations and
assignments, let us skim over the happenings of the
short period following.

John Taylor returned to Liverpool following the
April conference. Brethren who had previously been
baptized were ordained Priests and Elders, and they
assisted him in his ministry. Frequent outdoor meetings were held in the parks, on the street, or wherever
a few would gather. Public halls were rented. Baptisms increased—as did opposition. Meetings were
often disturbed, but the disturbance usually had only
the effect of better advertising the meetings. To gather
crowds, street meetings were held just before the hall
meetings; the listeners were then invited indoors.

In addition to this active ministry, Elder Taylor
was partly engaged in arranging the *Hymn Book* and
reading proofs for the *Book of Mormon* that was in the
process of being printed. By the July conference seventy members of the Church were raised up in Liverpool.

Parley P. Pratt also spent a full three months. It
is a matter of wonderment that one man could do so
much in so short a time. He had been selected editor
of the *Millennial Star* and also a member of the publishing committee. Let Parley P. Pratt account for his
own time in his own words—none will say that it was
not full:

"While the residue of the committee traveled in the ministry, I repaired to Manchester and commenced preparing to fulfill my new appointments.

"The first number of the *Star* was issued in May, 1840.

"While engaged in editing and publishing the *Star* I also preached the Gospel continually to vast congregations in and about Manchester, and the spirit of joy, and faith and gladness was greatly increased, and the number of the Saints was multiplied. I also assisted my brethren in selecting, compiling and publishing a *Hymn Book*. In this work was contained near fifty of my original hymns and songs, composed expressly for the book, and most of them written during the press of duties which then crowded upon me."—*Autobiography of Parley P. Pratt*, pp. 335-336.

The labors of Brigham Young, Wilford Woodruff and Willard Richards were also intense. They went to Herefordshire, and effectively followed up the remarkable work begun by Wilford Woodruff. One experience is related below in the words of Wilford Woodruff:

"The power of God rested upon us and upon the mission, in our field of labor in Herefordshire, Worcestershire and Gloucestershire. The sick were healed, devils were cast out, and the lame were made to walk. One case I will mention: Mary Pitt, who died later in Nauvoo, sister of William Pitt, who died years after in Salt Lake City, had not walked upon her feet for eleven years. We carried her into the water, and I baptized her. On the evening of the 18th of May, 1840, at Brother Kington's house in Dymock, Elders Brigham Young, Willard Richards, and I laid hands upon her head and confirmed her. Brigham Young being mouth, rebuked her lameness in the name of the Lord, and commanded her to arise and walk. The lameness left her, and she never afterwards used a staff or crutch. She walked through the town of Dymock next day, and created a stir among the people thereby; but the wicked did not feel to give God the glory."—Cowley's *Life of Wilford Woodruff*, pp. 119-120.

During this period Brigham Young labored in the

Herefordshire territory for about a month, chiefly in the neighborhood of Froome's Hill village—and village legends tell of him to this day. Among the places he visited are named Stanley Hill, Moorends Cross, Malvern, Ledbury, Marsden, Shucknell Hill, Dymock, and Lugwardine. At the last named place he wrote to the Prophet Joseph Smith, reporting his labors and asking concerning the advisability of publishing a British edition of the *Book of Mormon* and *Doctrine and Covenants,* and asking directions for emigrating Saints.

The Malvern Hills, a low range of mountains in southwestern England, are known for their soft beauty and varied hue. They skirt the region of Worcester and Ledbury. On one of the higher peaks, known as Herefordshire Beacon, lie the ruins of an ancient fortress or military camp, supposed to have been built and occupied by the ancient Britons of Siluria, and to have fallen before the sweeping onslaught of early Roman legions. To this historic place of solitude the brethren retired on May 20th, to counsel together, and with the Lord, for the purpose revealed by the following May 20th entry in the journal of Brigham Young:

"Brothers Woodruff, Richards and myself went on to the top of the Herefordshire Beacon, where, after prayer, we held a council and agreed, that since we had obtained 250 pounds from Brother John Benbow, and 100 pounds from Brother Kington towards publishing the *Book of Mormon* and *Hymn Book,* I should repair immediately to Manchester and join the brethren appointed with me as a committee, and publish 3,000 copies of the *Hymn Book* without delay. It was also voted that the same committee publish 5,000 copies of the *Book of Mormon,* with an index affixed. I started for Manchester (accompanied by Elder Kington a short distance) and went to Wolverhampton."—History of Brigham Young, *Millennial Star,* Vol. 25, p. 743.

Brigham Young reached Manchester on May 23rd,

calling, en route, upon Brothers George A. Smith and Theodore Turley, who had been laboring with success in Burslem and the Potteries generally. Elder Turley had only been released from Stafford jail on May 9th, "where," quoting Joseph Smith in the *History of the Church*, "he had been confined since his arrest on the 16th of March last, at the instigation of John Jones, a Methodist preacher, on the pretense of a claim arising under a partnership with another man fifteen years ago, before he left England; but the real object was to stop his preaching. He was without provisions for several days, but the poor Saints in the Potteries, on learning his condition, supplied his wants, some of the sisters actually walking upwards of twenty miles to relieve him. He preached several times to the debtors, was visited by Elders Woodruff, Richards, George A. Smith, A. Cordon and others, and was dismissed from prison on his persecutors' ascertaining their conduct was about to be exposed. This rather encouraged than disheartened the Elders, as I had told them on their leaving Nauvoo, to be of good courage, for some of them would have to look through grates before their return."*

The decision of the "Beacon Council" was approved by the other brethren, as soon as they were informed of it, and arrangements were quickly made for the printing of the *Book of Mormon*. The work of collecting and arranging the *Hymn Book* also progressed rapidly.

Meanwhile, Elders Woodruff and Richards continued their labors in the Herefordshire region. The work is summarized by Wilford Woodruff in a letter to America:

"We have held two conferences of late in the south of

*History of the Church, Vol. IV, pp. 127, 128.

England where I have been laboring; the first was held at the Gadfield Elm Chapel, in Worcestershire, England, June 14th. Elder W. Richards was with me; we had an interesting time; we organized twelve churches, and transacted much business; the other was held on the 21st of June, at Stanley Hill, Herefordshire, England. Elder Richards and myself conducted the meeting, or conference, with the help of God; and I never saw more business executed in one day, than on this occasion. We organized twenty churches; ordained 4 Elders, 7 Priests and 4 Teachers; baptized 10, confirmed 20, and blessed 20 children, besides a multitude of other business, and broke bread to several hundred Saints, etc. The work had been so rapid, it was impossible to ascertain the exact number belonging to each branch, but the whole number is 33 churches, 534 members, 75 officers, viz.: 10 Elders, 52 priests, and 13 teachers, all of which had embraced the work in less time than four months in a new field which I have opened in Herefordshire, Worcestershire and Gloucestershire, and the Church now in that place numbers over six hundred; and the work was never in a more prosperous state in that place, than at the present time. I have no doubt but what the churches in that place will soon number one thousand souls."
—*Times and Seasons*, Volume 1, p. 168.

The July 6th conference was held, but not in Preston, as had at first been planned. Members of the Church were numerous in Manchester; the *Millennial Star* office was there, and that city was centrally located for the branches; and so it was decided to hold the conference there. Carpenter's Hall, which would seat approximately fifteen hundred persons, was previously hired for regular meetings at a cost of £100 a year. There the conference convened and proceeded in order. Parley P. Pratt was chosen to preside. The other Apostles, with the exception of Orson Pratt, were in attendance. Well over twenty-five hundred members, and about eighty branches, were reported. Priesthood ordinations were recommended. The work of the publishing committee was approved, and the *Hymn Book* was unanimously accepted.

The call was sounded for volunteers to give their entire time to the ministry. Besides the missionaries from America, about fifteen of the local brethren offered their services, which were gladly accepted and used to advantage.

President Joseph Fielding and his two counselors, Hiram Clark* and William Clayton, were released from the duties of presidency, to enable them to give more time to the traveling ministry. Their labors in that capacity, extending over more than two years, were accepted and commended. This action left Brigham Young, as President of the Twelve, in charge of the Mission.

On the day following, a meeting of Church officers convened in the council room of the *Millennial Star* office, Oldham Road, Manchester, where missionaries were assigned to Scotland, Ireland, Newcastle-on-Tyne, Sheffield, Lancaster, and other territory in which they had already labored.

There were fruits in abundance to show for the labors of those eventful three months. The recommendations of the April conference had been fulfilled. The success enjoyed, if one may presume to analyze it, is attributable to at least three factors: First—and always—they were dependent on the Lord, and received and accepted His direction. Second, when there was work to be done, they did it, put it behind them, and tackled the next problem. Third—also important in missionary endeavor—they followed up their work.

---

*See p. 124, paragraph 3 of the minutes of the April 15th conference, for Hiram Clark's appointment to succeed Willard Richards.

CHAPTER 16

THE STORY OF THE "MILLENNIAL STAR"

The *Millennial Star,* official publication of the "Mormon" Church in England since May, 1840, has recorded the rise and progress of the Church of Jesus Christ of Latter-day Saints over a greater span of time than any other publication ever issued by this Church in its one-hundred and seven years of latter-day existence.

The *Star* has chronicled events, temporal and spiritual, under five Sovereigns of the British Empire and under all seven Presidents of the "Mormon" Church, including the Prophet Joseph Smith. When Queen Victoria was early displaying her superb British statesmanship and sagacity the *Star* was noting events of the Church and the world.

When Joseph Smith, the latter-day Prophet, was rounding out his work of "gathering the first harvest" and "strengthening the cause of Zion," the *Star* was recording the progress of events. When a murderous mob claimed the Prophet Joseph as its victim, the *Star,* with black borders, mourned the loss with those who loved the Prophet, and with just men everywhere.

When the first of more than fifty-two thousand Britons left home and country to take their chances with the Church of Jesus Christ in a new world and on new frontiers, the *Millennial Star* recorded their departure, and has continued to note the sacrifices and faithfulness of these men and women who chose principles before convenience, and truth before worldly possessions.

As nearly six thousand "Mormon" missionaries have quietly come and gone from British shores during the past century, the *Millennial Star* has noted their arrivals and departures, their successes and disappointments, their welcomes and persecutions, their testimonies and conversions.

When a misinformed British Press has attacked "Mormons" and "Mormonism," the *Star* has replied with facts. When a well-informed British Press has dealt fairly with the "Mormon" question, the *Millennial Star* has noted this fair treatment and has published its gratitude.

Among the editors and assistant and associate editors of the *Millennial Star,* oldest publication of the "Mormon" Church now in existence, have been numbered five of the seven Presidents of the Church, many of the General Authorities, and others of the Church's most worthy and brilliant writers and thinkers, including university presidents, eminent scientists, congressmen, professors, poets, lawyers, financiers and scholars.

The beginning of the *Millennial Star* dates back to the year 1840-41 when Brigham Young and a majority of the Twelve Apostles conducted their affairs in England as a Quorum for the first and last time. The action which brought the *Millennial Star* into existence and named it, is recorded in the minutes of a General Conference of the Church of Jesus Christ of Latter-day Saints, held in the Temperance Hall, Preston, Lancashire, England, on the 15th of April, 1840.*

In accordance with the commission from the Council of the Twelve, after the close of the conference, Elder Parley P. Pratt went to Manchester, and began preparations for the publication of the *Star.* Within a month he had all arrangements completed and was able to

*See pp. 124, 125.

issue the first number in the latter part of May, under date of May, 1840.

The purposes and policies of the *Star,* as set forth by its first editor, Apostle Parley P. Pratt, were incorporated within the "Editor's Address to His Patrons," which appeared in Volume 1, Number 1. Whether or not the aims and motives as first given have changed with the years the reader may best judge for himself by reviewing the printed address, which is here reproduced in full, unaltered as to wording or punctuation:

"Friends and Fellow-Travellers to Eternity,
"It is with heart-felt joy and satisfaction we have the pleasure of sending forth the first number of the *Millennial Star*—that luminary, which, rightly conducted, may be a means in the hand of God, of breaking the slumber and silence of midnight darkness, which, like a gloomy cloud, has long hung over the moral horizon —of dispelling the mists of error and superstition which have darkened the understanding and benumbed and blunted every great and noble faculty of the soul—and of kindling a spark of light in the hearts of thousands, which will at length blaze forth, and light up the dawn of that bright day which was seen afar off by holy men of old—the Sabbath of Creation.

"We trust this paper will prove a welcome visitor to the palaces of the noble, the mansions of the rich, the towers of the brave, and the cottages of the poor: that the sublimity of its truths, the splendor of its light, and the easy simplicity of its style and language, may, at once, interest and edify the learned, and instruct and enlighten those in the humbler walks of life.

"We are aware of the greatness of the undertaking, and of the solemn and awful responsibility resting upon us in conducting such a publication, as well as of the boundless field—the shoreless ocean—the fathomless deep upon which we have entered. We are truly sensible of our own weakness and inability to fill so important a station—to do justice to subjects so glorious and sublime, to themes so delightful, so divine: themes which have exhausted the eloquence of ancient prophets—the melody of inspired poets: themes, of which angels have tuned their sweetest notes—their sublimest effusions, in strains divinely new, the fulness yet untold.

"Sensible of our own inability, we shall carefully give heed to the sure word of prophecy as to a light which shines in a dark place, and seek for the inspiration of that Spirit which guides into all truth, and, which searches all things; yea, the deep things

of God. In so doing, we hope to be able to hold forth the truth
in a light so clear and evident, that it will commend itself to
every man's conscience.

"In our principles, we shall be obliged to come in contact with
many of the opinions, doctrines, and traditions of men; and have
to contend with many prejudices which now exist in the world,
growing out of the present and past unhappy state of religious
society. But we shall pursue a straightforward, bold, and fearless
course, without turning a hair's-breadth to the right or left from
the principles of truth, to court a smile or shun a frown. We shall
not be careful to inquire what will be popular or unpopular—what
will please or displease, but, what is truth; and when we discern
that a principle is true, and will benefit mankind, we shall publish
it, even if it were to come in conflict with the opinions of all
Christendom.

"If, at any time, we shall be under the necessity of answering
objections, correcting misrepresentations, or of entering into the
field of controversy with those who may differ from us, we shall
'contend earnestly for the faith which was once delivered to the
saints;' but at the same time, hold sacred the characters, regard
the rights, and respect the feelings of those who do not see with
us. 'The servant of the Lord must not strive, but be gentle—
patient towards all men.' 'In meekness instructing those who oppose
themselves.'

"In matters of doctrine, we shall contend for one Lord, one
faith, one baptism, one Holy Spirit, one God and Father of all; and
in short, for all the offices, ordinances, gifts, and blessings which
were set in order among the ancient saints.

"As to party names, we shall acknowledge no name as belonging to the people of God but that of Saints; a name which is older
than the flood. In relation to the Church of God in this age of the
world, we shall acknowledge no name but 'the Church of Jesus Christ
of Latter-day Saints.'

"In regard to prophecy, we shall contend for a literal application and fulfilment, according to the common usage of the language,
—according to the most plain, easy, and simple meaning of words
and sentences.

"As to 'Calvinism,' 'Arminianism,' 'Trinitarianism,' 'Unitarian-
ism,' 'Total-Depravity,' and a thousand other such-like terms,
which have confused, distracted, and divided the religious world,
we know of no such terms in the Bible, and therefore have nothing
to do with them.

"As to 'the powers that be,' we shall teach men to fear God,
honor and respect the laws, and all who are in authority, until
he (Christ) reigns, whose right it is to reign.

"As to temperance, we shall earnestly plead for men to be temperate in all things; and especially to beware of drunkenness and all its attendant evils and abominations.

"In our style, we shall endeavor to be plain and simple, as our principles are designed for the benefit of all classes of society. In short, we hope, by the aid and assistance of the Spirit of God, to comfort the mourner—to bind up the broken-hearted—to preach the gospel to the poor—to bring glad tidings to the meek; and 'that those who have erred in spirit may come to understanding, and those who have murmured may learn doctrine."

(*Manchester, May,* 1840.)

*"The size of the page, weight of paper, and general makeup chosen at the beginning have been continued until the present. It was issued first as a monthly of twenty-four pages, with cover, and bore the imprint, 'Manchester: Printed by W. R. Thomas, Spring Gardens, 149 Oldham Road.' The next three numbers were thirty-two pages each, and the next six numbers twenty-four pages each, making the number of pages in the first volume, three hundred and twelve. The last four numbers of the first volume were printed by W. Shackleton and Son, Duncie Place, Manchester.

"The first number (May, 1841) of the second volume, was printed by Dalton and Rigg, 61 Spring Gardens. After that the numbers bore the imprint: 'Printed and published by P. P. Pratt, 47 Oxford Street, Manchester, and for sale at the Emigration Office, 36 Chapel Street, Liverpool.' Before the volume closed, the publishing office was removed to Liverpool, 36 Chapel Street, and from that time until the removal of the European Mission Headquarters to London in March, 1933, the *Star* had been edited in that city.

"Volume II of the *Millennial Star* consisted of twelve monthly numbers, but each number contained only sixteen pages, making one hundred and ninety-two pages in the volume. Commencing with volume VI (June 15th, 1845) the *Star* was changed to a semi-monthly. That volume (Volume VI) only covered six months, the last number being dated December 1, 1845. Volume VII, also published semi-monthly, commenced with January, 1846, but like its predecessor, only covered six months. Volume VIII

---

*Adapted from "The *Star* and Its Prophesied Headquarters," by James H. Wallis, associate editor, *Millennial Star,* Vol. 95, No. 20.

covered the balance of 1846. Volume IX commenced with
January 1st, 1847, and closed with December 15th, 1847,
and consisted of twenty-four numbers. Volumes X, XI,
XII and XIII were also published regularly as a semi-
monthly periodical, each volume covering a calendar year.
But with the beginning of 1852, commencing with January
1st of that year (Volume XIV), the paper was changed
from a semi-monthly to a weekly periodical, and as such it
has been continued until the present time (1937). The
current volume being published is the ninety-ninth.

"Since 1852, when the paper was changed to a weekly
periodical, each volume has averaged about eight hundred
forty-two pages, and altogether the ninety-nine volumes of
the *Millennial Star* published from 1840 to 1937 inclusive,
contain more than seventy-five thousand pages of printed
matter, all the pages in the volumes being an average size
octavo.

"On two different occasions the very existence of the
Millennial Star has been threatened through lack of patron-
age. The editor intended to suspend the publication at the
close of Volume II, but upon the urgent appeal of the Scotch
saints and others, who promised and rendered financial aid, it
was continued. Early in 1843, agreeable to instructions
from the headquarters of the Church in Nauvoo, Illinois,
the publication of the *Star* was stopped temporarily, but
only for two months, after which it was continued, and the
back numbers issued, so that there was in effect no break
in the publication. In October, 1843, the *Star* had one thousand six hundred subscribers, but when the periodical was
changed to a weekly publication, January 1st, 1852, the
circulation was increased to about twenty-two thousand,
and the subscription price lowered from threepence to one
penny.

"Until 1861, the *Millennial Star* and other Church publications were printed by various firms in England, but in the
spring of 1861 arrangements were made by President George
Q. Cannon, according to the wishes of President Brigham
Young, for the printing and publishing of the *Millennial Star,
Journal of Discourses,* and other Church works and periodicals at the Latter-day Saint Mission Office in Liverpool.
Consequently, a printing press and the necessary machinery,
type and material was purchased, and the first number of
the *Millennial Star* was printed and published from number

42 Islington, Liverpool, commencing with number 17 of Volume 23, dated April 20th, 1861. The *Star* was printed from its own printing department from then until May 4, 1933, when, with the removal of mission headquarters to London, it came from the shop of Mr. James Foggo at 27 Park Lane, Liverpool, the plant having been leased to him."

The *Millennial Star,* important as it is in the century story of the British Mission, is, nevertheless only one of hundreds of publications that have been issued from the presses of the Church in Great Britain, and from private printing establishments under contract to the Church. Many first editions of important contributions to Church literature have been released from British presses before their appearance elsewhere.

Since the first British edition of the *Book of Mormon* in 1841, several editions of three of the four standard works of the Church—the *Book of Mormon, Doctrine and Covenants* and *Pearl of Great Price*—have come from British presses, in addition to an unnumbered and numberless mass of other books, pamphlets and tracts. The size and extent of some such editions shows in the record. Others are nowhere on record, and their number and extent may only be remotely estimated. President Heber J. Grant, prodigious distributor of literature, made the following report at the close of his term of Presidency over the European Mission:

"Today it is thirty-five months since I assumed the Presidency of the European Mission. The time has passed very rapidly. I have been busy and thoroughly enjoyed my labors. The mission was in splendid condition, and I have endeavored to maintain the high standard set by my predecessor. Since my arrival, nine hundred and sixteen missionaries have registered in Liverpool. In January, 1904, the property at 10 Holly Road was purchased as mission headquarters. It was a wonderful improvement over the old quarters at 42 Islington. On November 21, 1906, a splendid home at 295 Edge Lane, known as Durham House, was secured. During the eleven months ending November 30, 1907, there have been printed at the mission headquarters the following tracts and books: *Rays of Living Light,* 785,500; *Articles of Faith and Letter,* 600,000; *First Principles of the Gospel,* 463,000; *Is Baptism Essential?,* 534,000; *Is Belief Alone Sufficient?,* 286,000; *Glad Tidings,* 266,000; *Only True Gospel,* 162,000; *Baptism: How and By Whom Administered?,* 166,000; *Baptism for the Remission of Sins,* 144,000; *Universal Apostasy,* 89,000; *The Only Way To Be Saved,* 74,000; *Restoration of the Everlasting Gospel,* 60,-500; *Necessity of Revelation,* 56,500; *Why Is It?,* 39,000; *Character of the Latter-day Saints,* 11,500; *Bound Rays of Living Light,* 70,000; *My Reasons For Leaving the Church of England,* 20,400; *Was Joseph Smith Sent of God?,* 5,000; *Parry's,* 19,000.—From President Grant's Farewell Address to the British Mission.—*Millennial Star,* Vol. 95, p. 350.

For a century now "Mormon" missionaries have been distributing such literature, with its message of life and salvation, to the doors of the great and the lowly, and on the streets of the cities and the by-lanes of the countryside. Most of it has been freely given. Some has been sold at cost. While the condition of the record makes accurate estimation impossible, it is probable that the century has seen the distribution in Great Britain of no less than three hundred million tracts and ten million books and pamphlets. Some of this literature has been spurned; some has been ignored; some has been foolishly and wastefully passed out. But much of it has penetrated the hearts of honest, truth-seeking men and women and has started them upon a quest for further knowledge of God's will and purposes concerning men. Whatever of "Mormon" literature has gone unheeded in the British Isles, that which has reached its mark has paid sufficient rewards in human happiness and salvation to justify all of the money, labor and materials, with an inestimable balance still on the credit side of the ledger.

But to return to the "Story of the *Star*."

The foreman of the *Millennial Star* office was, from the first or very soon after, Mr. William L. Davies, who continued in charge for about thirty years, and under whom Elder James H. Wallis received his early training. Mr. Davies was succeeded by Elder H. J. Halton, who later went to Salt Lake City, Utah, but who was with the office for more than nine years, taking his departure for America, June 7th, 1900. He was succeeded by the efficient and faithful foreman, Mr. James Foggo, who served from May 25, 1900, until December 31, 1936, at which time the printing of the *Star* was placed under contract with the *Ludo Press*, 373 Earlsfield Road, London S. W. 18. With this change, under the administration of Dr. Richard R. Lyman, the *Star* was given a two-color cover and began, for the first time in its history, to accept a limited and selected type of advertising. It should be noted that for thirty-seven years under James Foggo, an issue of the *Star* was never late—not even during the World War, when he worked in an aircraft factory by day and set the type and printed the *Star* by night.

There have been a number of practical printers, typographers and pressmen called on missions to Great Britain, and it is known that several of these have at times served in the publishing department of the *Star*. Among them may be mentioned, Joseph Bull, Sr., Walter J. Lewis, Joseph Hyrum Parry, Joseph Bull, Jr., George C. Lambert, Edwin F. Parry, James H. Anderson and J. M. Sjodahl.

Brigham Young edited the *Millennial Star* for a

time, although his name never appeared in print as its editor. Elder Thomas Ward was the first associate editor of the *Star*, assisting Parley P. Pratt, and upon the return of Elder Pratt to the United States in October, 1842, Brother Ward was made editor-in-chief. Elder Reuben Hedlock subsequently arrived from Nauvoo, and became the presiding Elder of the Mission, but Elder Ward still continued editor of and principal writer for the *Star*, as he did also after Apostle Wilford Woodruff arrived in January, 1845, to preside over the Mission. In the following June, however, Elder Woodruff became senior editor, and Elder Ward, associate. In January, 1846, Elder Woodruff, having decided to return home, Elder Ward again became the editor.

On the arrival of Apostle Orson Hyde and John Taylor in October, 1846, to assume the presidency of the British Mission, the first named became editor of the *Star*. Word having been received that Elder Orson Spencer was dead, his obituary was published in the *Star* of January 1, 1847, and in the next issue Elder Hyde announced his own departure for America, and the appointment of Elder Franklin D. Richards to the presidency of the Mission and editorship of the *Star*. Elder Richards' tenure of office was very brief; he only remained to edit one number of the *Star*, and, indeed, his name was not even published as editor, but instead appeared the name of Orson Spencer, for, strange to say, he landed in England twenty-three days after his death had been announced, and enjoyed a privilege which most mortals are denied—that of reading his own obituary.

The names of the editors and associate editors of the *Millennial Star* subsequent to this time and until the present, are listed in the Appendix.

Nearly a century has passed since the publication of the *Millennial Star* was started, ten years after the organization of the Church, and during one of the most trying periods of its history. As set forth on the title page of the first volume, each one subsequent has contained "a great variety of useful information in regard to the doctrine, principles, rise, progress, success, opposition, persecution, etc., of the Church of Jesus Christ of Latter-day Saints, and of the great work of God in these last days, with a faithful record of the signs and judgments which are beginning to be shown forth in the heavens and in the earth."

Each week of every year the *Latter-day Saints' Millennial Star* goes forth in British lands as an expounder of doctrine, as a teacher of lofty precept, a bearer of timely news, a minister of comfort and cheer, a messenger of good will, and as a herald of salvation. It has recorded prophecies and their fulfillment; it has been the first place of appearance of some of the great works of "Mormon" literature, and of some of the most enduring and best beloved "Mormon" hymns. The *Star* has felt the pulse of the Church and its people, and has reflected, in truth, what it felt.

What events future issues of the *Millennial Star* will be called upon to record, no man knows, but that these and all other world events will be in accordance with the words and prophecies of the prophets of God, both ancient and modern, is a solemn and invariable certainty. That all such events will continue to be recorded in fact, and interpreted in the light of truth, is a sacred tradition of nearly a century's standing, from which the oldest current publication of the Church of Jesus Christ of Latter-day Saints may not depart.

CHAPTER 17

IRELAND HEARS THE GOSPEL

The Lord's latter-day work was well started in England and Scotland. There was work enough to keep all hands busy—and to spare—on the English side of the Irish Sea; but there were millions in Ireland still waiting in darkness, thousands of whom were prepared for the advent of truth. The privilege of carrying Gospel tidings to those who waited on the "Emerald Isle" fell to the lot of Elder John Taylor.

The Church in Liverpool was growing rapidly. There were demands upon every available hour of Elder Taylor's time; but to say unqualifiedly that John Taylor was popular in Liverpool would be to utter an untruth. True servants of the Lord are seldom popular with great majorities. Those who did seek his ministrations, however, sought earnestly, as if their soul's salvation depended upon it—which, indeed, was the case. It is plain, however, that this wholesome popularity did not extend to the gentlemen of the clerical garb. Of them he wrote:

"We called upon many of the leading ministers of different denominations, and delivered our testimony to them. Some received us kindly, some otherwise; but none would let us have their chapels to hold forth in. They were so good in general, and so pure, that they had no room for the Gospel. They were too holy to be righteous, too good to be pure, and had too much religion to enter into the kingdom of heaven."—*Times and Seasons*, Volume 2, p. 404.

Early in the month of July, 1840, Elder Taylor engaged for one year, one of the largest and finest halls

in Liverpool—the Music Hall, on Bold Street, with seating accommodations for approximately fifteen hundred
people. In this hall a lecture series was to be given by
Elder Taylor. Following its acquisition and before the
lectures were scheduled to begin, a brief week or two
was available for the introduction of the Gospel into
Ireland.

James McGuffie, obviously Irish, was among those
who were early baptized in Liverpool. He was well
acquainted and connected in the village of Newry,
County Down, Ireland. It is not at all unlikely that
Newry was the village of his birth and the home of
his youth, although we are not definitely told so. This
Brother McGuffie and Brother William Black were the
traveling companions of John Taylor on his first official
visit to the "Emerald Isle" as an ambassador of the
Gospel of Jesus Christ.

Taking leave at Liverpool from a large group of
Saints who had gathered to the docks to bid them farewell, these three sailed out of the River Mersey into
the Irish Sea on July 28th, 1840. Seven months earlier
there had been no member of the latter-day Church of
God in the world-famous port of Liverpool; now there
were scores, eager to assist the work and its servants,
and thankful for their own knowledge of the life-giving
message.

On the day after sailing, the three reached Newry,
a village among the hills of rural Ireland, some thirty odd
miles in a southerly direction from Belfast. The influence of Brother McGuffie, with the help of the Lord,
placed the courthouse at the disposal of the brethren.
The village bell-ringer was dispatched to give notice of
the pending meeting, an unusual meeting, which was to
be held at seven o'clock that evening. The news spread,

and had its effect. Between six and seven hundred nearby residents gathered at the appointed hour, and there Elder John Taylor preached the first public Gospel discourse in Ireland. One such discourse satisfied the curiosity of most of the congregation. The meeting that was announced for the following evening was attended by a few only, and the time was largely spent in friendly and informal discussion.

Following the second night's meeting in Newry, it was decided that other places should be visited. Accordingly, the next morning Brothers McGuffie and Black, with a Mr. Thomas Tate, a Liverpool acquaintance, accompanied Brother Taylor in a jaunting-car on a trip through rural Ireland. The first evening they reached the region known as the four towns of Bellimacrat, and preached in the barn of an obliging farmer, Mr. Willie, by name.

The next day they proceeded on foot in the direction of Lisburn, still accompanied by Mr. Tate, who, as John Taylor had previously prophesied, was to be the first person baptized in Ireland. As they walked along country lanes on that fresh summer morning, the spirit of truth and understanding was their companion. John Taylor expounded the eternal purposes of God for the welfare of man. All doubt departed from Mr. Tate, and, as they topped a hill, at the foot of which lay Loch Brickland, a sudden conviction of truth led him to exclaim: "See, here is water; what doth hinder me to be baptized?"—Acts 8:36.

Nothing hindered. The party drew near the lake shore. With John Taylor, Thomas Tate entered the water and was baptized—the first fruits of the Gospel in Ireland.

Further activities were carried on in the town of Lisburn. There Elder Taylor preached several times in the market place to audiences of gratifying numbers. Interest in the latter-day work was manifest throughout County Down. Nor had the efforts in Newry been futile. Before Elder Taylor left Lisburn, word came that Brother McGuffie, who had returned to the village, had begun to baptize.

John Taylor intended to begin activities in the city of Belfast, but appointments previously made called him soon to Scotland and back to Liverpool. He took boat from Belfast to Glasgow on August 6th, 1840, having labored in Ireland only ten days. But the work begun in that brief period has endured and prospered even until now.

Following a hurried trip, during which he preached on several occasions, Elder Taylor broke away from the Scottish Saints, under protest, to return to Liverpool and deliver his lectures, which were conducted as arranged, and which were attended by appreciative audiences. Two reverend gentlemen of our previous acquaintance—Mr. Robert Aitken and Mr. Timothy R. Matthews, and their disciples—were the chief disturbers of order at the gatherings. They used all the methods known to the unscrupulous in attempting to break up the meetings and discredit the missionaries—but the work has outlived them and their memory in the world.

Elder Theodore Curtis, who had formerly labored in New York, arrived in Britain during the summer of 1840, and was assigned to take up the work in Ireland. At the October 6th conference, 1840, he represented the Hillsborough Branch of five members—the first branch of the Church of Jesus Christ of Latter-day Saints in Ireland. A few months later Elder Taylor reported by letter to the Prophet Joseph Smith that Elder

Curtis had taken up the work in Belfast, and that the Church in Ireland numbered nearly thirty.*

Since that first thirty were brought out of the world, many thousands from the "Emerald Isle" have joined the Church of Jesus Christ, of whom thousands have emigrated.

From out of Ireland, as a lad, with a widowed mother, came Charles A. Callis, of the Council of the Twelve. Born at Dublin, Ireland, May 4, 1865, he was baptized in Liverpool at the age of eight years, and later, at the age of ten, emigrated with his mother to Utah in October, 1875, where he qualified himself for a legal career. All other pursuits he gave up in response to a call to serve the Church as a missionary, to which exalted pursuit he has devoted the best years of his mature life, and his example typifies the loyalty that the Irish Saints have given to the Church of Jesus Christ. One such mission carried him back to Ireland to preach the Gospel in his native land.

Despite this ancient land's turbulent religious and political history, the purposeful step of "Mormon" missionaries has sounded in the cities and across the shamrock countryside, bringing stalwart, courageous men and women into the Church, whose memories are honored by a worthy and loyal posterity, who are proud of their Irish lineage and grateful for their Gospel heritage.

---

*Times and Seasons, Volume 2, p. 401.

CHAPTER 18

GOSPEL TIDINGS TO THE ISLE OF MAN

The stir occasioned by the Gospel introduction to the Isle of Man may well be said to have been inversely proportional to the size of that land dot in the Irish Sea. The Isle, which measures only thirty odd miles in length by about twelve in width, as early as 1840 boasted a population of more than 47,000 inhabitants, many of whom were searching and waiting for truth.

The visit of Gospel messengers there was neither unpremeditated nor hastily planned. In all probability it was in John Taylor's mind to go there at the outset of his mission. He expressed his intention at least as early as the spring of the year 1840, nearly six months before the undertaking was under way, during a conversation with Mr. Radcliff, agent for the Bible Society and Superintendent of the School of Arts in Liverpool. On that occasion a Miss Brannan from the Isle of Man had been present and had expressed her displeasure at Elder Taylor's views of the outside religious world. Before parting, that worthy missionary told Miss Brannan that he proposed a visit to the Isle, and should be pleased to call on her household; to which she replied that she would be pleased to see him, but not as a religious teacher, unless his views were as those of other preachers of her acquaintance.

This provoked a firm but gentlemanly rebuke from John Taylor to the effect that he would visit the Isle of Man with or without her approval; that others would accept his message whether she did or not, and that her request that he be like other ministers, put him in

mind of the Prophet Micah, who, when he was advised
to speak as the other prophets of king Ahab, replied:
"As the Lord liveth, even what my God saith, that will
I speak."*   It is not likely that John Taylor, outstanding
as a gentleman, used just these words in just this abrupt
manner, but it was not characteristic of him to leave
any room for doubt in the minds of his auditors as to
the import of his message.

Admittedly, John Taylor had at least two good
reasons for paying the long contemplated visit to Manx
land.   They may be classed under the general heads—
sentimental and altruistic.   To be entered under the
first head is the fact that the Isle of Man was the
place of birth and scene of the girlhood of Leonora
Cannon, beloved wife of John Taylor.   There the Cannon manor had held place for many generations.   But
a more important consideration is to be placed under
the second head—the proclamation of the Gospel was
John Taylor's sole purpose for being in Great Britain,
and surely the beautiful Manx Isle with its thousands
of upright men and women was worthy the message of
life.   At least so felt John Taylor in the late summer
of 1840—and it is now a matter of historical certainty
that he was led aright.

The actual departure for the Isle occurred on September 16th, from Liverpool. On that day, accompanied
by Elder Hiram Clark and Brother William Mitchell,
an early convert in Liverpool, John Taylor sailed for
Douglas and arrived in that principal Isle of Man city
on the following day.   The fresh scenes that presented
themselves, and the fond memories they recalled, stirred
the poet soul of Elder Taylor as he first viewed the
place of Leonora's girlhood; his language flowed with
fervor and eloquence:

*Life of John Taylor, by B. H. Roberts, p. 82.

"Thou hast passed through trials, Nora, but thou shalt rejoice! Thou hast been driven from thy home for the truth's sake, but thou and thy children shall have a home in the kingdom of God! Thou hast suffered the bereavement of thy husband—the tender association has been severed—that others may be made partakers of endless life; but thou and thy husband shall yet reign together in the celestial kingdom of God. A few more struggles and the battle will be fought, the victory will be ours, and with the redeemed out of every nation we will sing: 'Glory and honor, and power, and might, and majesty, and dominion be ascribed to Him that sitteth upon the throne, and to the Lamb, forever and forever'."— *Life of John Taylor*, by B. H. Roberts, p. 90.

So much for sentimental considerations.

Within a day or two after their arrival, it was decided that Brothers Clark and Mitchell should take up their labors in Ramsey, the northern city of the Isle, and that Elder Taylor should remain in the town of Douglas. Before the company of three parted for service, they retired to a secluded field a short distance on the road from Douglas to Ramsey, and united in petitioning the Giver of all good gifts for the success of the work in hand. At the foot of a tree on which Elder Taylor carved their initials, they each placed a stone in remembrance of their covenants with the Lord, and devotion to His work. Brother William Mitchell was here ordained a Deacon. Elders Taylor and Clark blessed each other in turn. The Spirit of the Lord attended them, and approved; for they spoke in tongues and prophesied and sang songs of praise, and parted company rejoicing.

Returning the short distance to Douglas, John Taylor began at once to make his mission and message known. Visits to associates of his wife's youth, in addition to the many friends that his own attractive personality quickly won, soon lengthened the list of homes

in which he was welcomed. After preliminary activities
had aroused sufficient interest to justify the action, he
rented the Wellington Rooms, the largest and finest hall
in Douglas, with seating accommodations for a thousand persons. This distinctly bold stroke had the effect
of a gauntlet thrown down, upon the pseudo-religionists
of the Isle; and from then on the Manx activities of John
Taylor took on a controversial aspect—in printed
pamphlet, in private correspondence, in the public press
and in public debate. Of this "controversial period"
John Taylor wrote as follows, in a letter to the Prophet
Joseph Smith:

> "I hired a large room capable of containing one thou-
> sand persons and commenced delivering lectures; great ex-
> citement prevailed, and a persecuting spirit soon manifested
> itself. I held a discussion with one man, a preacher, which
> had a tendency to enlighten the eyes of the public. Another
> wrote in the papers, and I answered him; another published
> pamphlets, and I answered them; another delivered lectures,
> and I answered them; and I finally challenged any of them
> to meet me before the public and prove the *Book of Mormon*
> and my doctrine false if they could, but this they were
> afraid to do, and gave up the contest. I see, sir, more clearly
> every day the impossibility of overturning the principles
> of truth by any of the foolish dogmas or lame reasoning
> of this present generation, and how should they? for God has
> revealed it, and His arm supports it."—*Times and Seasons*,
> Vol. 2, p. 401.

But John Taylor was not without friends during
this period of intense feeling. Many volunteered themselves as his champions; they arose in his behalf at
public gatherings; his replies to the press were accorded
place with the attacks of his opponents; audiences at
public gatherings were sympathetic, and his activities
were well reported. Excerpts from the story of one
public encounter as it appeared in the *Manx Liberal* of

October 4th, 1840, is a notable example of the treatment he received from the press:

"On Friday evening last, while Mr. Taylor, who professes to be a missionary from the Latter-day Saints, was lecturing in the Wellington Market Hall, in this town, he was interrupted in a very indecorous manner by a party of Primitive Methodist preachers, and a young man of the name of Gill, who is both an itinerant bookseller and a Wesleyan Methodist local preacher, who ever and anon kept annoying him, until at last they so far confused the meeting as to stop the lecturer. There and then, in the fury of their zeal, they appeared ready for combat, but certain individuals possessing more discretion than religious intolerance, quelled the rage of the 'disorderlies' and showed the impropriety of such a proceeding, by stating that the room was Mr. Taylor's—that they had met for the purpose of religious worship, and ought not to be disturbed—but if they conceived that the speaker had advanced anything contrary to the word of God, they had no doubt but that Mr. Taylor would meet them if they appointed a time and place for public discussion.

"To this the lecturer consented, but at the same time gave them to understand that he was not favorable to disputation. Next day Mr. Taylor received a letter from Mr. Hamilton, charging him with having "misquoted the word of God; with having mutilated it, added to it, and taken from it; with having uttered blasphemy; and with endeavoring to decoy souls to perdition;" all of which Mr. H. declared himself ready to prove if Mr. T. would meet him at seven o'clock on Monday evening, in the Wellington Market Hall. Mr. Taylor accepted of the challenge on condition that each party should be allowed to choose his own chairman—that Mr. Hamilton should speak first—and be allowed one hour, and that he (Mr. T.) should have one hour to repudiate the supposed charges, and that each should have an additional half-hour to reply.

"Mr. Hamilton having approved of the conditions, on Sunday Mr. Taylor announced the intended discussion to his congregation, and on Monday evening, at the time appointed, the large room was completely filled with persons anxious to witness the coming conflict betwixt the two champions.

"All preliminaries being over and chairmen chosen, Mr. H. was called to defend his charges. He instantly arose and commenced his harangue by showing what a clever fellow he had been, what he had done, and by inference, what he was still able to do. He said that he once took part in a similar discussion, and so effectual were the weapons of his oratory that his antagonist died within three days, and that on a subsequent occasion he was equally successful. This, as might be expected, raised some excitement in the meeting, and created some alarm for the safety of his opponent, who seemed doomed to fall beneath the fatal influence of his death-striking logic. But as he proceeded, it soon became apparent that he was a mere braggadocio, possessing no qualifications save ignorance and presumption. His countenance void of every trace of intelligence—his common-place expressions abounding with tautology—the stiffness of his attitude—the inaccuracy of his language and the monotony of his tone—all indicated his utter inability to effect his purpose, so that the missionary had nothing to fear from the inoffensive weapons of the harmless Hamilton. However, he managed to occupy his hour in the delivery of one of his favorite sermons on the origin, nature, and design of the Gospel, but made not even the most distant allusion in reference to the gross and unfounded charges he had pledged himself to prove.

"Mr. T. being called, arose, and expressed his surprise that no proof of the charges laid against him had been attempted; but as he was allowed an hour, he would have to imitate the example of his friend, and preach too. His opponent had said much about the Gospel, he too believed it to be the 'power of God unto salvation to every one that believeth;' but it was the Gospel of Jesus Christ, and not a part, but the whole of the Gospel. Mention had been made of different sections of the Church; he did not believe that the Church of Christ was divided into sections. The Holy Spirit did not inspire one party with one opinion and another party with another opinion; God was not the author of confusion; there was one God, one faith, and one baptism. All the different sections of the Church, as they were called, originated in the observance of the opinions of men rather than the Word of Eternal Truth. As the Gospel was unchangeable, and its Author no respecter of persons, the Church at the present day ought to be the same, with regard to its offices, gifts, and privileges, as in the apostolic age. Mr. T. having strenuously defended the above sentiments, then turned to Mr. H. and contended that the section to which he (Mr. H.) belonged was not established on apostolic principles, and that its ministers were not called according to the ordinance of God."

*   *   *   *   *

"The time agreed to for the discussion having expired, the following motion was about to be put to the meeting—"Resolved: That as Mr. Hamilton has neither proved, nor attempted to prove, any of the charges made by him against Mr. Taylor, this meeting believes that they are utterly false, and consequently indefensible." This motion, had it been put, would have been carried by an overwhelming majority. But this was not permitted, for at that moment Mr. Gill, the chairman for Mr. H., sprang on his feet, and dancing mad, "half sung, half screamed," to the following effect: "As I have been implicated as one of the offenders on Friday evening last, I have a right to vindicate my conduct. We met here to discuss certain topics, but precious little has been said. It was I who wrote the letter charging him with having mutilated the word of God, with having added to and taken from it, with having uttered blasphemy, and with having labored to decoy souls to perdition, and I can prove it! and I can prove it! and I can prove it!" Here his voice was drowned by cries from all parts of the room of "shame, shame"—"put him down"—"put him out," mingled with hisses and groans. The tumult having subsided, he made an attempt to give out the doxology, when "no! no!" from a hundred voices assailed his ears. Then Mr. Taylor, who had conducted himself during the meeting both as a gentleman and a Christian, gave out the doxology, and concluded with prayer, after which the meeting quietly dispersed."—*Millennial Star,* Vol. 1, pp. 178-180.

Following is a sample of the newspaper correspondence that John Taylor was called upon to meet. It appeared in the *Manx Liberal* of October 14th, ten days later than the one reprinted above:

"Sir, I feel rather surprised and chagrined that the modern delusion, viz., 'Mormonism,' should have made such rapid strides in this town, hitherto considered exempt from the many systems of irreligious creeds which abound in England, America, and elsewhere. I had thought that the powerful and argumentative addresses of the dissenting ministers would have checked such a gross piece of imposition in its infancy, and thus prevented the great mass of our town's people from becoming dupes of designing knaves, 'and being led away by every wind of doctrine.' Above all, I imagined that the two pamphlets issued by that holy, religious and devout man of God, Mr. Hays, Wesleyan minister (to which connection I have the happiness and honor to belong) would have been quite sufficient to prove the fallacy of such a system, and prevent its further spread. But, sir, alas! the case is quite the reverse; numbers continually flock to the Wellington Rooms, and listen with eagerness to the principles there advocated. The members of our society (Methodists) seem to be most conspicuous in sanctioning and promoting this vile and abominable doctrine.

"Oh, sir, the result to our connection will be dreadful; the havoc tremendous. Just think of the majority of our *leading* and intelligent men aiding and abetting a cause of this description! Oh, sir, lamentable and heart-rending to witness the beaming countenances, and smiles of approbation displayed recently at Taylor's meeting! I could enumerate a host of our members who regularly attend those anti-Christian meetings." * * *

Just who were the first persons to be baptized in the Isle, and the exact date of baptism, are details that are

not given in any readily available accounts; but suffice
it to say that many were baptized, and in a small measure
at least, John Taylor was permitted to see the fruits of
his labors before he left these shores. In February,
John Taylor wrote to the Prophet Joseph Smith:

"I went to a country place on the Island and sat down
in the chimney corner, and talked to a few neighbors who
came in, and baptized eight and confirmed them the same
night, before I left them, nor would they wait until the morning."—*Times and Seasons*, Vol. 2, p. 402.

Elder Taylor spent between two and three months
on the Isle. His labors were followed, beginning November 16th, by those of Elder J. Blakesley, who arrived
from America early in the month. He and Elder Hiram
Clark labored together for a time. On Christmas day,
1840, the two met in Douglas with the brethren who
had been baptized, and formally organized the Isle of
Man Branch, with John Barnes as presiding Elder, and
John Mills, a Teacher, as branch clerk. The meeting
was held at the home of Brother John Cowells with
whom the missionaries lodged in Douglas. At this time
the membership of the branch was reported at about
forty. Two months later it had grown to seventy.

Elder Clark remained until January 8th; Brother
Blakesley until February 16th, 1841. One of the local
brethren from Liverpool carried on missionary activities
for a time after that date—possibly Brother William
Mitchell.

Some stalwart stock of the latter-day Church of
Christ was cradled on that picturesque Isle of the Irish
Sea, which for many generations had been the home of
the Cannons, the Quayles and the Cowleys, and of other
stalwart truth-seekers who had the courage of their
convictions.

CHAPTER 19

THE GOSPEL GOES TO LONDON

"The far-flung *British Empire* has but one heart—London!"

In the autumn of 1840, when three Latter-day Saint missionaries undertook to introduce the Gospel of Jesus Christ in its midst, the great metropolis was scarcely a shadow of the city that has now relentlessly enveloped so many of its neighboring towns and villages. In that year it had less than two million inhabitants. In this year it boasts more than eight millions. And yet, its substantial attractiveness and its peculiar advantages were probably greater by contrast and comparison with the rest of the world then than now.

There comes to mind the question: Why was not London chosen to be the British starting point of the Lord's latter-day work in 1837? Was it not the world's largest city and virtually the world's capital—the logical place for Church headquarters in its hemisphere? Was it not the most likely place to which men, bearing a message for all people, left to their own devices, would first direct their footsteps and begin their work? Were there not more people there to be reached with minimum travel and time expenditure? Was it not everything that is usually accounted desirable in such circumstances?

Undoubtedly London was all this and had all these advantages, and more. And, had the work been directed solely by the judgment of men, London would probably have been the starting point of the Lord's latter-day work in Great Britain. But unfortunately, or perhaps fortunately, it frequently happens that men's ways are not the Lord's. The work began in Preston, Lancashire, took root, gained strength and numbers for more than three years, before it spread to London. It is now a matter of history that this procedure was desirable and successful.

The London visit had been projected long before it was undertaken. At the 1840 April conference it was broached. At the July 6th conference it was planned and authorized. By then, branches of the Church were flourishing in many parts of England, and in Scotland, Ireland, Wales, and on the Isle of Man.

It was well that three seasoned missionaries—Heber C. Kimball, George A. Smith and Wilford Woodruff— were chosen for this task of many difficulties and many possibilities, of many discouragements and accomplishments. Such obstacles and indifference as they faced would have checked men of less faith and experience. Without the help of God, even such men would have been powerless to accomplish so great a task.

Following the British general conference of the Church in July, 1840, Wilford Woodruff and George A. Smith left quickly for the Herefordshire region, where they labored and preached, sometimes together, sometimes independently, for nearly a month. In early August they were joined by Heber C. Kimball. On the 11th of that month they began slowly to move London-ward. By the 17th they had reached Leigh, having baptized and organized en route. Leigh to Cheltenham by coach on the 17th, a night at Cheltenham, forty miles through Oxfordshire by coach, and a railroad journey from Farmington Station to the Great Western Terminus, brought them to the British metropolis at about four p. m. on August 18th, 1840—the first Latter-day Saint missionaries to visit London in official capacity.

They traveled to the center of the city by omnibus, and from there directed their steps to No. 19 King Street, Borough, the home of Mr. William Allgood, whose wife was a sister-in-law to Elder Theodore Turley. Mrs. Allgood cordially welcomed them, fed them, and directed them to the King's Arms, King Street, Borough, where they were comfortably lodged.

The next few days were days of orientation. The brethren saw much that was see-worthy in London. They called on preachers. They made friends and acquaintances. They directed many inquiries and surveyed the ground, always with an eye single to the great cause that brought them there.

Superficially, London must have changed much, but the real London—the punctuating points, the landmarks, the admirable, indescribable features that distinguish London from the world—seem almost to have changed little or not at all. A twentieth century reader can readily follow and feel the descriptions written by those worthy London missionaries of 1840, as they saw what was to be seen, and what is still to be seen in London:

London Bridge, the Thames, the Houses of Parliament, Buckingham Palace, Westminster Abbey and the British Museum, each drew its share of comment. St. Paul's impressed them. Regent Street received deserved attention. Chancery Lane was paid a visit. All Soul's Church was noted. Piccadilly, Leicester Square and Oxford Street were included in the London itinerary, and the city was viewed from the top of Christopher Wren's monument, built as a reminder of the great fire of 1666, which they were charged sixpence to ascend. No, that indescribable personality of London could not have changed much.

Defending the practice of "seeing what there is to see"—if, indeed, it needs defense—a letter written to

Brothers Robinson and Smith of the *Times and Seasons,*
dated London, October 28th, and signed by Heber C.
Kimball, George A. Smith and Wilford Woodruff,
opened with the following paragraph:

"As we consider it perfectly consistent with our calling,
with reason and revelation, that we should form a knowledge
of kingdoms and countries, whether it be at home or abroad,
whether it be ancient or modern, or whether it be of things
past, present, or to come, whether it be in heaven, earth or
hell, air or seas; or whether we obtain this knowledge by
being local or traveling, by study or faith, by dreams or by
visions, by revelation or by prophecy, it mattereth not unto
us; if we can but obtain a correct principle and knowledge
of things as they are, in their true light, past, present, and to
come. It is under such a view of things that we are endeavoring to avail ourselves of every opportunity in our
travels among the nations of the earth, to record an account
of things as they pass under our observation; extracts of
which we may forward to you from time to time, which may
not be uninteresting to your readers."—*Times and Seasons,*
Vol. II, p. 261.

In all their goings and comings the brethren were
interpreting their experiences in terms of their work—
seeking opportunities to present their message publicly
or privately. They called upon Reverend J. E. Smith,
of Lincoln-in-Fields. They attended meetings at Zion's
Chapel and heard Reverend Robert Aitken of the Aitkenites preach. Of him Wilford Woodruff wrote: "He
delivered a powerful warning to the Gentiles, and presented some of the most sublime truths I ever heard
from a sectarian priest; but he was building without the
foundation."* Mr. Aitken was a brilliant and living
illustration of the profound truth that eloquence alone
neither converts nor saves.

On August 24th the brethren moved their lodgings
to Mr. Robert Merryfield's, No. 15 Gloucester Row,

---

*Cowley's *Life of Wilford Woodruff,* p. 122.

Grange Road. Having settled in more permanent and satisfactory quarters, from then on their work was more consistent and deliberate.

Following a practice that proved so successful in many other cities, on the 25th the three attended a meeting of the Temperance Society, whose hall was located on St. George's Road, near the Elephant and Castle. They introduced themselves as missionaries from America. Responding to an invitation, George A. Smith addressed the gathering. His remarks, appropriately, were chiefly upon temperance and the Word of Wisdom, which, though brief and informal, may be accounted the first Gospel discourse publicly delivered in the British metropolis.

The brethren sought and obtained permission to rent the hall for a public meeting. September 7th was settled upon as the first available or suitable date.

In the meantime, the brethren, not quite satisfied with the one appointment they had obtained, continued diligent search for other openings. Baptist ministers and Methodist meetings were favored with calls—whether the recipients deemed such calls favors or not. Many religionists and many church bodies and proprietors of halls had—and exercised—the opportunity of refusing sought-for privileges to the Latter-day Saint missionaries of London. Two days after the first visit to the Temperance Hall, the brethren called again and by request Wilford Woodruff and George A. Smith spoke briefly in turn, and announced their meeting in that place for the 7th of the coming month.

Encouragement was conspicuous by its absence. London, the center of so much that goes on in the world, was obdurate, indifferent, unresponsive. The dwellers there seemed to be caught in the worldly whirl that slackens not its pace for the things of eternal worth.

London was stubborn! But finally the hoped for opening
came, and is recorded thus in the *History of the Church*:

"Elders Kimball, Woodruff and George A. Smith, after
having spent ten days visiting the clergymen and preachers
and others of the several denominations, asking the privilege
of preaching in their chapels, and being continually refused
by them in a contemptuous manner, they determined to
preach in the open air, Jonah-like; and accordingly went to
Smithfield Market—to the spot where John Rogers was
burned at the stake—for the purpose of preaching at 10 a. m.,
where they were notified by the police that the Lord Mayor
had issued orders prohibiting street preaching in the city. A
Mr. Connor stepped up and said: 'I will show you a place
outside his jurisdiction,' and guided them to Tabernacle
Square, where they found an assembly of about four hundred
people listening to a preacher who was standing on a chair.
When he got through another preacher arose to speak. Elder
Kimball stated to the first clergyman: 'There is a man present
from America who would like to preach;' which was granted;
when Elder George A. Smith delivered a discourse of about
twenty minutes, on the first principles of the Gospel, taking
for his text Mark 16:16, after which Elder Kimball asked
the preacher to give out another appointment at the same
place for the American Elder to preach; when he jumped
up and said: 'I have just learned that the gentleman who
has addressed you is a Latter-day Saint; I know them; they
are a very bad people; they have split up many churches,
and have done a great deal of hurt.' He spoke all manner
of evil, and gave the Latter-day Saints a very bad character,
and commanded the people not to hear the Elders, 'as we
have got the Gospel, and can save people without infidelity,
socialism, or Latter-day Saints.'

"Elder Kimball asked the privilege of standing on the
chair to give out an appointment himself. The preacher said:
'You shall not do it; you have no right to preach here;'
jerked the chair away from him, and ran away with it. Several of the crowd said: 'You have as much right to preach
here as he has, and give out your appointment;' whereupon
Elder Kimball gave out an appointment for three o'clock
p. m., at which time a large congregation was gathered.

"After opening the meeting by singing and prayer,
Elder Woodruff spoke about thirty minutes, from Galatians

1:8, 9, upon the first principles of the Gospel. Elder Kimball
followed upon the same subjects. The people gave good attention, and seemed much interested in what they had heard.
The inhabitants who lived around the square opened their
windows to four stories high; the most of them were crowded
with anxious listeners, which is an uncommon occurrence.
The meeting was dismissed in the midst of good feeling.

"Mr. Henry Connor invited the Elders to his house.
Soon after they arrived here, Elder Kimball felt impressed
to return to the place of preaching. When he got there
he found a large company talking about the things which
they had heard in the afternoon, and they wished him to
speak to them again. He did so, when several persons invited him home with them. While Elder Kimball was
preaching, several persons came to Brothers Woodruff and
Smith to converse on doctrine, when Mr. Connor offered
himself for baptism.

"Monday, August 31st, Elder Kimball baptized Henry
Connor, watchmaker, 52 Ironmonger's Row, London, in
Peerless Pool, being the first baptized in that place, and con-
firmed him the same evening."—*History of the Church*, Vol.
IV, pp. 182-184.

These were the first open-air meetings in London—
the predecessors of unnumbered thousands that have
since been conducted there by Latter-day Saint missionaries, of which many thrilling and colorful tales could be
told, and from which many additions to the Latter-day
Church of Christ have come.

Tabernacle Square, Hyde Park, and other London
open-air stands, for nearly a century have seen "Mormon" missionaries raising their voices in testimony to
the passing and lingering millions who live in the world
metropolis.

Henry Connor, the first of a large London harvest,
was soon followed by others of his family and by many
not of his kin.

CHAPTER 20

FURTHER LONDON LABORS

Following the first London baptism Elders Kimball and Smith paid a visit to the township of Deptford. During their absence a Mr. Panther, of 17 Wharf City Road, Basin, director of a Methodist Chapel, extended to Elder Wilford Woodruff the use of a schoolhouse at Bowl Court, 137 Shoreditch, for the next Sunday. On the appointed day, September 6, 1840, the three brethren repaired to the schoolhouse and held morning services, each speaking in turn. By evening, after the brethren had held an afternoon open-air meeting in Tabernacle Square, they returned to the schoolhouse to continue with appointed meetings and found that Methodist ministers had protested their use of the schoolhouse and refused its further occupation by "Mormon" missionaries. The action of those reverend gentlemen, hasty as it was, did not come soon enough to prevent four people receiving a testimony of the truth in that place, each of whom applied for baptism.

The evening of the next day, the 7th, had been set apart for the Temperance Hall meeting. Numerically speaking, the meeting scarcely justified itself. Only about thirty attended. Wilford Woodruff addressed the small gathering for about an hour, and was followed by Heber C. Kimball. The use of the hall for the one meeting cost the missionaries seven shillings and six-pence—a considerable sum for that hall, for that day, and for those men.

The time soon drew near for the brethren to leave London temporarily to attend the general conference in Manchester. Wilford Woodruff writes:

"On September 9th I paid my bills, called upon friends in company with Brothers Kimball and Smith, and on the day following I parted from the brethren and friends in London to return to Herefordshire. We had spent twenty-three days in the great Babylon of modern times and had found it harder to establish the Church there than in any other place we had ever been. We had baptized one man, and ordained him a Priest; six others had given in their names to be baptized on the following Sunday; and at this time there was some little prospect of the Reverend Robert Aitken receiving the work. I therefore left London, feeling that our mission and labors had not been altogether in vain." —Cowley's *Life of Wilford Woodruff*, p. 126.

Elders Kimball and Smith visited the Reverend Robert Aitken. He was much disturbed at this time by "Mormon" doctrine, admitted that it was reasonable and scriptural, but had so long tampered with contrary doctrines that his mind was in a state of confusion, and he feared to be deceived further. Not long after his early meeting with "Mormon" missionaries he returned to the clerical garb of the orthodox Church of England, from which order he had broken away.

Brothers Kimball and Smith tarried in London some days longer. Brother Kimball was suddenly stricken with a most severe case of cholera that threatened his life, but by the blessings of the Lord he recovered overnight and the next morning, Sunday, September 13th, he baptized four persons, according to previous appointment. On the 29th of the month the two brethren left for Manchester. The London Branch, as it was designated, was represented at the general conference, Carpenter's Hall, Manchester, October 6th, by Heber C. Kimball, and it was there reported as having a membership of eleven—the result of nearly a month's toil of three spiritual giants in the world's largest city.

Six of the Twelve were present at the October

conference, and increases in the membership of the Church of Jesus Christ were reported from every field represented.

On October 8th a meeting of the Council of the Twelve convened at the home of Willard Richards, No. 1 Chapman Street, Manchester, with Brigham Young presiding. Among other items of business it was "voted that our publishing office be removed to London *as soon as circumstances will permit.*"*

By this recommendation it appears that as early as 1840 the Twelve realized that London was the logical place in which to locate the publishing office, which office was then British Mission headquarters, and later became European Mission headquarters. The subsequent story of the British Mission tells us that this recommendation was not carried out until British and European Mission headquarters were moved to London early in 1933, under the direction of Dr. John A. Widtsoe, with the approval of the First Presidency.

Soon after the October, 1840, conference the publishing office and the general mission office were moved to Liverpool, where they remained until 1929, when the British Mission Office was separated from the European office and moved to Birmingham. Later, in 1933, both British and European headquarters moved to London. There seems to be little doubt that one major consideration favored the establishment of the office in Liverpool in the 1840 decade. That city then held undisputed first place among European shipping towns, both as a port of entry and embarkation for goods and passengers, and the emigration business of the Church attained tremendous proportions in the few decades following 1840.

---

*History of the Church, Vol. IV, p. 218.

But that day has passed. Emigration is no longer a consideration, and the years have taken from Liverpool much of her passenger traffic. Always much of the Mission business has of necessity been transacted in London, and many of the early publications bear the imprint of London presses.

So much for the 1840 recommendation of removal to London.

The following comment on London labors is extracted from a letter dated October 12th at Manchester, signed by the first London trio, Heber C. Kimball, George A. Smith and Wilford Woodruff:

"We have baptized eleven only, in the city of London, but through faith and the mercy of God we ere long expect a harvest of souls in that place; but we are willing to acknowledge, that in our travels, either in America or Europe, we have never before found a people from whose minds we have had to remove a greater multiplicity of objections or combinations of obstacles, in order to excite an interest in the subject and prepare the heart for the reception of the word of God, than in the city of London.

"While conversing with the common people concerning the Gospel we found their highest attainments to be: 'Why, I go to church or chapel and get my children christened; what more is necessary?' When we conversed with the learned, we found them too wise to be taught, and too much established in the traditions of their fathers to expect any change in the last days. While conversing with the ministers of the various orders of the day upon the principles of the Gospel, they would inform us that the ancient order of things was done away, and not longer needed; and some of them had preached forty years the good old religion, and God was with them, and they needed no more revelation, or healing the sick, or anything as manifest in the days of the Apostles, for we can get along without them in this day of refinement, light and knowledge.

"When we arose to preach unto the people repentance, and baptism for the remission of sins, the cry of 'Baptist! Baptist!' would be rung in our ears. If we spoke of the Church and body of Christ being composed of Prophets and

Apostles as well as other members: 'Irvingites! Irvingites!' would immediately dash into the mind. If in the midst of our remarks we even for once suffered the saying to drop from our lips: 'The testimony of Jesus is the spirit of prophecy.' 'O, you belong to Johanna Southcote,' would be heard from several places at once. If we spoke of the second coming of Christ, the cry would be 'Aitkenites!' If we made mention of the Priesthood they would call us 'Catholics.' If we testified of the ministering of angels, the people would reply: 'The Irvingites have their angels, and even the Duke of Normandy is ready to swear that he has the administering of angels every night.'

"These salutations, in connection with a multitude of others of similar nature, continued to salute our ears from day to day, until we were about ready to conclude that London had been such a perfect depot of the systems of the nineteenth century that it contained six hundred three score and six different gods, gospels, redeemers, plans of salvation, religions, churches, commandments (essential and non-essential), orders of preaching, roads to heaven and to hell; and that this order of things had so affected the minds of the people that it almost required a horn to be blown from the highest heavens, in order to awaken the attention of the people, and prepare their minds to candidly hear and receive the doctrine of one Gospel, one faith, one baptism, one Holy Ghost, one God, and one plan of salvation, and that, such as Christ and the Apostles preached. But notwithstanding this, we do not feel discouraged concerning the work being perfected in London, but firmly believe that many souls will embrace the fulness of the Gospel there, though it will be through faith, diligence, perseverance and prayer."—*History of the Church*, Vol. IV, pp. 222-223.

On October 10th, George A. Smith returned to his labors in the metropolis. Wilford Woodruff joined him in the course of a week, and the two took up their lodgings at No. 40 Ironmongers Row, St. Lukes. "Everything was costly," remarks Wilford Woodruff, "and we found that with the greatest economy we could not do with much less than a pound per week each. What few Saints there were in London were very poor, and unable to assist us. Most of the means used in my labors in London were supplied by my converts in Herefordshire."*

The extreme exertion occasioned by much vigorous open-air preaching on the streets and in the squares and parks of London caused frequent bleeding of the lungs to George A. Smith and seriously impaired his health and his work. He was counseled by his brethren to retire to less strenuous labors in Staffordshire for a time. He departed November 10th and left Wilford Woodruff to carry on alone. Elder William Pitt from Dymock joined Brother Woodruff, but soon left for Ipswich, the county seat of Suffolk, where he introduced the Gospel.

There seems to be no accounting for the variety of men to whom the Gospel appeals and whom it holds. Among the London friends of the missionaries were numbered tradesmen, professional men, seamen, and others of many classes—all caught and held by the spirit of the message of life. Dr. William Copeland, connected with the College of Surgeons, Brother William Hulme, captain of a small river vessel, ministers, and men and women in flourishing and in poor circumstances were among those who first were friendly and later were baptized.

Late in November Brigham Young and Heber C. Kimball were welcome intruders on the solitary labors of Wilford Woodruff. They arrived in London on November 30th—Brigham Young's first visit to the British metropolis. Brothers Kimball and Woodruff undertook the pleasant task of "showing him London." He was swung around the usual circuit and made acquainted with things worthwhile. In his private journal

*Cowley's *Life of Wilford Woodruff*, p. 130.

Brigham Young describes those brief days with a practical enthusiasm and humanness so characteristic of
him. The high points of London were his when he left.
On December 1st at Barratt's Academy Brigham Young
preached his first Gospel sermon in London. Ten days
later he departed for Cheltenham, and left London in
the capable hands of Brothers Kimball and Woodruff.

During the second week in December four persons
were baptized—Mr. and Mrs. Morgan, with whom the
missionaries lodged, Christopher Smith, their appren-
tice, and Henry Connor, Jr. This now commonplace
occurrence—the Gospel acceptance by people with
whom the missionaries live—has been repeated countless hundreds of times in the history of Latter-day Saint
missionary activity. That such was the case, spoke
eloquently then, as it does today, for the gentlemanly
conduct and circumspect lives of the missionaries.
Those with whom they have shared roof and board and
to whom daily habits have been revealed, have known
that their lives are in keeping with their precepts, that
their doctrine applied makes manly men—in short, that
they are what they profess to be—servants of the living
God. Having been so touched by intimate knowledge,
many have accepted truth, and, almost without exception, all have become firm friends.

A minister of the Independent Order, Reverend
James Albion by name, encountered the missionaries,
attended some of their meetings, and invited the brethren to his home, which invitation they accepted on more
than one occasion. Having heard the Gospel of the
Master from their lips, the Reverend Albion offered
the use of his chapel, which would seat about one thousand persons. On the first Sabbath after this unusual
offer the brethren accompanied the Reverend Albion
to his morning service and were introduced to the church

committee. Reverend Albion announced to his congregation that the missionaries from America would occupy his pulpit on the following Sabbath. Brothers Kimball and Woodruff then returned to their afternoon and evening meetings with the growing body of London Saints. Following the evening meeting the Reverend Albion sought them at their lodge and told them that he had announced their appointment for the next Sabbath at his further meetings that day, and that he had told his congregation that he was a Latter-day Saint, that he intended to be baptized at the hands of the missionaries, and that he would henceforth not be considered one of their number unless they were baptized into the true Church of Christ with him. Reverend Albion not only had conviction of truth, but also had what so many of his rank and office have lacked when they were faced with loss of livelihood—the courage of his convictions. The results of his astounding profession of faith were divided opinions and a divided congregation.

Despite opposition, the appointment on the following Sunday at the Church presided over by Reverend Albion was filled by the missionaries. At the evening services of that day, the final Sabbath of the year 1840, the brethren addressed the largest London congregation that they had had the privilege of standing before indoors since their arrival. A mixed audience, including ministers and lay members of many sects, heard them. Wilford Woodruff spoke about an hour. A Wesleyan minister arose, in bad taste and temper, and ungracefully opposed him. Both congregation and church committee detected the minister's spirit, and the latter refused him permission to speak again in their place of worship.

Three days more brought the close of the year

1840, and another, the opening of 1841. The brethren believed absolutely in starting the New Year right— they baptized two persons on New Year's Day and raised the number of the London congregation to twen- ty-one. Among those baptized later in the month of January were Dr. William Copeland, the Reverend James Albion and members of his family, a Mr. Hender, three more members of the Morgan family with whom the missionaries lodged, and four persons from Wool- wich, who had applied for baptism after once hearing Heber C. Kimball preach, and who had that night wan- dered up and down the Thames embankment until after nine o'clock seeking a suitable place for baptism, but the ice and mud on the river bank prevented. The next day Heber C. Kimball took them to the public baths in Tabernacle Square, to which they seem to have had ready access, and performed the ordinance.

A package containing twenty completed copies of the first British edition of the *Book of Mormon* and two dozen copies of the *Hymn Book* reached the London missionaries on February 8th, 1841. Immediately they went to Stationer's Hall and in the name of Joseph Smith, Jr., secured the first British copyright to the *Book of Mormon*, leaving in consideration three shil- lings in money and five copies of the book.

At about this time in our narrative of early London labors another leading character makes his appearance —Lorenzo Snow, later to become President of the Church, but then only a humble traveling Elder. He received his mission call at his home in Illinois in the early spring of 1840. Means to travel were not his, but by exhausting every available resource, borrowing at heavy interest and trusting the Lord for the rest, he procured the wherewithal to start upon his mission, and after many colorful experiences, not the least of

which was a forty-two day deck passage on turbulent
seas, he landed in Liverpool, visited the branch there,
and a few days later traveled to headquarters in Manchester, where he arrived October 21st, 1840.

Of his stormy voyage Elder Snow wrote:

"I did not feel surprised that men, women and children
who had not learned to trust in God wrung their hands in an
agony of fear and wept. My trust was in Him who created
the seas and defined their bounds. I was on His errand—
I knew that I was sent on this mission by the authority He
recognizes, and, although the elements raged and the ship
swayed and trembled amid the heaving billows, He was at
the helm, and my life was safe in His keeping."—*Biography
and Family Record of Lorenzo Snow*, p. 49.

From October to February Elder Snow's time and
strength were divided chiefly among Manchester,
Birmingham, Greet's Green and Wolverhampton. He
arrived in London on February 11th, 1841. Elder William Pitt arrived the following day. On February 14th,
Valentine's day, 1841, the first London conference was
held and an organization effected. The following extract of minutes is given by Wilford Woodruff:

"I give here the minutes of the first London conference, held
at the Academy, 57 King's Square, Goswell Road, February 14,
1841:

"There were present of officers of the Church, Elders H. C.
Kimball, Wilford Woodruff, Lorenzo Snow, and William Pitt,
besides four priests. The meeting was called to order by Elder
H. C. Kimball, at 2 o'clock p.m., Sunday, the 14th of February,
1841, when it was moved by Elder Kimball and seconded by Elder
Pitt that Wilford Woodruff be the president of the conference.
Moved by Elder Kimball and seconded by Elder Woodruff, that
Dr. William Copeland be the clerk. Carried unanimously. The
meeting was then opened by singing, and prayer by Elder Kimball.
The president then called for the representation of the branches of
the London conference. The Church at Bedford was represented
by Priest Robert Williams, containing forty-two members and one
priest; seven removed and two dead. The Church at Ipswich, represented by Elder William Pitt, consisted of twelve members, one

elder, one priest, and one teacher. The Church at Woolwich, represented by Priest John Griffith, consisted of six members and one priest. The Church at London, represented by H. C. Kimball, consisted of forty-six members, one elder and two priests; excellent prospect of continued increase. Moved and seconded by Elders Kimball and Woodruff, that James Albion be ordained an Elder; moved and seconded by Elders Kimball and Snow, that Thomas Barnes be ordained a teacher; moved and seconded by Elders Kimball and Pitt, that Robert Williams be ordained an elder to oversee the Church at Bedford; moved and seconded by Elders Robert Williams and William Pitt, that William Smith, at Bedford, be ordained a priest; moved and seconded by Elders Kimball and Pitt that Richard Bates be ordained a priest in the Woolwich branch; moved and seconded by Elders Robt. Williams and Wm. Pitt that John Sheffield be ordained a teacher at Bedford; moved and seconded by Elder Kimball and Brother Griffith that Brother A. Painter be ordained a teacher at Woolwich. These motions were carried unanimously, and those present were ordained under the hands of Elders Kimball, Woodruff and Snow. Afterward, Elder Kimball moved and Elder Woodruff seconded, that Elder Lorenzo Snow be appointed president of this conference, and to take the superintendency of the Church in London. Much valuable instruction was given by Elders Kimball and Woodruff in relation to the duties of official members, after which it was moved by Elder Kimball and seconded by Elder Snow that this conference be adjourned till Sunday, the 16th day of May, 1841; after which the conference closed. Wilford Woodruff, president; Dr. William Copeland, clerk.

"During this conference meeting, we also broke bread with the Saints, and confirmed four new members. At half-past six in the evening we met again, and had the largest congregation which had assembled at our preaching place. One person came forward for baptism. This was a day which we had desired long to see; for we had labored exceedingly hard to establish a Church in London, and at times it seemed as though we would have to give it up; but by holding on to the work of our Divine Master and claiming the promises of God, we were now to leave an established London conference with a prosperous Church planted in the metropolis, under the care of our beloved brother, Lorenzo Snow."—*Cowley's Life of Wilford Woodruff*, pp. 136-137.

From the time of its formal organization the activity of the Church in London was forward-moving. Soon after the conference both Heber C. Kimball and Wilford Woodruff left London and traveled northward by different routes, to make preparation for their coming

departure for America.   Lorenzo Snow spent most of
his time there until his departure early in 1843.   At the
April, 1841, conference in Manchester he reported a
membership of one hundred thirty-seven in the district.
A London conference, attended by Elder Lorenzo Snow
and Apostle Orson Hyde, was held on May 16th, 1841,
and the London Branch alone was then reported as
having seventy-four members and "good prospect for
increase."   By the general conference of April, 1842,
a membership of four hundred was reported in the London District.

Since that day there have come into the Church
from out of London's myriad streets and dwellings,
thousands of loyal Britons.   Records show that the
London District at one time numbered as many as
2,647, and those who have emigrated from there make
up a considerable portion of the great army of men
and women who have left England to live their lives
in the valleys of the western mountains.   Within
the corporate confines of greater London have been
organized many branches of the Church, and "Deseret,"
the spacious "Mormon" center located at High Road,
South Tottenham, London, England, was for years,
until its disposition in 1927, a gathering place and clearing house for the Saints and traveling Elders, from
the United Kingdom and the Continent.

As the Thames has slipped its slow way under London Bridge, as the Tower of London has silently looked
on and noted the progress of events, as Big Ben has
relentlessly ticked away a century of time, so "Mormonism"—the Gospel of Jesus Christ—has taken firm
root in the world's great and time-honored metropolis.

CHAPTER 21

QUEEN VICTORIA ACCEPTS A
BOOK OF MORMON

In the story of the British Mission, Queen Victoria holds a place of particular significance and genuine affection. It is worthy of more than passing note that she had ascended the throne but three weeks before the first "Mormon" missionaries set foot upon the shores of England. And the day on which these men arrived in Preston, where first they preached their message, (July 22, 1837) was the day of a general Parliamentary election, called for by the Queen at the beginning of her reign, and an election banner," "Truth Will Prevail," was accepted by these first "Mormon" missionaries as a favorable omen.*

Nearly four years later, after the work of the Church had taken firm root in British soil, Brigham Young, who had directed the publication of the first British edition of the *Book of Mormon,* arranged, before his departure from England in April, 1841, for copies of it to be richly bound for presentation to Her Majesty Queen Victoria and the Prince Consort.

It fell to Lorenzo Snow's lot to make the presentation, which he did before leaving London in 1842. The presentation was made to Her Majesty Queen Victoria and His Royal Highness Prince Albert, through the politeness of Sir Henry Wheatley. Tullidge records:

"It is said that her Majesty condescended to be pleased with the gift. Whether she ever read the *Book of Mormon*

---
*See pp. 23-24.

is not known, although if the presentation did not altogether fade from her memory, 'Mormonism' became sensational enough to provoke even a monarch to read the book, if for nothing better than curiosity."—Tullidge's *History of Salt Lake City*, p. 103 of "Biographies."

In an album of Lorenzo Snow's, now a prized possession of his descendants, is an autograph of Queen Victoria's. Whether or not it was a souvenir of this occasion is not now known.

The circumstances surrounding this presentation brought forth from the pen of Eliza R. Snow, Lorenzo Snow's sister, and a highly gifted "Mormon" poetess of the past century, a poem of twelve four-line stanzas written to Queen Victoria, which was widely published in that day, after appearing first in the *Times and Seasons*.

Queen Victoria has been greatly honored and spoken of with respectful affection by the members of the Church of Jesus Christ of Latter-day Saints, both in America and abroad, as have been all of the five British Monarchs of the century under whose benevolent protection the Church has been so graciously treated and so notably successful throughout the British Empire. Queen Victoria, King Edward VII, King George V, King Edward VIII and King George VI have ruled Britain's world-wide dominions during the ten decades in which "Mormonism" has grown and prospered under the British flag, Victoria ascending the throne but three weeks before "the Gospel came to Britain," and George VI being crowned but a few weeks before the century turns to begin a second cycle of years of "Mormon" activity in this Empire of righteous purpose and prophetic destiny.

CHAPTER 22

THE RESTORATION PROCLAIMED IN WALES

To the south and west of England lies the traditional homeland of a proud and ancient Celtic people, whose language and customs and traditions as a race and nation are time-worn and honored. In this old and fair land of the ancient Druids, in this kind and charming land of music and minstrelsy, has been nurtured a sterling and hardy race of men and women in whose hearts there is melody and in whose souls there is courage and high regard for honest and useful toil.

Gradually being absorbed in language and in territory by England, there persists nevertheless in the Welsh race something which sets them apart from all other British subjects and something which causes them yet to remain peculiarly patrons of Saint David.

To this hardy land of an honest people the message of the Gospel restoration found its way during the very early years of the history of the British Mission. Because in the minds of the uninitiated there is no very sharp dividing line between England and Wales, the facts concerning the earliest proclamation of the Gospel in the latter place have been somewhat beclouded, but latest research has brought to light the following:

The first converts to "Mormonism" in Wales were made through the preaching of Elders from America and local missionaries, who labored in Liverpool and vicinity, and who, in 1840, crossed over the River Mersey into Cheshire and thence into North Wales. Among these were Elders James Burnham and Henry Royle, who arrived in Liverpool for mission labors in the spring of 1840. These labors led to the organization of the Overton Branch in Flintshire, North Wales, in the fall of 1840, which branch consisted of 32 members when first reported. Later, Elder James Burnham on December 13, 1840, writing from Wrexham, North Wales, said: "The brethren at Overton have baptized 56 converts, and some more are ready."—*Journal History of Welsh Mission.*

It is a matter of record also that John Needham, a local Priest, was sent in 1840, to labor in Monmouth-shire, South Wales, where he baptized several Welsh people in the winter of 1840-41.

At a general conference of the British Mission held in Manchester, England, Oct. 6, 1840, Elder Henry Royle and Priest Frederick Cook were appointed to labor in Cly, Flintshire, Wales. We find nothing re-corded regarding their labors in this district, and there-fore the Overton Branch stands as the first organized in Wales, so far as our record is concerned. At a general conference of the British Mission held at Manchester, England, April, 1841, it was resolved that the branches of the Church in Liverpool, Isle of Man and Wales (Overton, Harding and Elsmere) be organized into one district, to be called the Liverpool Conference.

At this same conference, Elder James Burnham re-ported 117 members of the Church in Wales, mostly in the Overton Branch.

The work continued to spread toward South Wales, and William Henshaw and others began active missionary operations there. The Pen-y-darren Branch, a village near Merthyr Tydfil, was organized March 25, 1843.

The labors of Elder Henshaw and those with him resulted in the organization of other branches; namely, Beaufort, Rhymney, Tredagar, Merthyr Tydfil, and Ab-erdare, which branches originally belonged to the Bir-mingham District, but which were organized as the

Merthyr Tydfil District, April 6, 1844, at a general conference of the British Mission held at Liverpool on that date. This district later became the Glamorganshire District.

So colorful and dynamic and personally zealous a figure was Captain Dan Jones, that there has been a misconception in some quarters concerning the part he played in the opening of the work in Wales. While Captain Jones was one of the greatest and most effective Gospel messengers ever to cross the borders of that land, and while he did much to organize the work of the Church there and to place it on a permanent basis, the facts remain that several "Mormon" missionaries had preached in Wales, and a considerable Church membership raised up, before the advent of Dan Jones.

Captain Dan Jones was born August 4, 1811, in Flintshire, Wales, the son of Thomas and Ruth Jones. Unusual for his day, he received a college education. He emigrated to the United States about 1840 and found his way to what were then the Western States, and finally settled in Nauvoo.

In his early thirties we find Dan Jones as the owner and captain of a small river steamer, the *Maid of Iowa*, on which he transported many emigrating Saints who were then moving up the Mississippi River to Nauvoo. Frequent meetings and dealings with the "Mormons" impressed him. In April, 1843, he carried from St. Louis to Nauvoo a company of English converts who were traveling under the direction of Parley P. Pratt and Levi Richards. The circumstances surrounding this voyage led to the first meeting of Dan Jones and the Prophet Joseph Smith, on which occasion it was that the Prophet stepped up to him and said: "God bless this little man."

On May 11, 1843, about a month after Dan Jones had joined the Church, he was invited to attend a meeting of the Quorum of the Twelve held in Nauvoo. Present on this occasion were Brigham Young, Heber C. Kimball, Parley P. Pratt, Orson Pratt, Orson Hyde, George A. Smith, John Taylor and Wilford Woodruff. At this meeting, Captain Jones, who had been previously designated by the Prophet for this purpose, was told to prepare himself for a mission to Wales. He was then in his thirty-second year.

Shortly after their first meeting, the Prophet had purchased from Captain Jones a half interest in the *Maid of Iowa,* and Captain Jones began running the boat as a ferry between Nauvoo and Montrose. When the Prophet Joseph was arrested at Dixon the following June, Captain Jones with a force of armed men navigated the river for the purpose of intercepting steamboats operated by those who might be intent upon kidnaping the Prophet to take him into Missouri. In May, 1844, the Prophet bought out the entire interest in the *Maid of Iowa* and then Captain Jones was ready for his mission to Wales. However, the most tragic and bitter circumstance in Church history delayed his departure— the martyrdom of the Prophet Joseph Smith and his brother Hyrum, the Patriarch.

When the Prophet started for Carthage June 24, 1844, Dan Jones was one of the brethren who accompanied him. During the evening of June 26, 1844, in Carthage jail, the night before Joseph and Hyrum were murdered, Hyrum Smith read and commented upon extracts from the *Book of Mormon* pertaining to the imprisonments and deliverances of the servants of God for the Gospel's sake. Brother Joseph bore a soul-penetrating testimony to the guards concerning the divine authenticity of the *Book of Mormon,* the restoration of the Gospel, the administration of angels, and the establishment of the kingdom of God upon the earth, for the sake of which he was then incarcerated in that prison, and not because he had violated any law of God or man.

The brethren retired late.   Joseph and Hyrum occupied the only bedstead in the room, while their friends lay side by side on mattresses on the floor. Willard Richards sat up writing until his last candle left him in darkness.   The report of a gun fired close by caused Joseph to rise, leave the bed, and lay himself on the floor, with Dan Jones on his left, and John S. Fullmer on his right.   Joseph laid out his right arm, and said to John S. Fullmer: "Lay your head on my arm for a pillow, Brother John;" and when all was quiet they conversed in low tones concerning the prospects for their deliverance.

The Prophet gave expression to several presentiments that he had to die, and said: "I would like to see my family again," and "I would to God that I could preach to the Saints in Nauvoo once more."* Brother Fullmer tried to rally his spirits, saying that he thought the Prophet would often have that privilege, and Joseph thanked him for those assuring remarks.

Soon after, Willard Richards retired to the bed which Joseph had left, and when all were apparently fast asleep, Joseph whispered to Dan Jones: "Are you afraid to die?"

Captain Jones said: "Has that time come, think you? Engaged in such a cause I do not think that death would have many terrors."

Joseph replied: "You will yet see Wales, and fulfill the mission appointed you before you die."†

---

*p. 601, Vol. VI, *History of the Church.*
†Ibid.

It was the following year, however, before Captain Jones left Nauvoo on his mission to Great Britain,
because of delay caused by the unsettled conditions
among the Saints after the martyrdom. He left Nauvoo
with his wife, in company with Wilford Woodruff and
his wife Phoebe, Hiram Clark and his wife, Elder
Leonard W. Hardy, and others.

"At a special General Conference held in Manchester,
England, shortly after his arrival, President Wilford Woodruff rose to remark that inasmuch as Brother Dan Jones had
been sent on a special mission to Wales by the Prophet
Joseph when he was still living, he, Wilford Woodruff,
wished to see that appointment acknowledged by that conference; as he considered it a just and highly important
appointment, because Brother Jones was 'the only person
we had in this country who could speak, read, write, and
publish in the Welsh language.' He therefore proposed
that he receive the sanction of the meeting in his appointment and that he preside over the Church in Wales."—
Millennial Star, Vol. 7, p. 7.

Thus the wishes of the Prophet Joseph Smith concerning Captain Dan Jones and his mission to Wales
were carried out after the Prophet's martyrdom, and
this native Welshman, with his fiery zeal and irrepres-
sible energy, found himself journeying back to his native
land for a different and more cherished purpose than
had carried him away from the shores of his fathers.

CHAPTER 23

CAPTAIN DAN JONES IN WALES

The question of his destination having been settled,
Captain Dan Jones lost little time in reaching the land
of his birth. He proceeded at once to Merthyr Tydfil,
where he organized himself and family, consisting of
Dan Jones and wife, into the Welsh District (Conference).

"At a general conference of the British Mission held in
Manchester April 16, 1845, Captain Dan Jones delivered his
first public discourse outside of Wales. When he arose to
speak, he was suffering from a severe attack of fever and
ague, and remarked that he believed it was the intention of
the evil one to prevent his speaking that evening, but he was
determined to bear his testimony in spite of every opposing
power. He said that he came not in the character of a dele-
gate; he represented no conference; for if he had but baptized one, he should be able to represent three. But he would
speak of a nation renowned in history, one of the most
ancient nations of the earth, who had never been subdued,
and to whom he hoped to be instrumental in bearing the
tidings of the work of God in the last days. He enlarged on
the characteristics of the Welsh people in a manner, and
with an eloquence, that told how ardently he loved his native tribe and his fatherland. He remarked that, for many
years, as a mariner, he had been in search of the principles
of truth—he had sought it in almost every clime—among the
red men of the woods, or the civilized denizens of the city;
but he found it not until he came in contact with the followers of the Prophet of the Lord, the 'notorious' Joseph
Smith; but of that despised individual he would bear his
testimony, and though he might feel more at home among a
tribe of Indians, or on the deck of a ship, than upon that
platform and before such an audience, yet he would not
flinch from bearing a faithful testimony to the character of
the Prophet of the Lord. He had been with him in the do-
mestic circle; he had been with him in peril and in prison,
and only left him about an hour before the murderous deed
of his assassination was perpetrated; and he had now come

in obedience to the counsel of the martyred Prophet, as a
messenger to his native land, to bear testimony of the work
for which his brother, the Prophet, had died, and which he
had sealed with his blood." ("We would here remark,"
records the *Millennial Star* correspondent, "that we are utterly incapable of doing anything like justice to the address
of Captain Jones, for though delivered while struggling with
disease, such was its effect upon ourselves, and we also believe upon others, that we ceased to write, in order to give
way to the effect produced upon our feelings.")—*Journal
History of British Mission,* April 6, 1845.

Sixty days later Dan Jones reported to the president of the British Mission that he was publishing
pamphlets and was busily engaged distributing them:

"I have more places to preach in around here than I
can possibly attend to. I have one Elder in this circuit besides myself. The prospect is good everywhere for a plen-
tiful crop of good souls ere long. I have two chapels now
in the neighborhood to preach in when I can. I intend publishing a Welsh magazine monthly to proclaim the everlasting truths of 'Mormonism' to Wales."—*Millennial Star,* Vol.
7, p. 63.

Such marvelous results attended his ministry, that
at a conference held in the city of Manchester May 31,
1846, the Welsh District was reported by Dan Jones
as consisting of 28 branches and 687 members, 378
new members baptized since the last conference. "He
reported that they had lately baptized the only remaining two of an active church of Baptists. They had now
the chapel, priest, and hearers. His conference at one
time extended to a presidency consisting of himself and
wife, but now it was nearly 700. He had been much engaged in publishing some six different pamphlets, illustrative of the principles of the Church or in defense of
the many false statements and calumnious reports in
circulation. It was his determination to sound the praise
of that man of God, Joseph Smith, with whom he had

lived, among mobocrats, even up to the hour of the Prophet's death."—*Millennial Star,* Vol. 7, p. 187.

The gifts of the Spirit of God were wonderfully manifested in the labors of Captain Dan Jones. In a letter to the President of the British Mission, written at Merthyr, July 24, 1846, he wrote:

"Since I left you, I have been preaching on my way through the principal towns of eight counties. One circumstance in particular is worthy of note, because of the power of God it manifested thereby. In one place a young man who had a sore leg—past cure by the doctors—upwards of twenty pieces of bone having been worked out of it, and he not able to walk without a crutch since a year last Christmas. When he believed the Gospel, I told him he would be healed if he would obey; he walked about a mile with crutches. By the river side we prayed that he might be enabled to dispense with his crutch, and he walked into the water without it—out again, and home—and so far as I have heard has never used it since. I carried his crutch home through the town on my back, the man telling them that he was healed, but strange to say they would neither believe him nor their own eyes, but cried out impostors, etc., and that he might have walked before! although they knew better; but, however, the man got a blessing, and when I left, the wounds in his leg were closing finely, and free from pain. Two others, a priest and a Saint, were miraculously healed by the power of God publicly, yet for all that, there were none but the Saints that would 'return glory to God!'."—*Millennial Star,* Vol. 8, p. 40.

Fourteen months after Dan Jones arrived to open up the work to which he was appointed by the Prophet Joseph Smith, a remarkable showing was made at a conference held in Merthyr Tydfil, March 15, 1847. He reported 102 baptisms for three months, making the total number of Saints in Wales to be 900. On the 16th day of the same month Captain Dan Jones was appointed to preside over the Merthyr Tydfil District in addition to his presidency over Wales. This district included the branches of Beaufort, Rhymney, Tredagar, Merthyr Tydfil and Abedare.

When Captain Jones returned to Merthyr Tydfil July 8, 1847, he says:

"The whole place appeared to be in as great an uproar as Mars Hill of old. The first salutation after my arrival, was an invitation from the Mayor to defend myself against charges. When I reached his worship, he was in a hasty stew, reading a long catalogue of charges which were at the head of a lengthy petition to banish us from the limits of the city; attached were names of the clergy, reverends, doctors, lawyers, and deacons, and, following, the names of their deluded followers. After a dozen attempts I succeeded in hearing my own voice, and proceeded to defend myself against their charges, one at a time. The first was blasphemy. 2. Infidelity. 3. Saying that the end of the world was at hand, thereby scaring people out of their senses—taking them to a foreign country, and selling them as slaves, etc., etc. You'll be surprised to hear that the chief magistrate had been made to believe these lies so firmly, that he had actually made his arrangements to put me in prison, which he told me to my face! But I had weathered too many storms to give up the ship so soon. I reasoned with him until he pledged himself to befriend me. He summoned the aldermen, and I had a broadside with each of them in turn. I was alone amidst all the lions of the city, yet I was uppermost at every turn, until it was after midnight. Their clergy, my accusers, had refused to toe the mark. When I cited them to the treatment which we received in our native land, and among the graves of our fathers, for our religion, there was hardly a dry face in the vast assembly, even the sergeant of police who had presented, and big nobs who had signed the petition, wept like babes. The mayor had ordered the police and reporters there, and they never were in a more suitable place of worship!"—*Millennial Star,* Vol. 9, pp. 299-300.

At the close of the year 1847 Dan Jones reported:

"In regard to the press department in Wales, alone I have continued the *Welsh Star* monthly, and increased its circulation to about 1,200. I have published in the past year ten other pamphlets besides, containing in all about 850,000 pages 12 mo., many of which win their way into every circle of society, and make 'Mormons' from every grade—the priests, protestant and catholic, not excepted.

"I have been much afflicted with some disease like the pleurisy, but, through the kindness of our Father and the prayers of the Saints, I am now able to walk out a little. Since you were here, I have written and published three pamphlets of 52 pages each, and some smaller ones, besides my publication, *Udgorn Seion,* to which cause I attribute principally my illness, and which hints to me that I have published about enough for the present. I have published in Welsh the *Compendium,* or book of references (288 pages), illustrative of the doctrines of the Church."—*Millennial Star,* Vol. 10, p. 121.

In a letter to Orson Pratt, president of the British Mission, dated Merthyr, January 6, 1849, he says:

"The last Welsh General Conference, which was held last Sunday, December 31, 1848, and following days, was much the largest and most interesting of any other; our hall, which will hold two thousand people, was so crowded before the morning service commenced that we had to engage another hall nearly as large, which was also soon filled to overflowing, and continued for two days with but little intermission. Scores had come from one to two hundred miles; all the hotels, taverns, and private lodgings in the town, so far as I have heard, were thronged like an Egyptian fair; yet order, union, and love were so characteristic of the Saints throughout, that the Babylonians were astonished.

"The statistics of the morning at this conference meeting showed the total number of branches in Wales to be 55, and 17 new branches organized; including 156 elders, 180 priests, 147 teachers, 67 deacons. Baptized since last conference 1,001; total members 3,603; total baptized last year, 1,939; which will average nearly 1,000 a year since I have been in Wales, with brighter prospects for the future. This fills my soul with joy and gladness unspeakable, because the Lord God of Joseph so abundantly fulfills the predictions of the devoted martyr on my head; and because I hear my own kin and nation rejoice in the blessing of heaven, and show forth the wonderful power of God in the language and land that gave them birth; and in the prospects of a heaven on earth in Zion.

"I have changed the name of our monthly magazine at the end of the 4th volume to be *Zion's Trumpet*, have increased its circulation to 2,000, and have increased its size to eight pages, for the same price as before.

"All kinds of lying stories that the father of lies and his emissaries can invent are being told of me: such as, that I am going to take this company over and sell them as slaves. I am called a swindler, thief, and everything but what I really am; even this is preached out of pulpits, and published in the religious magazines of the day unblushingly; and when I walk the streets I am frequently gazed at as though I had hoofs and horns; and, with the fingers of scorn pointed at me, they say, 'there is the man who is taking all the property of the Latter-day Devils, and is going to sell them as slaves,' etc.

"Furthermore did I prove that I was so far from deserving the accusation of taking people's money, that I bore my own expenses and my family's, to come from a distance of nearly 6,000 miles, to preach for nothing to my own kindred; —that I have preached in all the principal towns of the Principality without having a night's lodging, or a meal's victuals, unless I paid for them; and that I have not to this day even asked, or laid any plans to be remunerated; and furthermore I had it to boast of, that I not only came here but intend to pay my own and family's expenses back again to Zion, without levying one collection for that purpose on the Saints. I seek not money for reward, but the riches that fade not away."—*Millennial Star*, Vol. 11, p. 38.

At the close of 1848 complete statistics for Wales were reported as follows: 12 conferences, 100 branches, 426 elders, 239 priests, 221 teachers, 119 deacons, with a total membership of 4645. Elder Jones sailed from England February 26, 1849, after being released from his Welsh mission. He sailed from Liverpool on the *Buena Vista* with 249 Welsh Saints on board. The company arrived in Kanesville, Iowa, in May, 1849, and crossed the plains in twenty-five wagons, with Dan Jones as captain.

After the arrival in the Valley the so-called Welsh

settlement was formed on the west side of the Jordan River, but most of the Welsh Saints subsequently became residents of the Fifteenth and Sixteenth Wards, Salt Lake City. The arrival of the Welsh company under Captain Jones virtually marked the introduction of Welsh blood and influence into the Church.

In August, 1852, Captain Jones was called on a second mission to Wales, during which he again performed a mighty work among his countrymen. He published again the *Udgorn Seion*. Returning from this mission in 1856, he had charge of a large company of 703 emigrating Saints, who crossed the Atlantic in the *Samuel Curling*, sailing from Liverpool, July 6, 1856.

Captain Dan Jones later moved to Provo, where he resided until the time of his death, which occurred there on January 3, 1861.

In his Gospel labors Dan Jones was an eloquent and rapid speaker, having both English and Welsh completely at his command. With his forceful personality and colorful language, it is said that he could hold his audience spellbound for hours at a time.

Directly and indirectly he was the means, in the hands of the Lord, of converting thousands of his kindred and countrymen, and while he was by no means the first missionary to preach the Gospel restoration in Wales, he will probably always be known as the "father of the Welsh Mission." From his native land have come two past conductors of the Tabernacle choir —John Parry and Evan Stephens—and much that is cherished in "Mormon" music; and since he took the first company of 249 Welsh emigrants to the Valley of the Great Salt Lake in 1849, there have continued to come from that ancient land and noble people, men and women who have brought into the Church the useful talents and superior culture of a great and hardy race.

CHAPTER 24

BRIGHAM YOUNG AND THE TWELVE DEPART

The Apostles of the Lord Jesus Christ in 1840-41 were not men who were wont to stay in one place longer than was needful—no more than have they been before or since. Their mission was to bear special witness to the world, and when the business at hand was reasonably well taken care of in any particular part of the world, it was their practice to leave the work in charge of capable, truth-loving men, and move on to organize the work of the Lord in other fields.

And so, having gone to Great Britain in obedience to the word of the Lord and in furtherance of the world-wide mission of the Church, and having there accomplished their purpose by organizing and permanently establishing the work of the Gospel restoration in Great Britain, it was decided that these men should depart, even as they came, further to pursue the business of the Master. Their families in America needed them; but what was more important was the fact that their work as a Quorum was done in Great Britain, and the Church—their Prophet and their people—needed them sorely at home.

To the casual reader or listener mention of the name Brigham Young calls to mind the Pioneer movement, Utah, "Mormonism" and associated ideas. By few people is this great prophet-leader thought of in connection with England. Comparatively few, indeed, in Great Britain, are aware that he spent an active year of his eventful life in England—a year of organization and notable achievement, and a year of deep import to the British Mission and to the Church as a whole. And it is not to be lost sight of that his abilities as an executive and organizer—the same abilities which made him the West's greatest colonizer—were of inestimable value in laying the permanent foundations for the century's work in the British Mission.

Four British Mission conferences were held while Brigham Young and a majority of the Twelve were in England. Much business was transacted at these times, and resident brethren who volunteered their entire time for the work of the Lord were sent throughout England, Scotland, Ireland and Wales with the few missionaries that came over from America.

Early in April, 1841, nine of the Quorum of the Twelve Apostles (Willard Richards had been ordained, and Apostle Orson Hyde had previously arrived) met together in Quorum capacity in the city of Manchester. Arrangements were made for seven of the nine to return to America. Parley P. Pratt was left in charge of the Mission, and Orson Hyde was bound for Jerusalem. A Mission conference convened on April 6th, 1841, to which hundreds came and at which thousands of Church members were represented. On the twentieth day of April, 1841, Brigham Young, with six other Apostles and one hundred thirty Saints, went aboard the sailing vessel *Rochester*. As a Quorum they had been in England but one year and fourteen days. Brigham Young's report of the labors and progress of that period follows:

"It was with a heart full of thanksgiving and gratitude to God, my Heavenly Father, that I reflected upon His dealings with me and my brethren of the Twelve during the past year of my life, which was spent in England. It truly seemed a miracle to look upon the contrast between our landing and departing from Liverpool. We landed in the spring of 1840, as strangers in a strange land and penniless, but through the mercy of God we have gained many friends, established Churches in almost every noted town and city in the Kingdom of Great Britain, baptized between seven and eight thousand, printed five thousand *Books of Mormon*, three thousand *Hymn Books*, two thousand five hundred volumes of the *Millennial Star*, and fifty thousand tracts, and emigrated to Zion one thousand souls, established a permanent shipping agency which will be a great blessing to the Saints, and have left sown in the hearts of many thousands the seeds of eternal truth, which will bring forth fruit to the honor and glory of God, and yet we have lacked nothing to eat, drink or wear: in all these things I acknowledge the hand of God."—*Millennial Star*, Vol. 26, p. 7.

Parley P. Pratt remained in the mission at this time until October 20, 1842, and under his direction the work continued to grow and prosper. When he left to return to America he notified the Church in Britain through the pages of the *Millennial Star* that their presiding officer would be Thomas Ward, with Elders Lorenzo Snow and Hiram Clark to assist him as counselors in "the office of the General Presidency of the Church in Europe." For his successors he hoped that "the officers and members in the several conferences will uphold and support these men in their high and holy calling, by the prayer of faith and by a willing, submissive and teachable spirit," and that the officers in turn, "will conduct and counsel in all things according to the mind of the spirit and according to the counsel which will be given them from Nauvoo from time to time, by the Quorum of the Twelve or the First Presidency."*

Bearing his testimony of the divine authenticity of the *Book of Mormon* and of the reality of the Gospel restoration, Parley P. Pratt further recommended in his farewell message "that the first principles of the Gospel

---

Millennial Star, Vol. 3, p. 110.

be fully and constantly taught, and the spirit of discussion and contention avoided as far as possible; for he
that hath the spirit of contention is not of God, but is
of the devil."*

With the departure of Parley P. Pratt, the last of
the Apostles had left Great Britain who, in 1840, went
there to meet and conduct business as a Quorum. With
this departure ends the eventful introductory period
of the Gospel to Great Britain. The work was only
fairly started and nearly a century has intervened.
Since that day the message of the Gospel restoration
proclaimed by "Mormon" missionaries has been felt in
one way or another in virtually every city, town and
village of Great Britain. In like manner the stories and
details of the subsequent periods and of the taking of
the Gospel to Leeds, Newcastle-on-Tyne, Norwich,
Hull, Bristol, Nottingham, Sheffield, Woolwich and
Cornwall and all the regions round about will some day
be collected and printed, but in this volume there remains space only for the broadest summary of what
has transpired since 1842.

Brigham Young and his associates, by using their
God-given faculties, by trusting in the Lord, and by
working with all diligence, placed the British Mission
on a permanent basis. Since the first "Mormon"
missionaries went to Great Britain, more than one
hundred and twenty-six thousand persons in that land
have embraced the Gospel and cherished it in their
hearts, and many of them and their children and their
children's children have returned and are returning to
their kindred and countrymen in the United Kingdom
to bear witness of the restoration of the Gospel and of
the joy that this truth brings to the souls of men.

*Millennial Star, Vol. 3, p. 110.

CHAPTER 25

A CENTURY WITH THE BRITISH PRESS

Reaching out from the Strand, London, in a more or less indefinite direction, but, for all that, in the same direction in which it has reached out these many and uncounted generations, is Fleet Street, a narrow artery through which pulses the life-blood of the world's newspaper industry. While modern structures devoted to the time-honored business of news dissemination punctuate Fleet Street here and there today, its essential character could not have altered much during the century since "Mormon" missionaries first set foot upon British shores.

For some apparently unknown reason Fleet Street, with its immediate crossroads and bylanes, has enfolded unto itself these multi-many years immortal "pliers-of-the-pen" and "printers-of-the-printers'-ink." Milton, Samuel Johnson, Oliver Goldsmith, Samuel Pepys, Richard Lovelace, Dickens—and even Ben Jonson and William Shakespeare—are all names, with many more unmentioned, that are inseparably connected, in one way or another, with this great "home of the British press," in which have been guarded the highest ethics of the writing and publishing professions. And the ethics and practices which are cherished in London's Fleet Street are transmitted and reflected in all the British provinces.

British fair-play and honest appraisal are notable characteristics of the British press, and during their century's sojourn in the United Kingdom, "Mormon" missionaries and members of the Church of Jesus Christ of Latter-day Saints have not long or often been without spokesmen and champions in their time of need. Some of the world's greatest newspapers—British newspapers —have cried against obvious unfairness, have answered attacks with counter attacks, have replied to falsehood with facts.

On the other hand, for the sake of the record's accuracy, it must not be left unsaid that the British press, being an institution of man's devising and of human operation, has, both in isolated cases and for general and protracted periods, acceded to misinformed public opinion, or bowed to the will of opposing factional interests, whose accusations have at times been in the nature of willfully dishonest and grossly untrue fabrications.

In short, the British press has been a fair and ethical institution, subject to those human frailties and failings which sometimes cause great newspapers to serve selfish interests, sometimes to reflect public opinion, and sometimes to proclaim boldly and fearlessly what they know to be truth, "let the chips fall where they may."

There may have been earlier instances of British press comment which do not, however, appear in any readily available record, but the first British newspaper recorded in the *Millennial Star* to have come to the defense of the "Mormon" cause was the *Manx Liberal*, which, in its issue of October 4, 1840, protested the interruption of a public meeting that was being conducted by John Taylor, and further reported the proceedings of the evening with trenchant irony and biting logic.* This same *Manx Liberal* on October 17th, 1840, published a reply by John Taylor in answer to an attack that had been made on the principles of "Mormonism" in an earlier issue by a contributor who signed himself "J. Curran."

*See page 159.

The *Millennial Star* first got around to the business of noting a direct attack in a British newspaper in its issue of November, 1840, when it quoted the following:

THE LONDON DISPATCH AND THE LATTER-DAY SAINTS

(From the *London Dispatch* of November 8th.)

"A new religious sect, from the United States, calling themselves Latter-day Saints, or 'Mormonites,' have just pitched their tents in Gloucestershire, for the purpose of plundering the ignorant people in the neighborhood of the palaces and cathedral of the Bishop of that diocese. These "Mormonites" are twelve in number, like the Apostles. They have a new Bible of their own, in which it is declared that they are the apostles and prophets of the Church of Latter Days, the only true and living church on the face of the earth; and as such, they tell the flocks of the learned clergy of the diocese of Gloucester and Bristol, that God has not revealed in the Bible all that is sufficient to salvation, and that they are commissioned to declare to them a new revelation, wherein is the fullness of the Gospel. This tale has been eagerly swallowed by the ignorant multitude.

"Captain D. L. St. Clair, a gentleman of the neighborhood, who has for some time been performing the work which ought to be done by the clergy, and attempting to reclaim them from the most degraded condition of human beings, gives this account of the success of the 'Mormonites': 'From my own knowledge,' says he, in a little tract addressed to these deluded people, 'they have plundered three families in Herefordshire, and left them in a state of the most abject poverty; one, a respectable farmer, has paid to them two hundred pounds; and two families in the parish of Basley have given them every shilling they possessed, and will probably be obliged to go into the union house, having nothing left but the clothes on their backs.' In corroboration of this statement, have they not obtained money from you? and what becomes of the money, sometimes amounting to 10 pounds a night, collected at their gatherings? We thought the followers of Southcote, and Irving, and mad Thom of Canterbury, were the most deluded of human beings; but, it appears, they are surpassed in ignorance and folly by the men of Gloucester, who believe in this new Bible, who give away their property to these false apostles, who are baptized anew in the hope that they shall live with Christ on the banks of the Mississippi, in glory and happiness for a thousand years!'

"We learn, in addition, that so late as the 29th of last month, ten poor persons were baptized in the parish of Boddington; and that upwards of 500 in the neighboring parishes have joined these humbug saints, and this, too, within from two to eight miles of the cathedral of Gloucester, whose Bishop has now two palaces to reside in, besides a prebendal house at Westminster, in Pear's Yard, and two rectorages, in all about 9,000 pounds a year. Has this Bishop, so well paid for attending to the flock, done anything to abate this ignorance? Is it not the fact that there are not fewer than eighty non-resident clergymen under him—that there are eighty-six in the commission of the peace—that, until lately, the Chairman of the Quarter Sessions was a reverend doctor—that at the Quarter Sessions there are frequently more clergy than laity at the dinner table; and that ignorance is so great, that not one adult in fifty of the rural population can read? Can we wonder that these unfortunate creatures are led away by 'every wind of doctrine,' and that the gaols and madhouses are filled with the victims of ignorance and superstition? The 'Mormonites' were wise in their generation in squatting upon this diocese, and in all probability their next remove will be to the diocese of Canterbury —the land of mad Thomites—celebrated for the number of its clergy, the vast income of its prelate, and the ignorance of its Christian population."—*Millennial Star,* Vol. 1, pp. 188-189.

In reply to this direct attack the editors of the *Star* printed in the same issue:

"We have published the foregoing entire, in order to give our readers a specimen of the wickedness, ignorance and folly of the editor of the *London Dispatch.*

"Can any man in his senses believe that in Gloucestershire there are twelve men living in tents, who have come all the way from America for the sake of 200 pounds from one man, and a few shillings from two or three others!

Their passage-money will cost.. 60 pounds
Their time as day-laborers for six months exclusive of
    board would be worth..288 pounds
Their clothing on such a mission.......................................120 pounds
                                                                        _____
    Total ....468 pounds

"All this, besides the toils, fatigues, self-denial, and hardships of such a journey, and the trouble and expense of returning again to America; and all this for the paltry sum of 200 or 300 pounds, and this plundered from poor people!

"Query. Why do not the laws put a stop to these twelve men's wicked proceedings? Is there no law against plundering in England?

"Again, 'these twelve men have a new Bible!' I have been a member of the Church of Latter-day Saints for upwards of ten years, and never before learned of their having a new Bible. The only Bible I have ever seen or heard of in use among them is the translation commonly called King James'. * * *

"As to this sect being a new one just started in England, commencing first in the region of Gloucester, it is utterly false.

"The Latter-day Saints have more than 200 native preachers, and perhaps nearer 500, in England, Ireland, Scotland, and Wales.

"They have been established in many parts of England for years. * * *

"As to money which Mr. St. Clair charges them of plundering or even of receiving in that region, it is utterly false, and could only have grown out of misrepresentation in regard to some funds which were obtained there from men who had it to loan without distressing themselves in the least. And this by a fair business transaction to raise a printing fund for the purpose of printing hymn books and other religious works. The greater part of this sum has been paid back, and the residue will be punctually paid according to agreement. * * *

"As to the Latter-day Saints preaching a new doctrine, it is a false charge. Everybody that has heard them knows that they preach faith in Christ, repentance towards God, and obedience to all the commandments of the Gospel. * * *

"But again to this plundering business. The Bishop with two or three palaces and 9,000 pounds a year, is a humble shepherd of the true fold, is he not? His scores of non-resident clergy and others, all supported by a salary, are not plunderers, are they? The Methodists, with an extra fund of between two and three hundred thousand pounds raised at the centenary of Methodism, are no robbers or plunderers, are they? No,—no,—it is this two or three hundred pounds, divided to twelve penurious missionaries (and this is a falsehood) that is the only plundering known in England, is it not?

"Now for education: Perhaps if the people of Gloucester and the neighborhood were taught a few lessons in reading and arithmetic they could be made to believe that the bishop and priests who are alluded to by the *Dispatch,* are going in the old way of Christ and His apostles; and that they should not suffer themselves to be led away from such true folds and such faithful shepherds, to follow after these men who are so extravagant as to live in tents, and require 200 pounds to support them after a journey of 5,000 miles. But after all, the people of that region are not so universally ignorant, for we circulate several thousand tracts, and four or five hundred of our periodicals among them. And besides this, we hold to a system of universal education among all classes and we intend to bring it into operation among the saints as soon as possible; and when properly taught, and enabled to read the Bible, if the editor of the *Dispatch* and Captain St. Clair can reclaim them back to the 9,000 pounds a year system, and make them think it is the Church of Christ, they are at liberty to do so.

"But I am inclined to think after all, that it is the captain and the editor who are led away and plundered by a set of false apostles and deceivers. I believe the people of the said parishes have too much common sense to be deluded by wolves in sheep's clothing.

"I must now close, after giving the story of Alexander the Great and the pirate.

"After Alexander had conquered the world, and robbed the treasury of all nations, a pirate was brought before him to be judged. Alexander enquired by what right he infested the seas?— By the same right, replied he, that Alexander conquers the world,— I am styled a robber because I command a small vessel, and you are styled a conqueror, because you command great fleets and armies. The monarch, struck with the justness of the comparison, dismissed his prisoner without further ceremony. This would be like the case of the hireling priests and the Latter-day Saints, if the charge of their plundering the 200 pounds were true, but it happens to be false. May God judge between us and our accusers." —*Millennial Star,* Vol. 1, pp. 189-190.

And so the British press, in its various moods, and "Mormonism," variously represented, were early introduced to each other, and since that day the relationship has continued without interruption with many attacks being countered and with many courtesies being exchanged.

At critical times, when the Church and its representatives were most in need of friends, great British journals have, in the name of justice and reason, befriended the cause. This was true during the time of the "Evarts' fiasco" when, on August 10, 1879, the United States Government, by its Secretary of State, William M. Evarts, issued a proclamation, approved by the Cabinet, to its Ministers in England, Germany, Norway, Sweden and Denmark, protesting against further "Mormon" emigration to America. The proclamation declared that bigamy in any part of the United States was a crime, and that the "Mormons" destined for Utah went there with the avowed purpose of violating the law. The proclamation recited the laws on the subject, with convictions thereunder, and declared the government's intention to prosecute everyone in Utah against whom evidence was obtainable of violating any law in this respect.

The proclamation further instructed the Ministers to lay a copy before the governments to whom they were severally accredited, and to represent, in the most friendly manner, that it would be an act of justice to their subjects—especially the female portion—to endeavor to dissuade them from yielding to the inducements presented by "Mormon" missionaries to settle in Utah, and that, as these "Mormons" come to the United States with criminal intent, the United States Government would deem it friendly on the part of those governments to regard the movement in this light, and act conformably. The Ministers were, moreover, to instruct the United States Consuls to aid them in procuring information for transmission to Washington as to the manner in which the "Mormon" Church is recruited from abroad. This letter was believed to be preliminary to Government action forbidding vessels from landing "Mormons" in its ports, in pursuance of its obligation to prevent the immigration of lawless people.

The document created quite an international breeze for a short time, and many appeared to think that emigration would really be checked. The Saints were undisturbed, however, and the tide of emigration continued to flow as uninterruptedly to Utah as if Mr. Evarts and his circular had never existed.

The press everywhere ridiculed the proclamation, and criticized the proposed method of procedure. The *London Times*, known as "The Thunderer," because of its fearlessness, denounced the idea of curtailing those "who have contravened no law,"* and the *London*

---

*London Times, August 12, 1879.

Examiner severely took Evarts to task in a scathing editorial entitled "The Mormon Embargo," from which
we extract the following:

"Finding themselves powerless to cope with the "Mormon"
pest, the U. S. authorities have issued a plaintive appeal to the
Governments of England, Germany, Norway, Sweden, and Denmark, begging aid in their troubles. The morality of this circular
is admirable; the logic is lamentable. It would be a gross infringe-
ment of the liberty of man or woman were he or she to be prevented going to any country simply because there might be a
suspicion against him or her in the direction of bigamy.   Such
an interpretation of any law would speedily put it in the power
of a despotic Government to prevent its subjects leaving their
native country at all. Mr. Evarts must be perfectly aware that
no "Mormon" is forced to commit bigamy—any more than he is
compelled to marry his deceased wife's sister—and that in reality
numbers of the most respectable inhabitants of Utah content themselves with one wife. Utah is an extensive territory, not one-half
peopled; immigration is required, and it is surely a remarkable act
of interference on the part of the Federal Government to prevent
in any way that portion of the United States attracting its proper
complement of settlers.   It is the duty of the Government to punish
offenders against the marriage laws, but not the office of any foreign
nation to prevent men with a suspected propensity for much
marrying from leaving the land in which they were born, but
probably cannot live. The truth, however, is that the United
States, after many years of unavailing effort, find themselves
utterly unable to crush the 'Mormons.'

"These folks have made the desert bloom like the rose, have
planted incorporated towns where thirty years ago there were only
Indian 'teepes;' by aid of irrigation, they have reared wheat instead
of sage brush, and by the universal consensus of all visitors pre-
served order and public morality in a manner strange to other
Western towns. In a word, the inscription over their principal
place of business expresses the leading idea in their life—'Zion's Co-
operative Mercantile Institution: Holiness to the Lord.' Even yet,
notwithstanding the influx of 'Gentiles' into the territory, the 'Mormons' are as seven to one, while the ingenious expedient of granting
female suffrage has rendered their voting power overwhelming.
In only one district, where the miners predominate, was there a
non-'Mormon' candidate returned at last election. Though the
country has a population legally entitling it to be admitted as a
State, Congress has hitherto been deaf to all petitions to that
effect, the Federal Government being anxious to keep in its own
hands the appointment of the Governor, the judges, and the other
chief territorial officials.

DESERET, 152 HIGH ROAD, SOUTH TOTTENHAM,
LONDON

London Headquarters of the Church from 1908 to 1927.
Generations of missionaries both lived and preached here.

BRITISH AND EUROPEAN MISSION PRESIDENTS (1837-1864)

Left to right, first row: Heber C. Kimball, Joseph Fielding, Brigham Young, Parley P. Pratt, Thomas Ward. Second row: Reuben Hedlock, Wilford Woodruff, Orson Hyde, Franklin D. Richards, Orson Spencer. Third row: Orson Pratt, Franklin D. Richards (second term), Samuel W. Richards, Franklin D. Richards (third term), Orson Pratt (second term). Fourth row: Samuel W. Richards (second term), Asa Calkin, Amasa M. Lyman, Charles C. Rich, George Q. Cannon. (See Appendix for individual dates.)

"It is not in the power of the United States, with any regard for the law, the Constitution, and the rights of man, to prevent 'Mormons' entering the country merely because they are suspected of polygamous views. In England there are several thousand 'Mormons,' and in Scandinavia quite as many. They hold their meetings publicly, and try to make proselytes. So long as they do not transgress the law of the land, there is not injustice enough in England to punish them."—*London Examiner,* August 16, 1879.

Contrasted with the foregoing is the experience of President Heber J. Grant as related before the Institute of Human Relations, Estes Park, Colorado, in early August, 1936, in which he speaks of his dealings with the British press during his presidency over the European and British Missions during the three years from 1904 to 1906, inclusive:

"Recently I was reading from Phil Robinson's book, *Sinners and Saints,* which reminded me that during the three years that I was in England as President of the European and British Missions, I never succeeded in getting into the newspapers one line in refutation.of lying and wicked things that were published regarding us, some of them too filthy to be mentioned.

"I went to London with a letter of introduction from a shipping firm with whom we had done business for fifty years, vouching for my honesty and integrity, and for the honesty and integrity of every man who had presided over the European Mission of the Church during the previous fifty years, and the assistant editor of the paper refused to publish anything. When I was told that the editor was not in, but the assistant editor, Mr. Robinson, would receive me, I had a thought, which I later used.

"After he dismissed me I went to the door, and took my 'two-story stovepipe hat off,' turned around, and pretended to have an idea, which idea I had when I was told that Mr. Robinson, the assistant editor, would receive me.

"I said, 'By the way; my letter was not to you; you are only the assistant editor, and I think the boy said your name is Robinson.'

"He said, 'That is my name.'

"I said, 'Do you know Phil Robinson?'

" 'Do I know Phil Robinson? Everybody knows Phil Robinson.'

" 'Was he the correspondent of the *London Daily Telegraph* during the Boer War, one of the two greatest newspapers—and I emphasized *greatest,* because his was not one of the greatest—in all London?'

" 'He was.'

" 'Would you believe anything he said?'

" 'Anything on earth.'

" 'Buy his book, *Sinners and Saints,* and you will find that everything you have published in your paper is a dirty lie.'

"In Phil Robinson's book, *Sinners and Saints,* he says that he is at the defiance of any man to find a single book, with one exception, written on the 'Mormon' question that is not absolutely untrue, because practically all the books on that subject were written by enemies of our people, and are unfair.

"In the book to which I refer, Mr. Robinson gives the 'Mormons' a fine certificate of character, and among other things says that he nearly choked to death for 'a drink' among the 'Mormons' while traveling three hundred and fifty miles to the south and a hundred-odd miles to the north, until after inquiring for a 'backslider' he was successful in finding a demijohn. After that he got along very well. He said he had always supposed water was for the cleansing of the body until he arrived in Utah, and there he found it was used for drinking purposes."—*Improvement Era,* Vol. 40, No. 7.

Perhaps the opposition during the period referred to above by President Grant, and immediately preceding and following it, may be accounted for by the fact that the missionary activities of the Church, numerically speaking, were more intense during this period than ever before or since. During the decade 1900 to 1910 the Church sent more missionaries from America to Great Britain than in any other decade of the century.* The resultant progress invited a mounting opposition which scarcely could help but be reflected in the press.

Of the years immediately following this period another account states:

"Later, during the administration of President Rudger Clawson, in an effort to stem the progress of 'Mormonism,' an anti-'Mormon' crusade was launched for the purpose of checking the missionary work of the Church. An anti-'Mormon' demonstration was held in the Holborn Hall, London, April 28, 1911, another in the Hope Hall, Liverpool, and a number of minor ones in various English cities.

"Scenes of violence and mobocracy were enacted at Birkenhead, Bootle, Heywood, Sunderland, Seaton Hurst,

---

*See Appendix, statistical table on missionaries by years.

Nuneaton, Birmingham, Bristol, London, and Ipswich. The Elders in most of these places were subjected to gross insults and in some instances to personal assaults, from which they suffered more or less personal injury. Indeed, Elder Albert Smith, a traveling Elder in the Birmingham conference, on leaving a meeting of the Nuneaton branch in May, 1912, was literally covered with tar and feathers. President Clawson himself was mobbed in Bristol on November 17, 1912.

"Speaking at an anti-'Mormon' meeting, Bishop Welldon, Dean of Manchester (Episcopal Church), said: 'I think the 'Mormon' propaganda ought to be put down in England. If the law is not strong enough to put it down, it ought to be reinforced.'

"Rev. Father Bernard Vaughan from his pulpit declared: 'The 'Mormons' should be taken by the scuff of the neck, rushed across our island, and dropped into the sea.'

"In this crisis, Mr. W. T. Stead, editor of the *Review of Reviews* (England), came to the defense of the missionaries and wrote as follows to the *London Daily Express*, which communication was published:

"The whole so-called crusade is an outbreak of sectarian savagery worked up by journalists, who in their zest for sensation appear to be quite indifferent to the fact that the only permanent result of their exploit will be to advertise and to spread the 'Mormon' faith among the masses, who love fair play, and who hate religious persecution none the less because it is based upon a lie."

"At this time in compliance with demands made by leading clergymen and other influentials the British Home Secretary, Winston Churchill, directed that a nationwide survey of the activities of the 'Mormon' missionaries be made. However, when pressed as to what action the British government intended to take against the 'Mormon' missionaries, he replied: 'I have not so far discovered any grounds for legislation in the matter.' "—*Improvement Era*, Vol. 40, p. 153.

While the years since that day, more than a quarter of a century ago, have not been without intermittent attacks of anti-"Mormon" feeling in the British press, the trend has definitely been toward something more nearly approaching an accord, until today and during

the years immediately past, the "Mormon"-press relationship in the British Isles is the best it has been during
the century.

In 1932 the *East Ham* (London) *Echo* said:

"Probably no section of the human race is more unfairly criticized, more libelled and slandered or more misunderstood by the
ignorant, than the members of the Church of Jesus Christ of Latter-
day Saints, or, as they are more popularly known—the 'Mormons.'

"Sensational fiction and crude films have created among the
uninformed in England, many queer impressions, and it was with
much interest that I approached Salt Lake City to learn for myself
something of the true nature of these people."—By Charles Eade,
Reprinted in the *Millennial Star*, Vol. 94, p. 342.

In 1933 the *Birmingham Weekly Post* said:

"Everywhere in Salt Lake City I found the 'Mormon' and
non-'Mormon' population working amiably together, the friendliest
of feelings existing between them.   Indeed, that is the amazing
fact that strikes the visitor—the impossibility of recognizing one
from the other.   As you wander about the city . . . you begin to
appreciate the sterling qualities of this once despised sect."—Harold
J. Shepstone, F. R. G. S., *Birmingham Weekly Post*, May 20, 1933.

In 1935 appeared these typical comments, reprinted from the *Improvement Era*, Vol. 40, No. 7:

". . . the 'Mormons' regard the Bible as one of their standard
works. In addition to the *Book of Mormon*, they read an inspired
work called, *The Pearl of Great Price*. . . . There are still lots
and lots of people waiting to be converted in England."—*London
Star*.

"No 'Mormon' smokes, drinks, or tastes tea or coffee."—
Yorkshire Post.

"Let us hope that readers will no longer look upon the 'Mormons' as decadent ministers, luring women to a shameful life in
Salt Lake City.   They are a clean-living band of young men,
anxious to convert Gentiles into God-fearing members of a pioneer
church. And they do it without reward of any sort."—*Liverpool
Evening Express*.

"The 'Mormons' are now regarded as honest, God-fearing
people who live according to clean, healthy tenets."—*Birmingham
Gazette*.

In 1936 have come these typical comments:

"Asking for no collections, infesting all their meetings with a spirit of cheerfulness, 17 young men—16 American and one Irish, are spending a month in Preston engaged in missionary work. . . . The Church has at present about 2,000 missionaries in various parts of the world.   Mostly young men, they volunteer for two years' service abroad, and then return to take up their former occupations."
—*The Lancashire Daily Post,* August 25, 1936.

Fifteen young missionaries of the Church of Jesus Christ of Latter-day Saints are at present staying in Northern Ireland. They are known as the Millennial Chorus, and tonight at 8:15 they are to broadcast some songs in the B. B. C. Northern Ireland programme. The chorus which possesses some very fine voices, will be under their conductor, Bertram Willis. Their visit to Northern Ireland is part of a two-year tour of the British Isles.—*The Northern Whig and Belfast Post,* November 6, 1936.

In 1937 have come such statements as this:

"Theirs is a Gospel of physical fitness as well as religion. No true 'Mormon' smokes, drinks alcohol, tea or coffee, eats meat, makes a habit of the cinema, or neglects his physical exercise. * * * These Latter-day Saints are expected to give a tenth of their income to the central fund."—*The London Star,* March 3, 1937.

And so the passing of the years and the decades has made a century which affords sufficient perspective to justify the conclusion that the present favorable relationship with the British press has been brought about by a long process of arriving at a mutual understanding. Being intensely British, Fleet Street and the provinces may have looked with some suspicion upon a movement which seemed at first glance to have its interests outside the British Empire, but with such fears having been allayed, there has come at least a partial realization that the Church of Jesus Christ of Latter-day Saints has only one motive, and that, to bring all men, let them live under whatsoever flag they may, to a knowledge and understanding of the ancient faith restored through the Prophet Joseph Smith, which is the Gospel of Jesus Christ.

CHAPTER 26

THE MEN WHO HAVE GONE TO BRITAIN

Seated in a conference of "Mormon" missionaries back in mid-January, 1928, at the then headquarters of the British and European Missions, 295 Edge Lane, Liverpool, the author, who was then serving as associate editor of the *Millennial Star*, critically observed the men who were there gathered at the invitation of Dr. John A. Widtsoe. These observations, jotted down on that occasion, were later published in the *Millennial Star*:

"As I write, seated before me are more than a score of men, the youngest of whom has barely reached his majority, the oldest of whom is grey-haired and well past the half century mark. By previous inquiry I learned that they or their parents or grandparents came from more than half the countries of Northern Europe.

"Judged by some standards, it would be difficult to find a more widely differing group of individuals gathered together. There are young men and old; married men and single; they have come from varied pursuits of life. Among their number are farmers, mechanics, business men, college students, engineers, stock-raisers, and professional men. From four to thirty months ago they were all engaged in those occupations.

"Each of these men is from six to seven thousand miles away from home; they left voluntarily; without exception they have received no monetary wage or other material compensation for their services, and, what is more strange, they have paid their own living expenses and have devoted their time and talents to labors ofttimes arduous.

"Another thing about them—as I look into their faces I see clear and steady eyes. I have heard them speak— they are happy and enthusiastic; they express good thoughts well. I have clasped the hand of each—they have firm, strong grips.

"Who are they? What brought them together? What is their work? Why do they pursue it?

"These men are 'Mormon' missionaries, so-called. The Gospel of Jesus Christ brought them together; some were the first of their families to join the Church of Jesus Christ; others represent two, three and four generations in the Church. Their work is to proclaim repentance to all the world, to proclaim the restored Gospel of the Master, the plan of life and salvation. They pursue their work diligently because they have burning testimonies within them of the truth of the message they bear—because the Spirit of the Lord is with them.

"As I look upon these men and reflect upon these things I am led silently to exclaim with reverent exultation: Thank God for such men! Thank God for the might of His latter-day work!"—*Millennial Star*, Vol. 90, pp. 58-59.

Essentially the same could be said for every gathering of "Mormon" missionaries in Great Britain since the beginning a century ago. And this great army of nearly six thousand—for such has been the number of "Mormon" missionaries who have gone to British shores—have an unprecedented record. Quiet, clean, earnest, sincere and law-abiding, they have won the respect of the servants of the Crown wherever they have gone, and this despite the perennial and persistent efforts, in times past, of certain class interests and misdirected individuals to penetrate every act of their lives and bring discredit to their names.

So far as the "hand of the law" is concerned, the worst that may be said of "Mormon" missionaries as a class is that they have at intermittent times and in diverse places, during the past century, been forced to seek police protection from mob violence. And to the credit of the British "Bobbie"—than whom there is no finer class of law enforcement officer in all the world—and in appreciation of his impartial devotion to duty, let it not remain unsaid that such protection has always been given when the need for it was known and the circumstances permitted.

The British Government, too, has exercised, as concerning "Mormon" missionaries and "Mormon" activities, those great fundamental principles of tolerance and justice which have contributed to the building of the world's greatest Empire. "Mormon" missionaries as a class have been accorded the privileges, courtesies and protection which the governments of great nations accord to the law-abiding citizens of other nations.

For a century now the Church of Jesus Christ of Latter-day Saints has sent a generous sampling of the flower of its manhood to the British Isles. From 1837 until 1850, when the Scandinavian Mission was first opened, the entire foreign missionary force of the Church was directed to Great Britain. With the spreading of the work to continental Europe there was a diversion of man power to other fields, but the British Isles have continued to receive, proportionately, a large share of the messengers of the restoration.

During the century thirty-three missionaries have laid down their lives in, or traveling to or from, the British Mission while serving in the Cause of the Master.* It has been the conviction of these men, and of those who have been bereaved by their passing, that no greater benediction could come at the close of life than to be found in the service of our Lord and Savior. And to Latter-day Saints there comes the comforting assurance that death is but an incident in an endless eternity of individual existence from which point all good things continue or resume in the Lord's own time.

Numerically speaking, the period of greatest missionary activity in Great Britain was during the decade from 1900 to 1909 inclusive, corresponding to the administrations of Platte D. Lyman, Francis M. Lyman,

---

*See Appendix for list of names.

Heber J. Grant, and Charles W. Penrose, during which decade the Church sent 1376 missionaries from America to Great Britain. The two most lean years so far as "imported" missionaries are concerned were 1917-1918, the closing years of the World War, during the administration of George F. Richards. Only one missionary arrived during those two years.

This trying war period, and the immediate post-war period, when necessary government restrictions on foreign missionary activity were sharply felt, was ably administered by Apostles Hyrum M. Smith, George F. Richards and George Albert Smith, whose experiences on this phase of British Mission history alone could well become the subject of a published volume.

Elder Hyrum M. Smith was presiding over the European Mission when the war broke out in 1914. Overnight, almost, all of the missionaries in the Swiss and German Mission, as well as France and Belgium, were advised to leave those countries. In Holland, Denmark, Norway and Sweden most of the missionaries were gone, and only a few were left to look after the property belonging to the Church. The missionary work was left to local people. Ship after ship carried the Elders home to the United States, where they were placed in the different missions in the states. With the departure of the traveling missionaries and with the great scarcity of British man power, President George F. Richards called upon a faithful and able corps of three hundred seventy-five British women to pursue the work. They conducted most of the missionary activities and rendered their reports to Mission headquarters, with the result that the years 1916 to 1919 saw virtually a doubling of tithes and very little decrease in baptisms.*

Bringing order out of the war chaos in the affairs of

---

*George F. Richards, April, 1932, *Conference Discourses*.

the Church in Great Britain and Europe, largely characterized the administration of Elder George Albert Smith.
His was a task of making friends with statesmen and
diplomats, of restoring confidence and rehabilitating a
broken down machine, with virtually no missionary man
power, and in a most marvelous manner did the Lord
manifest His power in several very trying and delicate
situations.

The presidency of Elder Orson F. Whitney, cut
short by illness, was followed by the administration of
President David O. McKay, whose presidency was preceded by a world-wide survey and good will tour for
the Church. President McKay's administration was one
of friend-making and vigorous proselyting. His kindly
nature, impressive personality and tireless energy
warmed the hearts of missionaries, members, and even
enemies, and the year 1923 set a record for baptisms
which has not been equalled since 1914.

The notable achievements of the administrations of
Dr. James E. Talmage, of Dr. John A. Widtsoe and of
Dr. Joseph F. Merrill, whose enviable ratings in the
scientific and academic world, and whose scholarly
attainments and personal abilities did so much for Mission organization and toward allaying the prejudices of
press and people, invite detailed comment. Likewise,
the present administration of Dr. Richard R. Lyman,
and of the recent British Mission presidents as distinguished from the European presidents, beckon the way
toward elaboration of statement. But at this stage of
our British Mission story we must largely shun the specific in favor of the general.

The century's work in the British Mission has
been generaled down through the decades principally by
forty-three different men, many of them men of international eminence in the fields of science, industry,

education, finance, and religion.*   Most of these have been General Authorities of the Church of Jesus Christ of Latter-day Saints, and all of them have been capable, sincere men of God.   Of the seven Presidents of the Church to date, six—excepting only the Prophet Joseph Smith—have labored in or presided over the British Mission.   Many others of the General Authorities of the Church have also presided over the Mission, some of them for two, three, and even four terms.   There have been fifty-three regularly appointed British and European Mission administrations, and six periods of temporary direction, during the century.*   Some of these men have served with one or two counselors, but most of them have served alone.   The record for the longest aggregate service as a British or European Mission president belongs to Albert Carrington, who, on four different missions, beginning in 1868 and ending in 1882, served a few weeks less than eight years.   The longest continuous term was that of Dr. John A. Widtsoe, who served five years and nine months from January 1, 1928 to October 1, 1933.   The shortest regularly appointed term was the first of the four administrations of Elder Franklin D. Richards, when he served sixteen days from January 15, 1847, to February 1, 1847.*

Of the men who have presided over the European and British Missions, since July, 1837, twelve are still living, as follows, in the order of their mission service: Rulon S. Wells, Heber J. Grant, Rudger Clawson, George F. Richards, George Albert Smith, David O. McKay, John A. Widtsoe, A. William Lund,† James H. Douglas,† Joseph F. Merrill,‡ Joseph J. Cannon,† Richard R. Lyman,‡ Hugh B. Brown.§

*See Appendix table of British and European Mission presidents.   †British only.   ‡European only.   §Appointment announced May 1, 1937.

Until the expansion of Church activity into continental fields, the responsibility of these men was limited to British Mission activity. With the opening of other European missions, beginning with the Scandinavian Mission in 1850, the responsibility of general supervision over the continental missions and mission presidents devolved upon the president of the British Mission, who then became president of the European Mission, in addition to the detailed responsibility for the progress of the work in the British Isles. Thus the president of the British Mission was also president of the European Mission comprising all ecclesiastical divisions in continental and insular Europe, and subsequently including Asia-Minor and South Africa. This practice of dual responsibility continued from 1850 until 1928, when, laboring under the crushing responsibility of directing the affairs of ten missions, Dr. John A. Widtsoe, then President of the British and European Missions, recommended to the First Presidency of the Church the appointment of a separate British Mission president, which recommendation was accepted, thereby giving separate identities to the British and European Mission presidents, which now leaves the presiding European representative of the General Authorities free to travel and confer in all Europe when and where the need is greatest. Thus, on December 11, 1928, Elder A. Wm. Lund arrived in England to become President of the British Mission, leaving Dr. Widtsoe and his successors up to the present time, Dr. Joseph F. Merrill and Dr. Richard R. Lyman, to serve solely as presidents of the European Mission.

Under the direction of these mighty men of God— the century's British and European Mission presidents— have labored the great and ever-changing army of almost six thousand "Mormon" missionaries who have gone to

Great Britain, and the uncounted host of local missionaries who have volunteered their services in their native land. A comparatively few have been women. Both schooled and unlettered, few have been wise in the ways of the clergy or trained in the traditional manner of the cloth, but all have been armed with the tradition of truth and with the Priesthood of God, which has enabled them to prevail against many more worldly-wise than they, and to reach, from every walk of life, the honest in heart.

Two by two, down cobbled city streets and over turfed country lanes, through poverty row and to the mansions of the great, in the market place, and at the family fireside, in season and out, they have passed their tracts, preached their sermons and voiced their testimonies, calling out the seekers after life eternal, tens of thousands of whom have responded.

Tolerant and respectful of the good works and sacred beliefs of all men and all religious organizations, these "Mormon" missionaries have nevertheless been solemnly obligated to proclaim that the Lord has established *one* divinely appointed way whereby men may attain salvation, and *one* lineage of Priesthood, whereby men may perform the essential rites and ordinances of the Church of Jesus Christ. And if there has been opposition to their message, it has been opposition born of refusal or unwillingness to believe that the Lord has spoken! That He has restored to earth His Church and Holy Priesthood; that He has reaffirmed the first principles of the Gospel of Jesus Christ as they were given in other dispensations; that He has sent out divinely commissioned servants to proclaim these principles. Such has been the message of the "Mormon" missionaries who have gone to Great Britain during the past century and such must ever be the message of every Latter-day Saint.

CHAPTER 27

THE MEN WHO HAVE COME FROM
BRITAIN

It was no less a personage than Charles Dickens
who, reconnoitering at the London docks on the banks
of the cargo-laden Thames, to see what he could see
of the world as it came and went in the salt-sprayed
black hulls of white-topped sailing ships, found himself
among "Mormon" emigrants leaving home and country
for a "strange" faith—a faith that had found its way
to their inmost hearts, even so completely that all else
the world had to offer seemed but a trifle to exchange
for the certain conviction that brought peace to them,
despite all else it brought of sacrifice and hardship.

And, seeing their deeds, but not understanding their
motives, Charles Dickens, who frankly came to discredit,
or ridicule or "expose" or to do whatever his findings de-
manded, wrote thus of what there met his eyes:

*"Behold me on my way to an Emigrant Ship, on a hot
morning early in June. . . Gigantic in the basin just beyond
the church, looms my Emigrant Ship: her name, the
Amazon. . .

"I go aboard my Emigrant Ship. I go first to the great
cabin, and find it in the usual condition of a Cabin at that
pass. Perspiring landsmen, with loose papers, and with
pens and inkstands, pervade it; and the general appearance
of things is as if the late Mr. Amazon's trustees found the
affairs in great disorder, and were looking high and low for
the will. . . But nobody is in an ill-temper, nobody is the
worse for drink, nobody swears an oath or uses a coarse
word, nobody appears depressed, nobody is weeping, and

---

*The reader will find delightful entertainment of the true Dick-
ens' variety by a reading of the complete "Mormon" episode
from *The Uncommercial Traveler*. The chapter title is "Bound for
the Great Salt Lake."

down upon the deck in every corner where it is possible to find a few square feet to kneel, crouch, or lie in, people, in every unsuitable attitude for writing, are writing letters.

"Now, I have seen emigrant ships before this day in June. And these people are so strikingly different from all other people in like circumstances whom I have ever seen, that I wonder aloud, 'What *would* a stranger suppose these emigrants to be!'

"The vigilant bright face of the weather-browned captain of the *Amazon* is at my shoulder, and he says, 'What, indeed! The most of these came aboard yesterday evening. They came from various parts of England in small parties that had never seen one another before. Yet they had not been a couple of hours on board, when they established their own police, made their own regulations, and set their own watches at all the hatchways. Before nine o'clock, the ship was as orderly and as quiet as a man-of-war.'

"I looked about me again, and saw the letter-writing going on with the most curious composure. Perfectly abstracted in the midst of the crowd; . . . Later in the day, when this self-same boat was filled with a choir who sang glees and catches for a long time, one of the singers, a girl, sang her part mechanically all the while, and wrote a letter in the bottom of the boat while doing so.

" 'A stranger would be puzzled to guess the right name for these people, Mr. Uncommercial,' says the captain.

" 'Indeed he would.'

" 'If you hadn't known, could you ever have supposed—?'

" 'How could I? I should have said they were in their degree, the pick and flower of England.'

" 'So should I,' says the captain.

" 'How many are they?'

" 'Eight hundred in round numbers.'

* * *

"Eight hundred what? 'Geese, villain?' *Eight Hundred 'Mormons.'* I, Uncommercial Traveller for the firm of Human Interest Brothers, had come aboard this Emigrant Ship to see what eight hundred Latter-day Saints were like, and I found them (to the rout and overthrow of all my expectations) like what I now describe with scrupulous exactness.

"The 'Mormon' Agent who had been active in getting

them together, and in making the contract with my friends, the owners of the ship, to take them as far as New York on their way to the Great Salt Lake, was pointed out to me. A compactly-made handsome man in black, rather short, with rich-brown hair and beard, and clear bright eyes. From his speech, I should set him down as American. Probably, a man who had 'knocked about the world' pretty much. A man with a frank, open manner, and unshrinking look; withal a man of great quickness. I believe he was wholly ignorant of my Uncommercial individuality, and consequently of my immense Uncommercial importance.

"*Uncommercial*. These are a very fine set of people you have brought together here.

"*Mormon Agent*. Yes, sir, they are a *very* fine set of people.

"*Uncommercial* (looking about). Indeed, I think it would be difficult to find eight hundred people together anywhere else, and find so much beauty and so much strength and capacity for work among them.

"*Mormon Agent* (not looking about, but looking steadily at Uncommercial). I think.—We sent out about a thousand more yes'day, from Liverpool.

"*Uncommercial*. You are not going with these emigrants?

"*Mormon Agent*. No, sir. I remain.

"*Uncommercial*. But you have been in the Mormon Territory?

"*Mormon Agent*. Yes; I left Utah about three years ago.

"*Uncommercial*. It is surprising to me that these people are all so cheery, and make so little of the immense distance before them.

"*Mormon Agent*. Well, you see; many of 'em have friends out in Utah, and many of 'em look forward to meeting friends on the way.

"*Uncommercial*. On the way?

"*Mormon Agent*. This way 'tis. This ship lands 'em in New York City. Then they go on by rail right away beyond St. Louis, to that part of the Banks of the Missouri where they strike the Plains. There, wagons from the settlement meet 'em to bear 'em company on their journey 'cross—twelve hundred miles about. Industrious people who come out to the settlement soon get wagons of their own, and so the friends of some of these will come down in their

BRITISH AND EUROPEAN MISSION PRESIDENTS (1854-1906)

Left to right, first row: Daniel H. Wells, Brigham Young, Jr., Franklin D. Richards (fourth term), Albert Carrington, Horace S. Eldredge. Second row: Albert Carrington (second term), Joseph F. Smith, Albert Carrington (third term), Joseph F. Smith (second term), William Budge. Third row: Albert Carrington (fourth term), John Henry Smith, Daniel H. Wells (second term), George Teasdale, Brigham Young, Jr. (second term). Fourth row: Anthon H. Lund, Rulon S. Wells, Platte D. Lyman, Francis M. Lyman, Heber J. Grant. (See Appendix for individual dates.)

BRITISH AND EUROPEAN MISSION PRESIDENTS (1906-1937)

Left to right, first row: Charles W. Penrose, Rudger Clawson, Hyrum M. Smith, George F. Richards, George Albert Smith. Second row: Orson F. Whitney, David O. McKay, James E. Talmage, John A. Widtsoe, A. William Lund (British Mission only). Third row: James H. Douglas (British Mission only), Joseph F. Merrill (European Mission only), Joseph J. Cannon (British Mission only), Richard R. Lyman (European Mission only), Hugh B. Brown (British Mission only—appointment announced May 1, 1937). (See Appendix for individual dates.)

Note: There have also been seven temporary British and European Mission presidents. See Appendix for names and dates.

own wagons to meet 'em. They look forward to that, greatly. . .

"After a noontide pause for dinner, during which my emigrants were nearly all between-decks, and the *Amazon* looked deserted, a general muster took place. The muster was for the ceremony of passing the Government Inspection and the Doctor. . .

"By what successful means a special aptitude for organization had been infused into these people, I am, of course, unable to report. But I know that, even now, there was no disorder, hurry, or difficulty.

. . . "There were many worn faces bearing traces of patient poverty and hard work, and there was great steadiness of purpose and much undemonstrative self-respect among this class. . . .

"I should say (I had no means of ascertaining the fact) that most familiar kinds of handicraft trades were represented here. Farm-laborers, shepherds, and the like, had their full share of representation, but I doubt if they preponderated. . . . Among all the fine handsome children, I observed but two with marks upon their necks that were probably scrofulous. Out of the whole number of emigrants, but one old woman was temporarily set aside by the doctor, on suspicion of fever; but even she afterwards obtained a clean bill of health.

"When all had 'passed,' and the afternoon began to wear on, a black box became visible on deck, which box was in charge of certain personages also in black, of whom only one had the conventional air of an itinerant preacher. This box contained a supply of hymn-books, neatly printed and got up, published at Liverpool, and also in London at the 'Latter-day Saints' Book Depot, 30, Florence street.' . . .

"I afterwards learned that a dispatch was sent home by the captain before he struck out into the wide Atlantic, highly extolling the behavior of these emigrants, and the perfect order and propriety of all their social arrangements. What is in store for the poor people on the shores of the Great Salt Lake, what happy delusions they are laboring under now, on what miserable blindness their eyes may be opened then, I do not pretend to say. But I went on board their ship to bear testimony against them if they deserved it, as I fully believed they would; to my great astonishment they did not deserve it; and my predispositions and tendencies must not affect me as an honest witness. I went over the *Amazon's* side, feeling it impossible to deny that, so far, some remarkable influence had produced a remarkable result, which better known influences have often missed.— From *The Uncommercial Traveller,* by Charles Dickens.

That this was not an ordinary emigration venture and that these were not ordinary men and women, the distinguished Mr. Dickens seemed to sense, but what perhaps he did not understand were the factors that made this differ from any one of hundreds of colonizing projects—what set these men and women apart from tens of thousands of emigrants who were continuously leaving for new frontiers. Mr. Dickens perhaps had not read, or, perchance, having read, had not perhaps comprehended the instructions given of the Lord, through the Prophet Joseph Smith, in 1830 and following, wherein He said:

"And, verily, verily, I say unto you, that this Church have I established and called forth out of the wilderness.

"And even so will I gather mine elect from the four quarters of the earth, even as many as will believe in me, and hearken unto my voice.

"Yea, verily, verily, I say unto you, that the field is white already to harvest; wherefore, thrust in your sickles, and reap with all your might, mind and strength."—*Doctrine and Covenants,* Section 33:5, 6 and 7.

"And it shall come to pass that the righteous shall be gathered out from among all nations, and shall come to Zion, singing with songs of everlasting joy."—*Doctrine and Covenants,* Section 45:71.

In accordance with these and other revelations, the Church began to gather unto itself truth-seeking men and women from an ever-widening circle, as its missionaries penetrated farther and farther on their world-wide mission of bearing witness of the Gospel restoration. And as testimonies of truth came to the humble and the honest in heart, so there fell upon them also the "spirit of gathering," the urge to comply with which made no sacrifice seem too great and no hindrance great enough.

When the first missionaries went to Britain, however, they were counseled not to preach immediately
concerning gathering.   The Church was undergoing
troublous times at home, and a great influx of dependent
people from foreign lands at that time would only have
added to their burdens.   And so, the beginning of "Mormon" emigration from Great Britain was delayed nearly
three years, until it could be properly organized under
the direction of Brigham Young and the Twelve when
they met and conducted the affairs of the Church as a
Quorum in England.

Accordingly, the first "Mormon" emigration from
Great Britain occurred June 6, 1840—the year after
Nauvoo was settled.   This first company, consisting of
forty souls, had been organized six days before, June
1, 1840, by Brigham Young, which date, it may be noted
in passing, was the thirty-ninth anniversary of his birth.
Of this occurrence the following paragraph appears in
the *History of the Church*:

"Saturday, June 6—Elder John Moon and a company of forty
Saints, to-wit: Hugh Moon, his mother and seven others of her
family, Henry Moon (Uncle of John Moon), Henry Moon, Francis
Moon, William Sutton, William Sitgraves, Richard Eaves, Thomas
Moss, Henry Moore, Navey Ashworth, Richard Ainscough, and
families, sailed in the ship *Britannia* from Liverpool for New York,
being the first Saints that have sailed from England for Zion."—
Vol. 4:134.

Of the arrival of this first company in New York,
the *Millennial Star* of September, 1840, comments as
follows:

"While thousands and tens of thousands are emigrating from
this land to America, New Holland, etc., hoping by their industry
to get a morsel of bread cheaper, and easier than they now do,
and thus escape the miseries of hunger which some are already
enduring, we rejoice that a few poor Saints find it in their hearts
and can get the means to do likewise.
"Elder John Moon and others who sailed from Liverpool
on the 6th of June, arrived in New York on the 20th of July (forty-

four days on the water) in tolerable health and good spirits, as we learn by Brother Moon's letter of the 22nd of July."

The Moon family and their connections, it will be remembered, were brought into the Church under unusual circumstances by Heber C. Kimball on his first mission to Great Britain.

The second emigrant vessel was the *North America*, leaving Liverpool for New York September 7, 1840, with two hundred souls on board. The third and last vessel to sail that year was the *Isaac Newton*, October 15, 1840, with fifty Scotch Saints. This vessel did not go to New York, but to New Orleans, a more direct route to Nauvoo, and at considerable less expense.

From that time, and as long as the emigration to Nauvoo continued, the main route of travel was direct from Liverpool to New Orleans, and from there up the Mississippi River to Nauvoo. President Brigham Young, and his brethren of the Twelve who were with him at the time, directed the emigration until April, 1841, during which time one thousand twenty Saints emigrated to Nauvoo.

Once "the gathering" had started, the desire of the British Saints to emigrate became a pressing and major consideration. Since the Church was not in a favorable financial condition either in Great Britain or America, the utmost cooperation and management of resources were required. There was the problem not only of transporting great numbers of people, but also the problem of caring for them and usefully absorbing them in harassed and persecuted communities when they arrived at the headquarters of the Church in America. It required the utmost wisdom and caution to keep such a situation from becoming completely out of control.

Relative to these matters, and before emigration was organized at its best, the Twelve wrote an epistle

"To the Church of Jesus Christ of Latter-day Saints, in the various Branches and Conferences in Europe" some months after they had left British shores to return to America. From this lengthy epistle, which speaks of economic conditions in a manner strongly savoring of the language of our own day, the following excerpts are quoted:

"Beloved Brethren,—We feel it our privilege, and a duty we owe to the great and glorious cause in which we have enlisted, to communicate to you at this time some principles, which, if carried into effect, will greatly facilitate the gathering of the Saints, and tend to ameliorate the condition of those who are struggling with poverty and distress, in this day when the usual means of support seem to be cut short, to the laboring classes, through the depression that everywhere prevails in the general business mart of the civilized world.

. . . "Many of you are desirous of emigrating to this country, and many have not the means to accomplish their wishes, and if we can assist you by our prayers and our counsels to accomplish the desires of your hearts in this thing, so far we will rejoice and be satisfied. You not only want to emigrate to this section of the earth, but you desire also to have some laudable means of comfortable subsistence after your arrival here, and this also is important. How, then, shall these things be accomplished, and your souls be satisfied? We answer, by united understanding, and concert of action. You all, or most of you, have trades or different kinds of business to which you have long been familiarized, and in which you would like to continue for the purpose of procuring a subsistence; and a great proportion of your occupation is such, that no employment can be had in this city or vicinity; for instance, there are no cotton manufactories established here, and many of you know no other business. You want to come here, and, when here, you want to continue your labors in your accustomed branches of business; but you have no means to get here, and when here there are no factories; and yet factories are needed here, and there would be ready market for all the fabrics which could be manufactured.

"Now comes the concert of action; if the church will

arise unitedly—if the brethren will individually feel that the great work of the Lord is depending on themselves as instruments, to assist in carrying it forward, and will unite all their means, faith, and energy, in one grand mass, all that you desire can speedily be accomplished. A short time only will elapse before you yourselves will be astonished at the result. and you will feel that your desires are more than realized. While the Saints are united, no power on the earth, or under the earth, can prevail against them; but while each one acts for himself, many, very many, are in danger of being overthrown.

"God has promised all things to those who love him and keep his commandments; then why be afraid that one should get a little more than another, or that one should gain, for a little moment, what another might lose, when Jesus has promised that the faithful shall be one with him, as he is one with the Father, and shall possess all things in the due time of the Lord; not by stealth, not by force, not by the sword, but by the gift of the Father, through faithfulness to his commands. . . .

"Had we means, we would not ask your aid. We would gladly send the ships of Tarshish to bear you across the great waters; we would bring you to our homes—to our firesides; we would provide you habitations, lands, and food, when you arrive among us. Our hearts are large enough to do all this, and a great deal more; but we have not the means. We have to labor for our own subsistence, as well as attend to those things which are laid upon us of the Lord, and which concern the whole Church as much as ourselves. It is not the will of heaven that any one should be put in possession of all things, without striving for them. . . ."—*Millennial Star*, Vol. III, pp. 17-20.

In the November 20, 1846, issue of the *Millennial Star* appears a lengthy "Memorial to the Queen, for the relief, by immigration, of a portion of her poor subjects," which asked for land grants and privileges in "Oregon territory."

The February 15, 1847, issue of the *Star* reports:

"The Memorial, measuring 168 feet in length and containing nearly 13,000 names has been forwarded to Her Majesty (Queen Victoria), together with a copy to each member of Parliament and

also to other distinguished individuals.   Tens of thousands await
the issue with prayerful solicitude and hope.   May He who holds
the hearts of sovereigns and the destinies of nations in His hands,
graciously incline Her Majesty to favor the Memorial."

"In most schemes by emigration [says Elder Orson Hyde]
hitherto approved and aided by government, great difficulty has
been found to induce the people of this country, to leave their native
isle; but we are prepared, and shall guarantee, to send twenty
thousand people of all trades, and from most districts in Scotland,
England and Wales, *at once,* or as soon as vessels can be found
to convey them."

The *Star* printed an acknowledgment of the receipt
of the Memorial from Lord John Russell, Prime Minister, in behalf of the Queen, and letters from members
of Parliament, but we find no further reference to any
action having been taken by the Parliament.

The establishment of the headquarters of the
Church in Great Salt Lake Valley automatically made
the "Great Basin" the gathering place for the Latter-day
Saints. But the securing of funds to transport so many
members of the Church, drawn mostly from the poorer
classes, and scattered over the United States and in
foreign lands, was a question of grave importance.
So in September, 1849, the Perpetual Emigrating Fund
Company was organized under the direction of President
Brigham Young. Donations of money, oxen, wagons,
foodstuffs and equipment were widely solicited to con-
stitute a fund whereby the poor might be gathered to
"Zion." The money advanced to individuals for transportation was considered as a loan to be repaid as soon
as possible after the arrival of the immigrants in the
"Valley." In the greater number of cases this obligation was honorably discharged. Years later many Utah
born children of those who had been beneficiaries of the
Perpetual Emigrating Fund, gladly made liberal donations to the fund, in order that their relatives abroad
might enjoy the blessings that awaited them in Zion.

The Perpetual Emigrating Fund Company was

legally incorporated by the Territorial Legislature of Utah on October 4, 1851, and at all times during its existence, functioned under careful supervision. It continued to operate as an emigration agency, collecting and disbursing funds, chartering ships, establishing purchasing agencies, and arranging for transportation of emigrants across the seas and the plains, in organized companies, and later by rail until 1887, when the company was dissolved by passage of the Edmunds-Tucker law, an act of Congress which, among other things, dissolved the Perpetual Emigrating Fund Company, the property of which escheated to the government. This act became a law without the signature of the President of the United States.

The British House of Commons took note of the "Mormon" emigration system in 1854, and, according to the *Edinburgh Review* of January, 1862, reported as follows:

"The select committee of the House of Commons on emigrant ships for 1854 summoned the 'Mormon' agent and passenger broker before it and came to the conclusion that no ships under the provisions of the Passenger's Act could be depended upon for comfort and security in the same degree as those under his administration. The 'Mormon' ship is a family under strong and accepted discipline, with every provision for comfort, decorum, and internal peace."

Such notices as the following were issued by the Church emigration office in Liverpool, usually from sixty to ninety days prior to sailing date:

"NOTICE TO INTENDING EMIGRANTS—We beg to inform the Saints intending to emigrate, that we are now prepared to receive their applications for berths. Every application should be accompanied by the name, age, occupation, country where born, and one pound deposit for each one named. Passengers must furnish their own beds and bedding, their cooking utensils, provision boxes. . . ." *Millennial Star,* Vol. 98, pp. 789-790.

The procedure from this point was essentially as that described by the " 'Mormon' Agent" to Mr. Dickens, the "Uncommercial Traveller." The following is typical of the frontier agent's instructions to these people:

"My assent will not be given to any Saint to leave the Missouri River unless organized in a company of at least fifty effectual well-armed men, and that, too, under the command of a man appointed by me. I will furnish at this point of outfit, for such as desire it, wagons, oxen, cows, guns, flour, bacon, etc. . . . One wagon, two yoke of oxen, and two cows will be sufficient for a family of eight or ten persons with addition of a tent for every two or three families."—*Millennial Star,* Vol. 98, pp. 789-790.

On the plains rigid regulations were needed for the welfare, protection and dispatch of a company so widely diversified and so strange to the mode of life they were undertaking. From the countries of northern Europe, from all the trades and professions and from homes of poverty and plenty came these men, women and children, taking with them such few cherished possessions as they could carry, but largely confining themselves to stern necessities—and oftimes not even those. Organized into companies of tens, fifties and hundreds, with horses, cattle, wagons and implements, they led a resolute life of self-discipline and community discipline. One company's instructions read:

"Resolved—First the horn shall be blown at four o'clock in the morning, when the people shall rise, and after the necessary preparations for starting, the horn will be blown again for the people to come together for prayers, and at half-past eight at night the horn will be blown again for evening prayers, which each family will attend in their wagons."—*Millennial Star,* Vol. 98, pp. 789-790.

On February 3, 1852, the first company of Perpetual Emigrating Fund emigrants arrived in Salt Lake City, Utah, from Europe, with thirty-one wagons; Abraham O. Smoot, captain. It was met by President Brigham Young and his counselors and by Captain Wm. Pitt's band, and a large company of Utah's leading citizens. This company brought across the plains the

remains of Elders Lorenzo D. Barnes and William
Burton, who had died while on missions in Great Britain.

In the fall of 1855, the financial strain of the season's
emigration program made it evident that the old plan
could not continue. Having already written a general
circular of information to the membership abroad, Brigham Young, as president of the Emigrating Company,
wrote to Franklin D. Richards, presiding in England,
Sept. 30, 1855, in part, as follows:

"I have been thinking how we should operate another year.
We cannot afford to purchase wagons and teams as in times past,
I am consequently thrown back upon my old plan—to make handcarts and let the emigration foot it with the necessary supplies,
and having a cow or two for every ten. They can come just as
quick, if not quicker, and much cheaper—can start earlier and
escape the prevailing sickness which annually lays so many of
our brethren in the dust. A great majority of them walk now even
with the teams which are provided, and have a great deal more
care and perplexity than they would have if they came without
them. They will only need 90 days' rations from the time of their
leaving the Missouri River, and as the settlements extend up the
Platte, not that much. The carts can be made without a particle
of iron, with wheels hooped, made strong and light, and one, or
if the family be large, two of them will bring all that they will need
upon the plains.

"If it is once tried you will find that it will become the favorite
mode of crossing the plains; they will have nothing to do but come
along, and I should not be surprised if a company of this kind
should make the trip in sixty or seventy days. I do know that
they can beat any ox train crossing the plains. I want to see it
fairly tried and tested, at all events, and I think we might as well
begin another year as any time and save this enormous expense of
purchasing wagons and teams—indeed we will be obliged to pursue
this course or suspend operations, for aught that I can see at the
present."—*Millennial Star*, Vol. 17, p. 813.

The suggestion of President Young was given
support by his associates, and in view of the enthusiasm
and impatience among the converts in Europe to come
to Utah under almost any conditions, the plan was announced in a letter dated October 29. It follows in part:

"Let all the Saints who can, gather up to Zion, and come while
the way is open before them; let the poor also come, whether they
receive aid or not from the Perpetual Emigrating Fund; let them

come on foot, with handcarts, or wheelbarrows; let them gird up their loins and walk through and nothing shall hinder or stay them.

* * *

"We propose sending men of faith and experience with some suitable instructions to some proper outfitting point, to carry into effect the above suggestions; let the Saints therefore, who intend to emigrate the ensuing year, understand that they are expected to walk, and draw their luggage across the plains, and that they will be assisted by the Fund in no other way."—*Millennial Star*, Vol. 18, p. 54.

Acting upon the instructions of the general officers of the emigrating company relative to the season's emigration, the *Millennial Star* for February 23, 1856, announced that Iowa City had been selected as the outfitting post for that year and that the emigrants would be forwarded from the port of landing to that point via the Chicago and Rock Island Railroad. The cost of transportation under the new plan for that year, was placed at nine pounds ($45.00) for each adult.

The disaster that befell two handcart companies late in 1856, many of whose number perished in Wyoming snows, was tragic, but the movement as a whole and the four thousand who walked the plains, must not be lost sight of. The experiment was not entirely without success and would likely have continued over a longer period, had not the westward extension of the railroad and the supplementary use of Church teams entered to lessen its operations and bring the handcart episode to a close in 1860.

Neither the dissolution of the Perpetual Emigrating Fund in 1887, nor any previous or subsequent difficulty until the United States immigration restrictions of recent times, halted the influx of British Saints to the headquarters of the Church. More than fifty-two thousand* of them have come during the years of the near-century since the inception of this unprecedented modern mi-

---

*See Appendix table of emigration by years.

gration. And they have brought to the Church loyal man power, and fine, clean British blood. They have brought, too, from every walk of life those skilled in the arts and the trades and the professions, and fine British capacity for adapting themselves to the vastly different environmental conditions of frontier life.

To membership in the presiding councils of the Church Great Britain has directly contributed eleven men, among them some of the most brilliant, capable and devoted champions and defenders of the faith that the century has produced.*

But besides this British contribution to the official leadership of the Church have come the great unrecordable contributions of the hosts of men and women throughout the decades. Uncounted scores of the most useful men and women this Church has had on its membership rolls were British-born, including the first designer and builder of the Tabernacle organ, one Tabernacle organist and five Tabernacle choir conductors.

A brief check-up of the current official Latter-day Saint Hymn Book reveals that the words of more than half of the 421 hymns it contains were written by British-born members of the Church, and of more than three-fourths of these hymns, the music was written by British-born members of the Church.

And so specific details of British contributions could be multiplied virtually without limit. These alone would more than justify the century's existence of the British Mission, and the cost in time, personal sacrifice and money that have been put into it.

But these tangible and material things, that may be listed and multiplied and evaluated in ordinary terms, are not the reason for the existence of the British or any

---

*See Appendix table of British-born General Authorities.

other mission of the Church.   The only justifiable reason is the salvation of human souls—the bringing of a conviction of truth to the hearts of men, and to their lives a transforming knowledge of the divinity of the Lord Jesus Christ and His plan for the joy and exaltation of men.   And for this cause have they come— from the coal mines of Wales, from the heather-covered hills of Scotland, from the midland mill towns, from the shamrock countryside of Ireland, from the labyrinths of Londontown, and from the sea-swept shores of all the Island Empire.

Some have come from material poverty to rise to material riches; some have left comparative ease to find penury and deprivation; some have remained as they were and as they are, to make their way still on British shores; some tossed on the seas; some walked the plains; some died before the journey was through—but all have found whatever price was asked and whatever cost was paid to be the greatest exchange of values this world has to offer, and that is why these men and women of a century's harvest in Great Britain have closely cherished the Gospel of Jesus Christ.

Such has been the spirit of the men and women who have come from Great Britain.   And those same traditional British qualities of character, that have meant so much to the Church of Jesus Christ in frontier lands, will go far toward building a strong and permanent Church organization in the British Isles, now that emigration is no longer encouraged.

CHAPTER 28

CHALLENGING CONCLUSIONS

The latter-day restoration of the Gospel of Jesus Christ, and the authority of the Priesthood wherewith its ordinances are administered, has been operative in Great Britain almost as long as it has in America— one hundred years out of one hundred and seven years. While speculation upon things that may never be known is an idle thing, nevertheless it is intriguing to think that but for the "spirit of gathering" and its attendant "mass" emigration of British converts, the "Mormon" Church in the British Isles might already have become numerically great even as it has in America. It is not difficult to believe this when one remembers that more than fifty-two thousand members of the Church have sailed from British shores in decades past, and they with their influence, and with their friends, and with their faithful posterity, would have made a mighty concourse in the United Kingdom.

When Heber C. Kimball and his immediate successors preached in British lands, the "field was white, already to harvest," and these noblemen of God thrust in their sickles and reaped gloriously. Since then there have been seasons of lean and seasons of abundance, with cycles that rise and fall. There have been as few as one hundred forty-seven converts reported in a year as compared with thousands at other times.* During periods of low yield there has been a feeling in some quarters that the British harvest was over. Unofficial talk concerning the closing of the British Mission has been heard in former years. But the writer knows of no law, natural or ecclesiastical, which would justify the

---

*See Appendix table on baptisms by years.

conclusion that one harvest may not be followed by another.

Salvation, after all, is an individual matter, and Wilford Woodruff's testimony to John Benbow and the United Brethren back in 1840, has little actually to do with the testimony of today's missionary to the confused twentieth century seeker-after-truth. Until the Lord speaks otherwise, bearing witness to all the world is the everlasting obligation of the Church of Jesus Christ of Latter-day Saints, and "all the world" must certainly include the present generation in Great Britain.

These and other challenging conclusions were reached in part as a result of a comparison of certain figures from the British Mission statistical report for a recent year, with certain current vital statistics of Great Britain, as follows:

There were approximately a quarter of a million people residing in the British Isles to every "Mormon" missionary. There were approximately 7,000 people residing in the British Isles to every member of the Church living in Great Britain.

But forgetting the existing forty-odd millions of population, and confining ourselves for the moment to a consideration only of annual births—the newcomers to the scene of life, so to speak—and the following astounding results appear:

There were approximately 2 persons born in Great Britain in a recent year to every door that was opened to a "Mormon" missionary; there were approximately 6 persons born to every Gospel conversation engaged in by a "Mormon" missionary; 9 born to every Gospel pamphlet distributed; 30 born to every family of investigators visited; 230 born to every *Book of Mormon* distributed; and approximately 3,000 born to every baptism into the Church of Jesus Christ of Latter-day Saints.

Challenging!

Who yearns for opportunity? Here it is in stag-
gering abundance! In the oldest mission of the Church
on the eve of a centennial celebration, our man power
and facilities do not reach even the newcomers to the
world-scene, to say nothing of the existing population.

How this problem is to be solved, no man knows.
The presiding authorities in the British field have made
notable strides in adapting missionary methods to modern conditions. The press, radio, sports, recreational
activities, and group efforts are supplementing the "tried
and true" methods of the early British missionaries, but
nothing will ever be effectively substituted for their he-
roic faith, and their diligence and unquestioning trust in
the Lord. The year 1936 saw a "Mormon" missionary
chorus, the Millennial Chorus, engaged to sing on radio
stations of the British Broadcasting Corporation, and in
British theatres. Numerous recent British press notices
are available praising "Mormon" baseball, basketball,
and other recreational activities, all of which are helpful
to the cause, and indicative of the diligence, initiative
and resourcefulness of the twentieth century missionary.
But the missionary of today is confronted with the task
of harmonizing "streamlined" methods with the ancient
faith and the preaching of fundamentals, without which
no man may serve the Lord effectively.

Another challenging situation is this: The record
of a century seems to indicate that there is little or no
relationship between the number of "imported" missionaries and the number of baptisms.* What are the
other elements affecting conversions and to what extent
may they be controlled or modified are questions that
may well bear looking into.

---

*See Appendix statistical tables on number of missionaries
and number of baptisms by years.

But the future of the Church in Great Britain does not depend wholly upon the activities and continuance of its "imported" missionaries. As indicated in the opening sentences of this concluding chapter, it is idle speculation to contemplate what might have been the destiny of the Church in Britain had there been no widespread emigration to America, but it is not idle speculation to contemplate what might yet be the destiny of the Church of Jesus Christ of Latter-day Saints in the British Isles, growing out of the united efforts of its present membership of more than six thousand souls.

Whether the traveling "Mormon" missionaries from America are called out of Great Britain tomorrow, or whether they remain there for the next hundred years, changes the fundamental situation not the least. The fact remains that unsettled world conditions and immigration restrictions mean that the Church must be built to flourish as a permanent institution in Great Britain. And every Latter-day Saint in the British Isles must strive toward that day when the Church of God shall be mighty in Britain, and when the spires of a Temple of the Lord shall pierce British skies, for "Zion is the pure in heart."

APPENDIX

BRITISH AND EUROPEAN MISSION PRESIDENTS
OF THE CENTURY

Heber C. Kimball—July 20, 1837 to April 20, 1838.
Joseph Fielding—April 20, 1838 to July 6, 1840.
Brigham Young—July 6, 1840 to April 20, 1841.
Parley P. Pratt—April 20, 1841 to October 20, 1842.
Thomas Ward—October 20, 1842 to November 1, 1843.
Reuben Hedlock—November 1, 1843 to February 4, 1845.
Wilford Woodruff—February 4, 1845 to October 3, 1846.
Orson Hyde—October 3, 1846 to January 15, 1847.
Franklin D. Richards—January 15, 1847 to February 1, 1847.
Orson Spencer—February 1, 1847 to August 15, 1848.
Orson Pratt—August 15, 1848 to January 1, 1851.
Franklin D. Richards—(second term) January 1, 1851 to May 8, 1852.
Samuel W. Richards—May 8, 1852 to June 8, 1854.
Franklin D. Richards—(third term) June 8, 1854 to July 13, 1856.
Orson Pratt—(second term) July 13, 1856 to October 4, 1857.
Samuel W. Richards—(second term) October 4, 1857 to March 6, 1858.
Asa Calkin—March 6, 1858 to May 19, 1860.
    Nathaniel V. Jones; Jacob Gates—(pro tem) May 19, 1860 to August 11, 1860.
Amasa M. Lyman, Charles C. Rich—August 11, 1860 to May 14, 1862.
George Q. Cannon—May 14, 1862 to July 25, 1864.
    Jacob G. Bigler—(pro tem) May 17, 1862 to August 10, 1862.
Daniel H. Wells, Brigham Young, Jr.—July 25, 1864 to August 30, 1865.
Brigham Young, Jr., August 30, 1865 to June 30, 1867.
Franklin D. Richards—(fourth term) June 30, 1867 to September 9, 1868.
Albert Carrington—September 9, 1868 to June 15, 1870.
Horace S. Eldredge—June 15, 1870 to June 6, 1871.
Albert Carrington—(second term) June 6, 1871 to October 21, 1873.
    Lester J. Herrick—(pro tem) October 21, 1873 to March 21, 1874.
Joseph F. Smith—March 21, 1874 to September 13, 1875.
Albert Carrington—(third term) September 13, 1875 to May 27, 1877.
Joseph F. Smith—(second term) May 27, 1877 to July 6, 1878.
    Henry W. Naisbitt—(pro tem) September 10, 1877 to July 6, 1878.
William Budge—July 6, 1878 to November 1, 1880.
Albert Carrington—(fourth term) November 1, 1880 to November 19, 1882.
John Henry Smith—November 19, 1882 to January 1, 1885.
Daniel H. Wells—(second term) January 1, 1885 to February 21, 1887.
George Teasdale—February 21, 1887 to October 6, 1890.
Brigham Young, Jr.—(second term) October 6, 1890 to May 4, 1893.
    Alfred Solomon—(pro tem).
Anthon H. Lund—May 4, 1893 to July 16, 1896.
Rulon S. Wells—July 16, 1896 to December 8, 1898.
Platte D. Lyman—December 8, 1898 to May 17, 1901.
Francis M. Lyman—May 17, 1901 to January 1, 1904.
Heber J. Grant—January 1, 1904 to December 1, 1906.
Charles W. Penrose—December 1, 1906 to June 9, 1910.
Rudger Clawson—June 9, 1910 to April 11, 1913.
    E. Taft Benson—(pro tem) April 11, 1913 to September 30, 1913.
Hyrum M. Smith—September 30, 1913 to September 7, 1916.
George F. Richards—September 7, 1916 to July 1, 1919.
George Albert Smith—July 1, 1919 to July 14, 1921.
Orson F. Whitney—July 14, 1921 to November 9, 1922.
David O. McKay—November 9, 1922 to November 1, 1924.
James E. Talmage—November 1, 1924 to January 1, 1928.
John A. Widtsoe—January 1, 1928 to October 1, 1933.
A. William Lund—(British Mission only) December 11, 1928 to January 15, 1932.
James H. Douglas—(British Mission only) January 15, 1932 to December 10, 1934.
Joseph F. Merrill—(European Mission) October 1, 1933 to September 24, 1936.
Joseph J. Cannon—(British Mission only) December 18, 1934 to July, 1937.
Richard R. Lyman—(European Mission) September 24, 1936, still presiding.
Hugh B. Brown—(British Mission only) Appointment announced May 1, 1937.

NUMBER OF BRITISH MISSIONARIES, BY YEARS*

1837-1839

1837	7
1838	0
1839	14
Total for three years	21

1840-1849

1840	5
1841	1
1842	2
1843	2
1844	10
1845	0
1846	19
1847	0
1848	12
1849	9
Total for the decade	64

1850-1859

1850	9
1851	8
1852	43
1853	24
1854	25
1855	13
1856	42
1857	21
1858	0
1859	5
Total for the decade	191

1860-1869

1860	48
1861	6
1862	19
1863	44
1864	33
1865	30
1866	30
1867	35
1868	15
1869	35
Total for the decade	295

1870-1879

1870	21
1871	20
1872	31
1873	31
1874	30
1875	50
1876	41
1877	58
1878	42
1879	57
Total for the decade	379

1880-1889

1880	86
1881	52
1882	68
1883	60
1884	52
1885	51
1886	65
1887	62
1888	64
1889	77
Total for the decade	637

1890-1899

1890	101
1891	127
1892	67
1893	79
1894	91
1895	71
1896	167
1897	98
1898	129
1899	191
Total for the decade	1121

1900-1909

1900	136
1901	66
1902	136
1903	111
1904	114
1905	120
1906	168
1907	151
1908	190
1909	184
Total for the decade	1376

1910-1919

1910	138
1911	146
1912	120
1913	126
1914	63
1915	42
1916	32
1917	1
1918	0
1919	20
Total for the decade	688

1920-1929

1920	46
1921	107
1922	68
1923	66
1924	82
1925	73
1926	80
1927	68
1928	90
1929	106
Total for the decade	786

1930-1937

1930	78
1931	41
1932	38
1933	43
1934	57
1935	49
1936	54
1937	30
Total for seven years to April 1937	390

Grand Total for one hundred years (to April 15, 1937)......5947

*Note—These figures represent traveling missionaries sent to Great Britain from other countries. They do not include the un-numbered thousands of British-born missionaries who have served while still being citizens and residents of their native land.

APPENDIX

BRITISH MISSION BAPTISMS BY YEARS

A record of the number who have been received into membership in the Church of Jesus Christ of Latter-day Saints through the waters of baptism during the past century in Great Britain.

1837-1839

1837	600
1838	727
1839	190

Total for three years 1517

1840-1849

1840	2326
1841	2883
1842	3216
1843	1195
1844	1762
1845	2505
1846	2354
1847	2918
1848	6520
1849	8620

Total for the decade 34299

1850-1859

1850	8017
1851	8064
1852	6665
1853	4603
1854	4530
1855	3711
1856	2947
1857	2405
1858	1298
1859	1064

Total for the decade 43304

1860-1869

1860	1928
1861	2067
1862	1517
1863	2231
1864	1910
1865	1246
1866	856
1867	1096
1868	2091
1869	1170

Total for the decade 16112

1870-1879

1870	793
1871	654
1872	466
1873	461
1874	530
1875	560
1876	691
1877	534
1878	718
1879	888

Total for the decade 6295

1880-1889

1880	843
1881	980
1882	848
1883	778
1884	537
1885	474
1886	374
1887	562
1888	344
1889	321

Total for the decade 6061

1890-1899

1890	239
1891	267
1892	336
1893	353
1894	364
1895	378
1896	347
1897	503
1898	539
1899	416

Total for the decade 3742

1900-1909

1900	488
1901	986
1902	581
1903	472
1904	602
1905	624
1906	676
1907	986
1908	1234
1909	938

Total for the decade 7587

1910-1919

1910	963
1911	482
1912	363
1913	376
1914	399
1915	298
1916	297
1917	319
1918	248
1919	166

Total for the decade 3911

1920-1929

1920	204
1921	243
1922	288
1923	333
1924	282
1925	168
1926	246
1927	171
1928	232
1929	182

Total for the decade 2349

1930-1936

1930	246
1931	245
1932	267
1933	153
1934	152
1935	147
1936	206

Total for seven years
to 1937 1416

Grand Total up to 1937 126,593

BRITISH MISSION EMIGRATION BY YEARS

A partial* record of the British members of the Church of Jesus Christ of Latter-day Saints who have left the mother country during the past century.

1840-1849
1840	290
1841	705
1842	1083
1843	475
1844	431
1845	276
1846	122
1847	133
1848	369
1849	1900
Total for the decade	5784

1850-1859
1850	1048
1851	990
1852	581
1853	1778
1854	2109
1855	2686
1856	2434
1857	1208
1858	122
1859	399
Total for the decade	12355

1860-1869
1860	665
1861	807
1862	1053
1863	1599
1864	1272
1865	515
1866	1132
1867	271
1868	1732
1869	878
Total for the decade	9924

1870-1879
1870	835
1871	688
1872	737
1873	881
1874	650
1875	389
1876	349
1877	669
1878	903
1879	812
Total for the decade	6913

1880-1889
1880	808
1881	1150
1882	1398
1883	1457
1884	804
1885	697
1886	644
1887	422
1888	392
1889	447
Total for the decade	8219

1890-1899
1890	347
1891	218
1892	283
1893	225
1894	86
1895	153
1896	100
1897	94
1898	112
1899	106
Total for the decade	4849

1900-1909
1900	135
1901	445
1902	253
1903	255
1904	270
1905	280
1906	363
1907	447
1908	324
1909	423
Total for the decade	3195

1910-1919
1910	555
1911	337
1912	
1913	
1914	
1915	
1916	
1917	
1918	
1919	
Total for the decade	892

1920-1929
1920	256

Grand total 52,387*

*Not included in this figure are an unrecorded and inestimable number who have left Great Britain individually or in small groups without their departure having been noted in any of the Church records or publications.

BRITISH-BORN GENERAL AUTHORITIES OF THE CHURCH

JOHN TAYLOR—Born November 1, 1808, at Milnthorpe, England, ordained an Apostle December 19, 1838, under the hands of Brigham Young and Heber C. Kimball. Sustained October 10, 1880, as President of the Church, at the age of 72; died July 25, 1887, at Kaysville, Davis County, Utah.

GEORGE Q. CANNON—Born January 11, 1827, at Liverpool, England; ordained an Apostle August 26, 1860, at Salt Lake City, Utah, by Brigham Young, at the age of 33 years, advanced to be First Counselor in the First Presidency October 10, 1880. Died April 12, 1901, at Monterey, California.

GEORGE REYNOLDS—Born January 1, 1842, at Marylebone, London, England; ordained a Seventy March 18, 1866; set apart as one of the first seven presidents, April 10, 1890, at Salt Lake City, Utah, at the age of 54 years. Died August 9, 1909, at Salt Lake City, Utah.

GEORGE TEASDALE—Born December 8, 1831, at London, England; ordained an Apostle October 16, 1882, at Salt Lake City, Utah, by John Taylor, at the age of 51 years; died June 9, 1907, at Salt Lake City, Utah.

BRIGHAM H. ROBERTS—Born March 13, 1857, at Warrington, Lancashire, England; ordained a Seventy, March 8, 1877; set apart as one of the first seven presidents October 8, 1888, at Salt Lake City, Utah, at the age of 31 years. Died September 27, 1933.

JOHN R. WINDER—Born December 11, 1821, at Biddendew, England; ordained a high priest, March 4, 1872, by Edward Hunter; sustained October 17, 1901, as first Counselor in the First Presidency, at the age of 80; died March 27, 1910, at Salt Lake City, Utah, at the age of 89 years.

CHARLES W. PENROSE—Born February 4, 1832, at London, England; ordained an Apostle, July 7, 1904, by Joseph F. Smith at Salt Lake City, Utah, at the age of 72; advanced to be second Counselor in the First Presidency December 7, 1911; and as first Counselor in the First Presidency March 10, 1921; died May 16, 1925, at the age of 93 years.

CHARLES W. NIBLEY—Born February 5, 1849, at Hunterfield, Midlothian, Scotland; ordained and set apart as Presiding Bishop of the Church, December 11, 1907, at Salt Lake City, Utah, at the age of 58; set apart as second Counselor in the First Presidency, May 28, 1925, at the age of 76 years. Died December 11, 1931, at Salt Lake City, Utah, at the age of 82 years.

JAMES E. TALMAGE—Born September 21, 1862, at Hungerford, Berkshire, England, ordained an Apostle December 8, 1911, by Joseph F. Smith, at Salt Lake City, Utah, at the age of 49 years. Died July 27, 1933, at Salt Lake City, Utah.

JOHN WELLS—Born September 16, 1864, in Carlton, Nottinghamshire, England; ordained a Bishop July 18, 1918, and set apart as second Counselor to the Presiding Bishop.

CHARLES A. CALLIS—Born May 4, 1865, at Dublin, Ireland; ordained an Apostle October 12, 1933, at the age of 68 years, by Heber J. Grant.

THE CENTURY'S EDITORS OF THE "MILLENNIAL STAR"

Parley P. Pratt........May 1840-Oct. 1842	F. D. Richards........June 1854-July 1856
Thomas Ward ....Jan. 1846-Oct. 1846	Orson Pratt...............July 1856-Oct. 1857
Wilford Woodruff....June 1845-Jan. 1846	S. W. Richards....Oct. 1857-May 1860
Thomas Ward............Jan. 1846-Oct. 1846	Nathaniel V. Jones..May 1860-Aug. 1860
Orson Hyde................Oct. 1846-Jan. 1847	Amasa M. Lyman....Aug. 1860-Jan. 1861
F. D. Richards......Jan. 1847-Feb. 1847	George Q. Cannon..Jan. 1861-Sept. 1864
Orson Spencer........Feb. 1847-Aug. 1848	Daniel H. Wells....Sept. 1864-Sept. 1865
Orson Pratt............Aug. 1848-Mar. 1850	Brigham Young, Jr...Sept. 1865-July 1867
Eli B. Kelsey............Mar. 1850-July 1850	F. D. Richards........July 1867-Sept. 1868
Orson Pratt............July 1850-Dec. 1850	Albert Carrington....Sept. 1868-June 1870
F. D. Richards......Jan. 1851-May 1852	Horace S. Eldredge..June 1870-June 1871
S. W. Richards....May 1852-June 1854	Albert Carrington....June 1871-Oct. 1873

Joseph F. Smith....March 1874-Sept. 1875
Albert Carrington....Sept. 1875-June 1877
Joseph F. Smith....June 1877-Aug. 1877
William Budge......July 1878-Nov. 1880
Albert Carrington..Nov. 1880-Nov. 1882
John Henry Smith....Nov. 1882-Dec. 1884
Daniel H. Wells....Jan. 1885-Nov. 1886
George Teasdale....Nov. 1886-Sept. 1890
Brigham Young........Sept. 1890-June 1893
Anthon H. Lund......June 1893-July 1896
Rulon S. Wells........July 1896-Dec. 1898
Platte D. Lyman....Dec. 1898-Aug. 1900
H. W. Naisbitt......Aug. 1900-June 1901

Francis M. Lyman....May 1901-Jan. 1904
Heber J. Grant........Jan. 1904-Nov. 1906
Chas. W. Penrose..Nov. 1906-June 1910
Rudger Clawson....June 1910-April 1913
Hyrum M. Smith....Sept. 1913-Aug. 1916
George F. Richards..Aug. 1916-June 1919
Geo. Albert Smith....June 1919-July 1921
Orson F. Whitney....July 1921-Nov. 1922
David O. McKay....Nov. 1922-Nov. 1924
James E. Talmage....Nov. 1924-Dec. 1928
John A. Widtsoe......Jan. 1929-Oct. 1933
Joseph F. Merrill..Oct. 1933-Sept. 1936
Richard R. Lyman....Sept. 1936-................

Note: Incomplete records of earlier years leave some doubt as to specific dates and exact status of editors.

THE CENTURY'S ASSOCIATE EDITORS OF THE "MILLENNIAL STAR"

1840-1849
Thomas Ward
Lyman O. Littlefield

1850-1859
Eli B. Kelsey
James A. Little
E. W. Tullidge
John A. Ray
Henry Whittall

1860-1869
Henry Whittall
George J. Taylor
Eugene Henroid
E. L. Sloan
William H. Shearman
John C. Graham
Joseph G. Romney
J. V. Hood
N. H. Felt
Aurelius Miner
Orson Pratt
Franklin D. Richards
Charles W. Penrose
George Teasdale
John Jaques

1870-1879
John Jaques
George Reynolds

James G. Bleak
S. S. Jones
John C. Graham
L. J. Nuttall
Edward Hanham
David McKenzie
Henry W. Naisbitt
John Nicholson

1880-1889
John Nicholson
Charles W. Stayner
Orson F. Whitney
George C. Lambert
George Osmond
Charles W. Penrose
B. H. Roberts
Thomas W. Brockbank

1890-1899
John E. Carlisle
James H. Anderson
W. B. Dougall, Jr.
John V. Bluth
Alfred L. Booth
Edwin F. Parry
Attewell Wootton

1900-1909
Attewell Wootton
Joseph J. Cannon
Walter M. Wolfe

Nephi Anderson
William A. Morton

1910-1919
William A. Morton
S. Norman Lee
Hugh Ireland
Thomas A. Brockbank
J. M. Sjodahl
Junius F. Wells

1920-1929
Junius F. Wells
William A. Morton
David L. O. McKay
George M. Hopfenbeck
F. Artell Smith
James K. Knudsen
Waldo L. Osmond
Richard L. Evans
Weston N. Nordgren

1930-1937
Weston N. Nordgren
Wm. D. Callister
James H. Wallis
Weldon C. Roberts
Dennis McCarthy
Richard S. Bennett
Wendell J. Ashton
Parry D. Sorensen

Note: Incomplete records of former years place in doubt the exact dates and status of some of the earlier Associates. For more complete details see the *Millennial Star,* Vol. 95, No. 20.

BRITISH MISSIONARIES WHO HAVE DIED WHILE LABORING IN OR TRAVELING TO OR FROM THE BRITISH MISSION

Lorenzo D. Barnes—died Dec. 20, 1842, Bradford, England.
James H. Flannigan—died Jan. 25, 1851, smallpox; buried in Birmingham.
William Burton—died, Edinburgh, March 17, 1851, chills and fever.
Levi Stillman Nickerson—died Dec., 1853, near Kanesville, Ohio, enroute to Great Britain, exposure.
William W. Major—died Oct. 2, 1854, London, chills and ague.
Robert W. Wolcott—died Feb. 27, 1856, England; smallpox.
Samuel F. Neslen—died May 13, 1858, Williamsburg, N. Y., returning from England; consumption.
John M. Kay—died Sept. 27, 1864, near Laramie, returning from England; mountain fever.
Martin Wood—died Oct., 1864, Weber Rver, Utah; returning.
George Sims—died Oct. 23, 1865, Platte River, drowning; returning.
Collins M. Gillet—died Aug. 20, 1866, Nebraska, returning.
Jesse Y. Cherry—died May 20, 1865, Nottingham; smallpox.
Brigham W. Kimball—died July 24, 1867, Nebraska, returning.
Anson V. Call—died Aug. 4, 1867, Rock Creek, Wyo., returning.
Ezra James Clark—died July 14, 1868, Fonda, N. Y., returning.
John Mace—died Jan. 19, 1869, Leeds, Eng.
Caleb Parry—died Sept. 19, 1871, Birmingham, England; smallpox.
Thomas Hunter—died Aug. 23, 1876, Scotland.
Edwin W. Street—died April 12, 1878, Beachwood, England.
Joseph E. Hyde—died July 3, 1878, at sea, returning.
William H. Butler—died Feb. 24, 1882, Birmingham, England.
Shadrach Jones—died June 24, 1883, Swansea, Wales.
Samuel T. Clarke—died Sept. 21, 1899, Wales; erysipelas.
David M. Muir—died Nov. 20, 1898, Lochgelly, Scotland; pneumonia.
Marvey Leon Angell—died Nov. 30, 1907, Halifax, England; pneumonia.
Griffith E. Williams—died Sept. 25, 1909, Tredegar, Wales; appendicitis.
Joseph Watson Maynes—died June 9, 1912, near Cheltenham; heart trouble.
Ralph H. Hendricks, died Feb. 24, 1913, Sunderland, England; hemorrhage.
Stewart Eccles—died Nov. 4, 1913, London.
John Alexander Maynes—died Oct. 14, 1925, Hull, England; pleurisy.
Wilford Orr Freckleton—died Feb. 27, 1917, Hull, England; spinal meningitis.
Herman Kerr Danielsen—died Mar. 9, 1919, Ireland; pneumonia.
Lawrence T. Heath—died June 2, 1932, Abbingdon, England; drowning.

INDEX

Aitken, Robert, Rev., "Exposes 'Mormonism,'" 42; Heber C. Kimball converts many of his congregation, 42.

Albertson, John, second British Patriarch, 131.

Albion, James, Rev., gives free use of chapel, 176; entertains Elders, 176; applies for baptism, 178.

Apostles, called by revelation to England, 85; revelation fulfilled, 87; majority meet in council, 119; business transacted, 125; recommend moving publishing business to London, 172.

Appendix, Mission Presidents, 242; number of British missionaries by years, 243; names of missionaries who have died, 244; total baptism for century, 247; British emigration by years, 248; British-born general Church authorities, 249; associate editors of *Millennial Star*, 250; editors of *Millennial Star*, 250.

Ballard, Melvin J., 3.

Baptisms, first British Mission, 32.

Bedford, Elders sent there, 35; nineteen baptized, 39; branch organized, 39.

Benbow, John, entertains Wilford Woodruff, 111; opens home to Gospel, 112; numerous baptisms, 112; advances 300 pounds to print *Book of Mormon*, 114; emigrates, 114; gives bond for the Prophet, 115; wife dies, 115; marries, 115; daughter born, 115; helps emigrate poor, 115; dies at Provo, 115; visit to Hill Farm by author, 116.

Birmingham, 94.

Black, William, missionary to Ireland, 151.

Book of Mormon, first British edition: copyright ordered secured, 125; money donated by John Benbow, 114; published in 1841, 145; first copies reach London, 178; other editions, 145.

British Government, extends courtesies to missionaries, 216.

British Parliament, investigates "Mormon" emigration, 232.

British Press, Fleet Street and Strand, 201; attitude toward "Mormonism," 202; first attack, 203; first reply by Parley P. Pratt, 204; *London Examiner* defends freedom of "Mormon" emigration, 208; W. T. Stead charges opposition to "Mormonism" as "sectarian savagery," 211; attempt to influence British Home Secretary meets with failure, 211; present favorable attitude, 213.

Brown, Hugh B., 219, 242.

Budge, William, mission president, 83, 242, 246.

Callis, Chas. A., 3; Irish birth, 154; Liverpool baptism, 154; emigration, 154; missionary activities, 154; British-born general authority, 246.

Calkin, Asa, mission president, 242.

Canada, gospel interest in, 15.

Cannon, George, visited by John Taylor, 96; parents and children baptized, 102.

remains in charge of mission,
199; released, 199; appoints
successors, 199; last apostle
to leave British mission, 200.

Preston, first branch organized,
33, 37; thousands hear elders
preach, 34; large number confirmed, 37; five branches organized, 52; 100 children
blessed, 52.

Reynolds, George, 246.

Richards, Franklin D., mission
president, 242, 246, 247.

Richards, George F., calls British women into missionary
service, 217; wonderful results, 217; mission president,
242, 247.

Richards, Jennetta, converted
and baptized, 36; first confirmation in Great Britain, 36;
Heber C. Kimball prophecies,
36; healed through administration, 131; married to Willard Richards, 71.

Richards, Samuel W., mission
president, 242, 246.

Richards, Willard, leaves for
England on day's notice, 14;
joins Heber C. Kimball, 16;
helped with money, 18; sails
for England, 19; arrives at
Liverpool penniless, 21; leaves
for Preston, 23; preaches in
Vauxhall, 26; experience with
devils, 30; sent to Bedford,
35; organizes branch, 39; re-
ceives counsel from Heber C.
Kimball, 53; ill health, 61;
first counselor in British presidency, 63; marries Jennetta
Richards, 71; his call to apostleship made known to him,
71; Twelve meet at his home,
94; visits John Benbow, 114;
ordained an apostle, 123.

River Ribble, first converts baptized in, 29; race to the river,
32; thousands witness event,
32; invalid carried to river,
33; baptized and healed, 33.

Roberts, Brigham H., 246.

Russell, Isaac, mission to England, 16; arrives in Preston,
23; seized by evil spirits, 29;
devil rebuked, 29; five thousand hear him preach, 34; sent
to Cumberland, 35; labors in
Alston, 51; sails for home, 65;
apostatizes, 72.

Scotland, first missionaries, 75;
hardships encountered, 77;
first baptisms, 78; elders mobbed, 80; Orson Pratt arrives,
80; gospel produces prominent
men, 82; fifty converts emigrated in third ship, 228.

Sheffield, 138.

Smith, Geo. A., leaves Nauvoo
for England, 121; arrives in
Liverpool, 103; labors in
Herefordshire and London,
164; delivers first Gospel sermon in London, 167; slow results, 168; attends Manchester conference, 171; returns to
London, 174; health breaks
down, 175; retires to Staffordshire, 175; sails for home, 198.

Smith, Geo. Albert, successful
work of mission rehabilitation
at close of war, 218; term of
office, 242, 247.

Smith, Hyrum M., adjusting
work of missionaries at outbreak of war, 217, 242, 247.

Smith, John Henry, mission
president, 242, 247.

Smith, Joseph Fielding, 3.

Smith, Joseph (the Prophet),
10, 11, 12, 13, 186, 187, 188.

Smith, Joseph F., mission president, 242, 246.